Recipes for a Happy (if Disorderly) Life

Muffins and Mayhem

Suzanne Beecher

A Touchstone Book
Published by Simon & Schuster

New York   London   Toronto   Sydney

Touchstone
A Division of Simon & Schuster, Inc.
1230 Avenue of the Americas
New York, NY 10020

Copyright © 2010 by Suzanne Beecher

First Touchstone hardcover edition June 2010

TOUCHSTONE and colophon are registered trademarks of Simon & Schuster, Inc.

For information about special discounts for bulk purchases, please contact Simon & Schuster Special Sales at 1-866-506-1949 or business@simonandschuster.com.

The Simon & Schuster Speakers Bu   ithors to your live event. For more information or to book an event contact the Simon   Bureau at 1-866-248-3049 or visit our website at www.simonspeakers.com.

Designed by Ruth Lee-Mui

Manufactured in the United States of America

10 9 8 7 6 5 4 3 2 1

Library of Congress Cataloging-in-Publication Data
Beecher, Suzanne.
   Muffins and mayhem : recipes for a happy—if disorderly—life / by Suzanne Beecher.
       p. cm.
   1. Cooks—Biography. I. Title.
   TX649.B443B44 2010
      641.5092—dc22
                                                                        2010006473

ISBN 978-1-4391-1287-8
ISBN 978-1-4391-4951-5 (ebook)

Contents

The Recipe for This Book   ix

Introduction: Does Anybody Else Feel Like This?   1

1. A Budding Chef   9

2. Main Street   15

3. Loose Wires   27

4. Pretending My Way to Success   46

5. Failure That Was Good Enough   55

6. The Boogeyman Just Might Be Under My Bed!   67

7. In-a-Pickle   77

8. A Not-So-Perfect Piecrust   86

9. Bull-Puckey, I Can Do This   95

10. Please, Give This Woman a Job!   102

11. He Loves Me, He Loves Me a Lot   114

12. Somebody Should Have Told Me About This!   131

13. Muffins and Mayhem   136

14. May I Please Have This Dance?   147

15. I Miss My Mother   157

16. Still In-a-Pickle and It's *Not* What Miss Manners Would Do   172

17. Home for the Holidays   183

18. Did Somebody Bring the Cookies?   203

19. Seasonings: The Ingredients of a Small-Town Girl   213

20. Writing the Recipe for My Life   219

One Last Note from the Author   229

Acknowledgments   231

Recipes

"Almost" Beef with Broccoli — 53

Amy's Piecrust — 94

Apple Cutout Sugar Cookies — 113

Basic Crepes — 156

Beef Stew — 76

Braised Shrimp with Vegetables — 130

Candy-Cane Cookies — 201

Chicken Crepes — 154

Chocolate-Chip Cookies — 212

Cinnamon Rolls — 44

Company Fare Pork Chops — 154

Crock Pot Dressing — 192

Dolly Madison Muffins — 146

Funeral Cake with Buttercream Frosting — 5

Grandma Hale's Deviled Eggs — 65

Grandma Hale's Stuffing for a Fifteen-Pound Turkey — 193

Hearty Chili — 65

Hot 'n' Sour Soup — 126

Lava Cakes — 6

Marinated Flank Steak — 135

Mother's Oatmeal Chocolate-Chip Cookies — 170

Mrs. Creswick's Frosted Meat Loaf — xvi

My Favorite Blueberry Muffins — 26

Never Fail Piecrust — 94

Northern Maine Oatmeal Bread — 125

Pickling Syrup — 182

Porcupine Meatballs — 14

Potsticker Sauce — 129

Potstickers — 127

Pumpkin Bread with Pumpkin Whipped Cream — 195

Ron and Virginia's Bread-and-Butter Pickles — 181

Ron's Goulash — 171

Shrimp Salad — 193

Skunk Beans — 194

Spaghetti Sauce — 100

Turkey Pie — 196

Whoops! Banana Bread — 84

Zucchini Bisque — 153

The Recipe for This Book

Almost every week my parents and I would go to Grandma and Grandpa Hale's house for Sunday dinner. Grandma Hale was the shutterbug in the family and I was always ready to pose.

I used to think I didn't have anything to say about my childhood. For the life of me, except for the bad complaining stuff, I couldn't remember a thing I did with my parents as a kid. Since I didn't want to lug *those* stories around with me the rest of my life, my mind would always go blank whenever somebody started talking about their warm and fuzzy childhood experiences.

"I remember when," somebody would begin . . . and from those three words would flow a precious childhood memory about the time they got caught sneaking in the back door of the movie theater, and they'd recite in vivid Technicolor every single detail, right down to what they were wearing when the manager called their parents to come and get them. I *hated* those people who told their cute little "I remember when" stories. Okay, I know I'm not supposed to say I *hate* anyone, so let's just say I was consumed with envy, jealousy, and disdain.

How did these people do it? How could they remember all of these things? And what the heck was wrong with me, that I couldn't?

So I took a quick inventory and discovered my one-dimensional childhood consisted of these four scintillatingly dramatic "stories":

1. I was born in Madison, Wisconsin. We didn't live there—we lived seventy-five miles away, in the small town of Cuba City, population 2,000—but my mother became very ill in the last six weeks of her pregnancy, so the doctor sent her to the big-city Madison hospital.

2. My parents and I lived in a trailer for a while—just long enough to save up money for a down payment on a house.

3. I had a green dress with a scratchy cancan slip underneath it. I think this was in the fourth grade.

4. When I was in eighth grade, the first round school building in the county (maybe even the state) was built in Cuba City. In the middle of the school year, we all packed up the stuff in our old desks and walked in a single-file pilgrimage from the old rectangular school building to the new round one.

The End

That's the short, happy childhood of Suzanne Beecher in 157 words, plain and simple. And boring, even to me.

So I accepted my fate as an adult deprived of a childhood. Or at the very least an adult deprived of those warm and fuzzy memories I should have been able to tap into when I wanted to go back home in my mind. But then it occurred to me that I'd always been ambivalent about going home anyway—not only in my mind, but in my car, too. At least it seemed that way. Whenever I planned a trip to see my parents, I'd get sick. I'm not kidding! Two or three days before I was supposed to leave, an illness would consume me: wheezing, sneezing, that all-over crummy feeling. Nothing serious, a twenty-four-hour virus sort of thing—but just enough "miserable" so I'd have to cancel my trip. My recovery period was amazing. And eventually I realized there was a pattern: As soon as the "magic hour" had passed and it was too late to go, no hope of getting back home in time for a weekend visit, I was cured.

So I asked myself: Really, what's the big deal? Who cares if I can't remember any cute childhood stories—didn't want to go back to measly podunk Cuba City, anyway. It was a stupid town, one of those blink-and-you'll-miss-it dots on the map. Cuba City meant nothing to me. My life is all about what happens to me now. Right?

But then Mrs. Creswick died. She was my girlfriend's mother. Everyone called her Purse, but I never used her nickname, or her real name, Priscilla. It seemed more respectful to address her as Mrs. Creswick.

When I heard the news that Mrs. Creswick had died, I realized I'd lost something precious from my past. Every kid needs a role model, and although I hadn't realized it at the time, Mrs. Creswick was one of mine.

I loved going to Mrs. Creswick's house because she made me feel special. She always made sure there was cottage cheese and those little cherry tomatoes in the refrigerator because she knew I loved them. Course I don't really know for sure—I was just a kid. Maybe she always had cottage cheese and tomatoes in the fridge—but she knew they were my favorite, so she'd set a plate in front of me every time I visited.

Mrs. Creswick was a great cook, and there was love in her kitchen. Whenever I got the chance, I liked to watch her make dinner. One afternoon she even taught me how to make her famous Frosted Meat Loaf. When I asked for a copy of the recipe, she helped me write it down on one of her recipe cards, along with personal tips on how not to burn the meat loaf when it was time to put it under the broiler. I still have the faded Frosted Meat Loaf recipe card today.

It was important for me to let someone know how special Mrs. Creswick had been to me. So I called her husband and my old girlfriend, gave them my condolences, and shared my childhood memory of the Frosted Meat Loaf. Then I dug out my old recipe card and started cooking. Mrs. Creswick would have been proud of me, because her Frosted Meat Loaf came out of the broiler just right.

Years ago I'm sure Mrs. Creswick thought she was simply giving me a recipe for meat loaf, and for a long time that's what I thought, too. But suddenly it was all so clear—the things that make me what I am today, the things I really like about myself, they all came from growing up in Cuba City. Remember the girl who was ambivalent about going home? Mrs. Creswick's meat loaf finally showed her the way.

So if a plate of cherry tomatoes and cottage cheese and a Frosted Meat Loaf recipe could leave such a big impression on my heart, maybe there were other little things in my life that I was overlooking?

I'm a daily columnist who writes about life, and after I wrote the story about Mrs. Creswick's Meat Loaf the tone of my columns changed. I guess what really happened is I wasn't afraid to open my heart and let readers see the real me. Now I freely write about the feelings I wrestle with every day—my father's final farewell apology, embarrassing moments like the day I was trying to make a big impression but suddenly realized a lint roller was stuck to my behind, trapping Mighty Roach in the middle of the night, and how I couldn't get back in the groove after my mother died even though we'd never been close.

When I opened up my heart to readers, they opened up their hearts to me. Hundreds of people email every day and tell me their stories. In fact, one woman's email, another Priscilla, inspired me to write this book. . . .

Dear Suzanne,

I have been following your Dear Reader column for several years now. I am so grateful you are willing to share with your readers a glimpse of your life, whether it's happy or sad.

Let me introduce myself: I am a 43-year-old mother of three children ages 8, 10, and 11. I have been diagnosed with late-stage metastasized lung cancer.

Knowing that I won't have the privilege of walking my three young children through their tough teenage years and adulthood, I want to prepare a scrapbook for each of them to fall back on when they are down and have no one else to turn to. When I was reading your column about the "writing inspiration" folder you keep, it strikes me to the core—that's exactly what I want to prepare for my kids. Something to inspire them to be the best person they possibly can, and to pick their spirits up on a rainy day when things feel out of control and they need to get themselves grounded again.

It will be greatly appreciated if you can share some pointers with me as to where to find these inspiring books, articles, quotes, etc. Thank you for your time!

> Yours sincerely,
> Priscilla

And my reply . . .

Dear Priscilla,

It's always a pleasure to hear from a reader, especially someone who has been reading with me for such a long time.

Some of the most precious things I own are the photo albums and recipe box that my Grandma Hale passed on to me. Whenever I thumb through the albums, or I'm following the recipe on one of Grandma's recipe cards, I feel like she's standing right beside me in the kitchen. It's such a comfort, and the memories come flooding in.

Making scrapbooks or journals you can leave for your children is a wonderful, loving thing to do. They are going to miss you, and you're right, there are going to be sad times in their lives when no one else but their mother could comfort them.

Pictures in a scrapbook with a caption underneath about why this was your favorite, or something about the day the photo was taken—your kids would love the photos. And when you make a list of books that have made a difference in your life, you could explain the reason why.

But Priscilla, I think the most important thing you can tell your children is what you are thinking, or were thinking. Write down what you were thinking on your first date (it doesn't have to be fancy), how it took you hours, maybe days, to figure out what to wear. How awkward your first kiss was. Tell them about the day you flunked your algebra test, how you worried that you might not make it into college, or why you felt you didn't need to go. Why you decided to say yes and get married. How did you meet their father? On days when you feel like a loser, what do you do to get yourself grounded again?

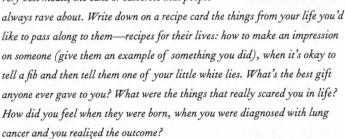

Create recipe boxes for your children and include your favorite recipes and stories. Leave your children a handwritten copy of the recipes for your very best meals, the cake or casserole that people always rave about. Write down on a recipe card the things from your life you'd like to pass along to them—recipes for their lives: how to make an impression on someone (give them an example of something you did), when it's okay to tell a fib and then tell them one of your little white lies. What's the best gift anyone ever gave to you? What were the things that really scared you in life? How did you feel when they were born, when you were diagnosed with lung cancer and you realized the outcome?

My mother died from lung cancer a year and a half ago. My son said that he asked my mother if she was afraid to die. She told him no, that she didn't think it would be quite this soon, but that she wasn't afraid. That statement has brought my son so much comfort. I know, because he's mentioned it to me several times.

There are things I wish I had asked my mother, and most of them begin with "How did you feel about . . . ?"

Don't weigh yourself down with the need to write fancy, just simply write. Pretend your kids are sitting in front of you and start talking. I can picture you leaving each one of your children a recipe box filled with recipes for cooking and recipes for their lives, written on 3 x 5 index cards.

Priscilla, I wish I could say something to make everything better. I'm so sorry. There is a quote I say out loud to myself when it feels like my world is falling apart and I need to get grounded. It always brings me at least a moment's respite. I'm saying it out loud for you today.

"If I knew the way, Priscilla, I'd take you home."

Priscilla did make recipe boxes for her children. Unknowingly, she left a gift behind for me, too. I didn't realize it until I wrote back to Priscilla, but for years I'd been creating my own recipe box, and the stories I discovered in it inspired me to write this book.

I've picked out some of my favorite dishes and recipes from my life—the stories that help keep me grounded in this unpredictable world, like Mrs. Creswick's Meat Loaf. Stories that remind me I'm okay, just the way I am.

Recipes are meant to be exchanged, so please share my book with your friends—and substitutions are allowed. Maybe there's a Mrs. Creswick hidden away in your heart, filed away in your own recipe box? My hope is by the time you're finished reading the recipes from my life, you'll be reliving some of your own, and if you're still looking, I hope you find that missing ingredient.

Mrs. Creswick's Frosted Meat Loaf

It's a one-bowl recipe. I keep a box of light disposable gloves in my kitchen for jobs like mixing a meat loaf. You can use a mixer, but I like to get my hands in the meat loaf. For the frosting, peel a couple of Idaho potatoes, or quickly mix up some instant mashed potatoes.

Meat Loaf

2 pounds hamburger
½ cup French dressing
½ cup dry bread crumbs
½ cup chopped onions
2 eggs
1 teaspoon salt
¼ teaspoon pepper

Meat Loaf Frosting

2 cups hot mashed potatoes
1 egg, beaten
½ cup Miracle Whip

Mix all meat loaf ingredients together. In a baking dish, shape into oval loaf. Bake for one hour at 350 degrees. Then mix frosting ingredients together, and frost meat loaf. Broil until slightly brown.

Introduction

Does Anybody Else Feel Like This?

Life isn't always about the serious stuff.

My recipe box gets a lot of use. It's filled with the necessities of life—stories to help keep me grounded and recipes for good stuff to eat, like the Funeral Cake—my favorite cake since I was a kid. I realize that may sound a little strange, but in Cuba City when I was growing up, whenever someone passed away, neighbors would take food over to the bereaved family so they wouldn't have to worry about cooking. Even if they didn't have much of an appetite, most likely there'd be a steady stream of friends and relatives stopping by their house, and this way they could offer their guests something to eat.

I made sure to tag along with my parents when they'd go to drop off a casserole and offer their condolences, because I was hoping to get a piece of the Funeral Cake. It was the absolute best chocolate cake I'd ever eaten and it always showed up at every grieving family's home in Cuba City. And when my mother died five years ago and friends and neighbors brought food over to her house, guess what showed up then, too?

The Funeral Cake.

What a surprise when I discovered that the Funeral Cake baker, the woman who'd been making my favorite cake all those years—a devil's food cake with a light buttercream frosting—was Betty, a shirttail relative of mine.

Frequently I thumb through my recipe box looking for a story to reassure me things are gonna be all right. I have good intentions, but more often than I like to admit, my life gets off course, so I spend a fair amount of time "fixing" myself. My feelings change daily, sometimes hour by hour. Blame it on a headache, blame it on some bad fish I ate for dinner, blame it on not getting enough sleep, or the hormones I'm juggling in this phase of my life called menopause, but one minute I'm a happy camper, and the next, I'm wondering what went wrong—isn't it time to take a nap?

Other days are amazing, and I'm certain I've finally found the perfect recipe for my life. Happy and contented, creative beyond my wildest dreams—things are cooking now—but I'll wake up the next morning and for some reason see myself on the cover of *Loser* magazine and it'll be time to get out my recipe box again. Time to find a recipe to assure me that even though things don't look promising at the moment, this is the recipe I followed in the past when life got scary but everything turned out fine.

I'm a complicated person, even to me. It's embarrassing to admit, but I spend a lot of time wondering *why*. I might wake up in the middle of the night trying to come up with possible reasons why the supermarket clerk kept giving me nasty looks when she was ringing up my order. I suppose it would be easier for me to figure out why I bother spending time wondering about such things and work on changing *me* instead.

But through the years, I've come to realize that I'll never be able to completely rid myself of that particular personality trait, and I'm not so sure I'd even want to. Because it's not always the "bad stuff" I review later on in my mind—I learn a lot from taking another look at the "good stuff," too. When I'm in the middle of a daily interaction, the little cues, mannerisms, and words that someone chooses might slip right by me. It happens all so fast. But when I think about the encounter later in the day and I write about it, visualizing and replaying how it all went down, I learn a lot about me.

The recipes from my life, each story teaches me something about myself. For example, this one reminds me why I don't always need to be the best.

The woman down the street is one of those wonderful people who is always planning something fun, and I say that with all sincerity, because I'd probably be a social recluse if it weren't for her invitations. So when she invited me to a neighborhood bake-off, I RSVP'd "yes." The only instructions: Be ready to serve by 6:30 p.m., and whatever you bring to the bake-off, make sure it contains chocolate or berries.

Knowing my neighbor as I do, calling it a "bake-off" could simply be her clever ruse for getting people to bake for her, because she's not a baker. Was there really going to be a first prize, or a judge, for that matter? Just in case, I decided to make Lava Cakes, which are best right out of the oven when the warm, gooey chocolate is running out of the center. It was a risky choice because of the timing, but they're impressive and they taste divine. My plan was to put the Lava Cakes in the oven at 6:10, bake them for thirteen minutes, and then head to the party. (My neighbor's house is only a three-minute walk away.)

I was thinking I should probably be feeling a little nervous, because when you're baking something at the last minute, there are no second chances. I might have had to show up empty handed, but surprisingly it didn't bother me, and that was a wonderful realization.

It's not that I don't usually lean toward risky choices, I do. In fact, some people would say that's part of my trademark. But in the past, whether

I acknowledged it or not, there was always a backup plan waiting in the wings—all the details worked out in advance, checked and double-checked, even for something as trivial as baking Lava Cakes. But this new loosey-goosey approach, I liked it. I think I could get used to feeling like this. There *was* a bake-off judge and a first-prize blue ribbon, but I didn't win it. A chocolate dessert that didn't require delicate timing came in first. You really need to eat Lava Cakes right out of the oven, so I came in an easygoing second—and it was quite all right with me.

Life isn't all about the serious stuff. When I need a good laugh—when I'm looking for the "funny" in life—I can find those stories in my recipe box, too. Here's one of my favorites.

I couldn't see clearly because I didn't have my glasses on and it was the middle of the night. But I was pretty sure that the big, blotchy mass running up the wall next to my bed wasn't there when I went to sleep.

Lights on!

Yell at husband! (He's in charge of things that scurry in the night.)

Pull covers over my head! (In case the blotchy thing goes airborne.)

Yes, we have an exterminator. But every now and then a critter gets through the outside bug barrier, as this roach—a really big roach—obviously did. He was bold, all right. He knew we'd seen him; he could have retreated, but he chose to stay put and defend his wall. Okay, this was war!

My husband's weapon of choice was a rolled-up newspaper, but I quickly reminded him that squishing the enemy on the wall would make for a messy cleanup job, possibly even touch-up painting. I suggested the vacuum cleaner instead. And after a fleeting chase, the vacuum did indeed suck that roach right up through the hose. Now safe and secure, I thought I'd drift right off to sleep. But I didn't.

Did you ever watch the *Mighty Mouse* cartoon show when you were a kid? I did, and for some reason the image of Mighty Mouse with his chest puffed out, flexing the muscles in his arms, was suddenly crystal clear in my mind. Now all I could think about was, *What if that roach spends all night in that vacuum cleaner bag, munching on yesterday's toast crumbs, and in the morning he crawls down the vacuum hose and emerges as Mighty Roach? He's not gonna be too happy.*

Lights on—again. Yell at husband—again: "You hold the vacuum cleaner hose upright, dear. I'll get the duct tape."

Yes, life is definitely entertaining at our house. My husband says he married me because he knew life with me would never be boring. I don't intend to let him down.

The Funeral Cake with Buttercream Frosting

½ cup vegetable shortening
1½ cups sugar
1 egg
½ cup milk
2 cups all-purpose flour
2 teaspoons baking soda
½ teaspoon salt
½ cup cocoa
1 cup boiling water
1 teaspoon pure vanilla extract

Cream shortening and sugar. Mix in the egg. Add the milk, alternating with the following ingredients that have been sifted together: flour, baking soda, salt, and cocoa. Stir in boiling water and vanilla. Bake at 350 degrees (grease and flour pans).

Loaf pan 13 X 9 X 2: 40 minutes
Two round 9-inch pans for a layer cake: 30 minutes
Cupcakes: 17 minutes

Buttercream Frosting

If you're making a layer cake, double this frosting recipe.

½ cup milk
2 tablespoons all-purpose flour
1 stick soft butter
½ cup granulated sugar

Mix together milk and flour. Cook over medium-high heat, stirring constantly until thick, then let the mixture cool. Cream together soft butter and sugar. Then whip the milk and butter mixtures together. Frost your cake or cupcakes and enjoy!

Suzanne's Lava Cakes

Makes 6 cakes

These cakes look very impressive, but they are super simple to make. I love them. I like to serve them with a scoop of vanilla ice cream on the side.

6 ounces bittersweet chocolate, chopped
10 tablespoons butter
1 teaspoon pure vanilla extract
3 large eggs
3 large egg yolks
1¼ cups powdered sugar, sifted
½ cup all-purpose flour

Preheat the oven to 450 degrees if you are baking the Lava Cakes immediately. Butter six ¾-cup ceramic ramekins.

Stir chocolate and butter together in medium saucepan over low heat. Stir in vanilla. Cool the mixture slightly. Whisk eggs, yolks, and sugar together in a large bowl. Add chocolate mixture and flour. Pour mixture into the prepared ramekins, dividing equally. Cover and chill if you're making the Lava Cakes a day in advance.

Bake cakes until the sides are set, but the center remains soft, about 11 minutes. (If you refrigerated the batter, you might have to bake them for up to 15 minutes.) You really do want the center soft and runny on the inside, so remove the cakes from the oven promptly—and don't second-guess yourself.

Immediately run a small knife around the edges to loosen the cakes. Then invert each cake onto a single serving plate.

1. A Budding Chef

Grandpa Hale built the kitchen cupboard for me, and that's my dog, Moochie, sitting on the floor hoping I'll spill.

I learned how to cook when I was eight years old and singing backup for the Monkees.

Mom and Dad worked every day, including Saturdays, and I was an only child, so the weekend chores were left to me. Every Saturday morning, before my mom left for work, she'd tape a list on the front of the refrigerator.

Susan, (my given name)

1. *Iron*
2. *Vacuum the living room and bedrooms*
3. *Dust everything*

4. *Clean the bathroom*

5. *Fix lunch*

NO playing outdoors until your work is done.

Love, Mom

I'd always get the work done, at least most of the time. But the "getting-it-done" part didn't start until about an hour and a half before my parents came home for lunch, because I'd get sidetracked by other important things. Like lip-synching with the Monkees.

Hey, hey, we're the Monkees
And people say we monkey around.

A bottle of Pledge was my microphone and a pair of my mother's high heels gave me that onstage look. I'd draw the curtains over the big picture window in our living room—I wasn't ready for an audience yet—then I'd slide back the cover of our dark wooden console stereo, put the Monkees' 33⅓ LP on the changer, click the switch, and when the needle dropped the magic would begin.

Sing a few tunes, then take a break to do a little dusting, pound the round steak—Swiss steak was on my lunch menu—brown the meat, add some onions and tomato sauce, and pop it in the oven just in time to do another set with the Monkees.

Timing is everything when you're onstage, and when you're cooking, too. If the backup "doo-wops" come in on the wrong beat, the song is ruined. If the meat doesn't have enough time to slow cook, it won't turn out fork-tender. Everything has a rhythm to it: peel the potatoes, set them aside; vacuum the floor, then open a can of peas and dump them into a saucepan—but they'll have to wait for their cue to start cooking because it's time to go back onstage.

Thirty minutes left before lunchtime: put the potatoes on medium-high; tilt the lid over the saucepan to let some of the steam out; set the table. Only fifteen minutes left: Open the drapes, turn down the music, take one last look around the house, and by the time my parents walk through the door, Mike, Davy, Mickey, Peter, and I have finished two curtain calls—our last number was "Forget That Girl"—and I'm in the kitchen smiling and stirring the peas when I hear the front door open.

"Hi, Mom, hi, Dad, lunch is ready."

Cooking was the one thing I seemed to do right when I was a kid. My parents never came right out and said, "Wow, that was a great meal, Susan," but they ate it and sometimes even went back for seconds, so it was implied that I'd done a good job.

But when other people tasted my Porcupine Meatballs at the church picnic and raved about what a good little cook I was, I believed them. And when the neighbor down the street asked me—just a kid in elementary school—if I would give her my recipe, I felt proud as a peacock. So even though making lunch started out as another dreaded chore on my Saturday list, cooking was something I really got to like doing—a "safe" hobby. Something I could be proud of.

I had to choose hobbies carefully when I was a kid, because my mother's rule was if you started something you were going to finish it. Even when I went to the library I only checked out thin books—just in case. So a hobby like knitting was totally out of the question. What if something went terribly wrong? From past experience I knew the routine—there wouldn't be any such thing as a practice, *learning-how-to-knit* sweater. If I tried to make a sweater, it wouldn't matter if there were twisted stitches, or if it ended up two sizes too big—I'd be wearing it to school anyway. "I paid good money for that yarn. You'll grow into it."

It was bad enough that I had to wear the jumper I made in home economics class to school. My wide-ribbed, dark green, corduroy jumper was cut from the same pattern as everybody else's. So even if I'd actually liked the stupid jumper, no way did I want to wear it to school. It would have been a fashion disgrace. Think about it—all twenty girls in my class showing up for school wearing a rainbow assortment of corduroy jumpers, all cut from the same pattern, on the same day? I don't think so.

But cooking was different. If my timing was off—if I did too many curtain calls to "I'm a Believer"—I could hide my mistake with a can of cream of mushroom soup. Cut the burnt part off the fried chicken, throw the dried-out meat into a casserole dish, mix a can of cream of mushroom soup with milk, pour it over the chicken, salt, pepper, then sprinkle half a can of French's French Fried Onions on top and instantly it was chicken casserole.

Cream of mushroom soup saved me from the taste of burnt chicken and ketchup saved me from the taste of liver. My mother didn't like to cook and it showed. Once every two weeks—at least!—she served liver. It was frightening. As soon as I saw Mom slicing up that big slab of liver into little liver servings, and dipping them in flour and heating up the oil—I got on the phone and started calling friends as fast as my fingers could dial.

"Have you eaten yet? Can I come over for dinner? I just got *Sgt. Pepper's Lonely Hearts Club Band* and I'll bring it along. You can even keep it for a week. Please? I really need to come to dinner."

If those calls didn't produce a liver reprieve, I'd plead with our neighbor to get off the party line, so I could start dialing friends of friends. "Hello there, I'm Ginger's best friend and she thought we should get to know each other. Have you eaten yet? By the way, I just got the new Beatles album. . . ."

Mom liked liver because it was cheap. It didn't matter that I hated the stuff. "This isn't a restaurant, I'm not a short-order cook." And of course the other half of that sentence was something about not wasting food and my mother's hard-earned money. So I had to sit at the dinner table until I ate every single bit of the liver and onions piled on the plate in front of me. Oh, did I forget to mention the onions? Not that they made the dinner any more palatable. The onions were cooked in the same pan as the liver.

Gagging produced no sympathy at the liver dinner table. My only salvation was ketchup. Dump lots and lots of ketchup on the liver, pinch my nose with two fingers, then shove as big of a piece of liver as I could get down my throat without choking, while listening to my mother lecture me on the cathartic "truths" of eating liver.

When my mother got a "truth" about something in her head, like liver, even if you could absolutely, positively, prove it not to be true—it didn't matter. Her truths were absolute. And my mother had a truism about ironing, too. Everything in our house that touched our bodies needed to be ironed, including socks, sheets, pillowcases, and even underwear. Why? "Because I said so."

I never understood the logic of it all, but I did it. Wash the clothes, roll them up while they're still wet, and freeze them—yes! Freeze them, even in the summer! So instead of playing softball on Saturday, it was my job to unroll those frozen stiffs and iron the wrinkles out of them.

Why didn't we just dry the clothes? Because my mother said it cost too much to run the dryer. And she even defended that "truth" when she had to buy a second freezer. The small freezer on the top part of our refrigerator didn't have enough space for the frozen peas and my dad's underwear, too! So Mom bought a new upright freezer and put it in the basement, and all we kept in it were our frozen clothes.

Wash the clothes, roll them up, freeze in the wrinkles, and buy a freezer whose only purpose was to freeze the sheets? Sounded crazy to me. But hey, I was just a kid—what did I know?

Old habits die hard, and I confess that today I continue to iron some of my clothes and pillowcases, too. And yes, if the sheets come out of the dryer with too many wrinkles I give them the once-over. But ever since I moved out of my parents' home, I'm proud to say I've never ironed anyone's frozen underwear.

Porcupine Meatballs

Serves 4

1 pound ground beef
½ cup uncooked instant rice
½ cup water
⅓ cup chopped onion
1 teaspoon salt
½ teaspoon celery salt
⅛ teaspoon garlic powder
⅛ teaspoon pepper
1 (15-ounce) can tomato sauce
1 cup water
2 teaspoons Worcestershire sauce

Preheat oven to 350 degrees. Mix meat, rice, ½ cup water, onion, salts, garlic powder, and pepper. Shape mixture into meatballs. Place meatballs in ungreased baking pan. Stir remaining ingredients together and pour over meatballs.

Cover and bake for 45 minutes. Uncover and bake 15 minutes longer.

Dresses, bows in my hair, ankle socks, and patent leather shoes, I loved to get dressed up. Clothes were definitely this girl's best friend when I was growing up.

It was a blessing and a curse and it sat right smack in the middle of Main Street. Everybody knew it as the Dime Store, but it was really called The Ben Franklin Store. My mother worked there when I was a kid. Today, whenever I see an old Ben Franklin Store I have to go inside, because to me it feels like home. Truth is, if it hadn't been for the Dime Store I never would have gotten to know much about my mother.

Mom wasn't much of a talker. When she did speak up, she rarely started a sentence with "I feel . . ." But after school when I'd stop by the Dime Store to say hi, I got to see the way my mother felt about something—her job. Work was the thing Mom did best. At the Dime Store she was self-assured, very confident in her abilities. But when it was time to go home at the end of the day, I think my mother felt a bit lost and out of place in the world.

Mom started out at the Dime Store as an inexperienced part-time clerk, but by the time she left thirteen years later, my mother *was* the Dime Store, at least in my eyes. Watching my mother all those years instilled in me the confidence that I could accomplish anything if I put my mind to it. If there's a will—and Mom always had plenty—there's a way. I know, because I learned it from my mother.

My favorite memory of Mom is her in the back room of the Dime Store surrounded by stacks and stacks of pink, green, and yellow Easter grass, woven baskets, toy shovels, colored eggs, and candy. She always made up the Easter baskets for the store. I guess when you think about it, my mother was Cuba City's Easter Bunny.

The Dime Store was a blessing not only because it brought me closer to my mother, but also because it acted as Cuba City's whatever-you-needed "general store." And it was an especially great place for me to get school supplies, because I got first pick at everything before Mom put it out on display.

But the Dime Store was my worst nightmare when it came time to buy school clothes. If my mother couldn't buy something at the Dime Store, then in her mind, I didn't need it.

My mother never understood fashion; she only understood her 20 percent employee discount. If I didn't have another store's coupon that matched it, then there was no discussion—the Dime Store's striped, short-sleeved shirt tucked into an A-line cotton skirt was going to be my "chic look" for school in the fall. This all seemed perfectly logical to my mother, because she was a woman for whom nothing in her closet *ever* went out of style.

But the "A-line Dime Store look" wasn't the look I had in mind when I was thumbing through the JCPenney catalog, circling the clothes I had my heart set on wearing. And the Dime Store look certainly wasn't going to impress my friends, either. So I got a babysitting job. Because early on I'd learned the most dependable recipe for getting what I wanted—at least from my mother:

🌀 Work hard, no "ifs, ands, or buts" hard.

🌀 Earn my own money.

🌀 Mix in a little extra housework for Mom on the side; only then would she bend her Dime Store rules.

Babysitting was an easy fifty cents an hour, because the two boys I took care of just wanted to play outside with the other kids in the neighborhood. So after I fixed them lunch and did some light housekeeping for their mother, I spent the rest of the afternoon sitting in the sun with lemon juice in my hair and listening to Neil Diamond. My hair was dark brown, but I desperately wanted to be a blonde, just like Sharon, the girl who lived across the street. Sharon was the reason my boyfriend dumped me, which convinced me that blondes really do have more fun.

My mother didn't care about my boyfriend problems and she wouldn't even discuss the possibility of letting me dye my hair, even though the Dime Store sold hair color. But an article in the June issue of *Teen* magazine came to my rescue. "Brunette and want to be blonde? Sit in the sun with lemon juice in your hair and it will get lighter." But it didn't get any lighter—it just got sticky. Squeezing lemons, singing along with Neil Diamond, *Cracklin' Rosie, get on board*; and secretly wishing something awful would happen to Sharon. It was a long hot summer. But the lemons did give me another moneymaking idea.

SUSAN'S ICE COLD LEMONADE. It was a simple beginning—a card table with a sign taped to the front of it, purple and green aluminum tumblers, and fresh-squeezed lemonade. But after the first day I didn't need the table or the sign any longer, because I learned one of the ingredients of a successful business—networking.

My dad worked as a mechanic at Dellabella's, the local Buick dealership, which was practically in our backyard. The lemonade business was slow because we didn't live on a busy street, but when I took my wares over to the garage where my dad worked, suddenly business was booming. Not only did my dad buy a glass of lemonade, but all of the other mechanics bought some, too. Dad said I couldn't continue to sell lemonade at the garage unless his boss gave the okay, so I mixed up a big glass of lemonade, added a bendy straw, and offered Mr. Dellabella a free sample. By the time I left his office, I'd secured a lemonade contract for the summer. I would be the sole supplier of ice-cold lemonade (twice a week) for all of Mr. Dellabella's mechanics and even for some of his new car-buying customers.

I have only fond memories of my lemonade business. So one day when I was driving around doing errands and I noticed two young entrepreneurs standing behind their lemonade stand, I just had to stop. The girls had a real sense of style and merchandising: bright yellow lemon slices were neatly stacked in a row on a cutting board and tall slender glasses surrounded a pitcher of lemonade in a semicircle. The pitcher was there for show, to whet the appetite. The real stuff was in a cooler, hidden away underneath the fancy lace tablecloth that covered their card table. The girls were even selling "add-ons"—blueberry muffins showcased on top of a real white china plate. Two smiling faces were beaming from behind their "counter" eagerly awaiting customers. So I stopped.

"What a nice stand! How much is your lemonade?"

"Four dollars," one of the girls quickly replied and her business partner chimed in, "and the muffins are three dollars and fifty cents each."

"Four dollars for one glass of lemonade?" I was dumbfounded. *School clothes must cost more than they used to. Four dollars?* I wasn't familiar with this neighborhood, but looking around at the very expensive homes, it was obvious I'd ventured into the high-rent district. This must be the Rodeo Drive version of a lemonade stand. *Four dollars?!* I wasn't even sure I had that much cash on me. It never occurred to me that a sentimental stop at a kids' lemonade stand would send me in search of an ATM.

When I was a kid, the going rate for a glass of lemonade was ten cents plus the occasional tip. But combined with the money I earned from baby-sitting, it was enough to order some of the JCPenney clothes I'd circled in the catalog. And whatever I couldn't afford, I'd borrow from my friends, especially when I needed an outfit for the Saturday night dance.

Almost every other weekend a live band played in the Cuba City school gymnasium—pretty amazing entertainment for a town of 2,000 people. Teenagers from the surrounding small towns, like Benton, Dickeyville, and Hazel Green, came to the dance, too. So I guess that's how they were able to sell enough tickets to pay for the band. When you're a kid, you don't think about those nasty profit-and-loss concerns. Instead, I worried about important stuff, like what I was going to wear to the dance.

It always took me at least a week of trying on clothes to find the perfect outfit. Because after I tried on everything in my closet I'd look in my friends' closets, too, and that's where I found it—in Judy Gallagher's closet. It was perfect for the dance: a square-necked, sleeveless, brown and yellow polka-dotted dress shorter than anything I owned, or had ever worn. It would never pass the school knee-length-or-longer dress test—they made you get down on your knees and if the bottom of your skirt didn't touch the floor, the principal sent you home to change. But this dress was the perfect length for the dance—I would definitely get noticed.

Unfortunately I got noticed *before* the dance. Judy brought the dress over to my house so I could try it on, and that's when my mother walked by and saw us dancing in the full-length mirror.

"Just where did you get *that* dress?" My mother seemed upset.

"Oh, it's not *my* dress, it's Judy's. . . ." but in the middle of trying to explain that Judy was lending me the dress for the dance, my mother had a meltdown and pretty much went berserk right in front of Judy.

"YOU'RE NOT LEAVING THIS HOUSE IN THAT DRESS! YOU LOOK LIKE A HUSSY! WHAT PARENT IN THEIR RIGHT MIND

WOULD EVER LET THEIR DAUGHTER WEAR SUCH A SHORT DRESS?"

"Well, Judy's mother would. She let Judy wear the dress to school last Tuesday." (This was the truth, but not the whole truth. I neglected to mention that Judy was several inches shorter than me.) "Anyway, this isn't a school dress, Mom, it's a dance dress."

"TAKE IT OFF. YOU'RE NOT WEARING THAT DISGUSTING DRESS ANYWHERE—AND THAT'S FINAL!"

Well, okay, I pretty much understood what was going on now. But how do you sort things out when your mother has just embarrassed you in front of your friend, and insinuated that your friend is a "hussy" because she wore *this* dress to school last Tuesday, and that your friend's mother is one of *those* mothers, because she let her daughter wear it?

I was furious with my mother. Judy ran out the front door before I could say anything to her. Mom embarrassing me in front of my friend, and that polka-dotted dress hanging in my closet, they haunted me for the rest of the week. It wasn't fair. My mother just didn't get it. After all, it was only a dress! What harm could come from wearing a polka-dotted dress to the dance?

So instead of going out the front door when I left for the dance Saturday night, I waited until my parents were distracted and then I climbed out my attic bedroom window, onto the roof, where it was only a short jump down to the ground. I brushed myself off, walked across our backyard, crossed over Main Street, and three blocks later I was at the dance, feeling pretty cool in Judy's short polka-dotted dress. My friends and I waited in line to buy our tickets, and when I went to hand my ticket to the man by the entrance—there stood my mother!

It still makes me queasy when I think about it today. My mother didn't say a word. She didn't have to. I knew what was coming and so did my friends. They gave me a commiserating look of sympathy. *Good-bye, so long, it was a nice childhood while it lasted,* because they knew my mother, and they knew I'd probably be grounded for the rest of my life. And it felt like I was. Six weeks later, I finally got to go to another dance. Just to be safe, I wore long pants.

Every year when the first few snowflakes showed up in Cuba City, they sent another horrifying fashion signal to my mother. It was time to get out the snow pants. My mother thought snow pants were functional. My friends and I considered them an embarrassment. No self-respecting, fashion-conscious elementary school girl would wear snow pants. But my mother didn't care. She made me wear them underneath my dress when I walked to school, so my legs wouldn't get cold.

I'd reason and plead with my mother for days about why I didn't need to wear snow pants—and every year I'd lose the argument. So I always did the next best thing. I'd leave the house with the snow pants on underneath my dress, but as soon as I crossed over Main Street, once I was out of sight from our house, I'd duck behind the repair business on the corner, take off the snow pants, fold 'em up, and wedge them in between my books.

Taking off my snow pants wasn't an easy thing to do because the pants wouldn't slip over my rubber boots. So I'd have to take off my boots, then pull off my shoes, take off the snow pants, put my shoes back on, retie them, and then put my rubber boots back on. It was quite a production and when there was snow on the ground, I had to hop on one foot and then the other so my socks wouldn't get wet. I felt pretty silly, but I'd always remind myself that it was my secret. Turns out it wasn't.

Years later when I was visiting my parents for the weekend, Mom had sent me to the grocery store for a couple of things. When I was standing in the produce section I heard someone in the next aisle. "Well, hello there," she said. "You're Virginia and Ernie's girl, aren't you? I remember you, but I wouldn't expect you to remember me."

Good thing, too, because I had absolutely no idea who this woman was.

"I used to live across the street from the repair shop on Main Street," she continued. "Every morning when you were a little girl I'd watch you duck back there and hide your snow pants. You were the cutest thing."

The woman was laughing now, but I wasn't. Even though I was in my thirties, I felt like I'd just been caught.

"It was always kind of sad to see the snow start melting," she said, "because that meant pretty soon your mother wouldn't make you wear snow pants."

I laughed nervously along with her, but I also recognized a familiar tense, worried feeling in my stomach. So I asked if she'd do me a favor.

"I realize I'm all grown up now and that it shouldn't matter," I said, "but could you please not mention this story to my mother the next time you see her?"

Thankfully she agreed.

At least snow pants meant the possibility of a snow day. And whenever there was the slightest chance that a big snowstorm was headed toward Cuba City I'd get up early in the morning, even before my parents, and turn on the local radio station to hear the verdict. It was like Lotto for kids.

"And now for the local school closings," the announcer would finally say.

Okay, this was it. I was hoping, wishing. The listings were in alphabetical order, so Cuba City was always near the top, but I could hardly stand the wait. I'd be down on my knees in front of the radio, practically praying as the announcer got closer to the *C*s.

"Please say it. Come on, come on, you can do it. Let me hear it." Finally the moment I'd been waiting for!

"Cuba City Schools will be . . . *(here it comes: yeah!)* . . . starting two hours late today."

You've got to be kidding! Two crummy extra hours? That was almost worse than going to school on time. Since the bus didn't pick me up and my parents both worked, that meant I'd have to spend part of those two hours wading through snowdrifts—in those stupid snow pants. And if that wasn't bad enough, my mother always added to my misery with one of her lists: "Susan, since you'll be going to school late this morning, vacuum the living room, do the dishes, and change the sheets on the beds before you leave."

Snow or no snow, there was one of those lists waiting for me every day after school, except on Fridays. After school on Fridays I always went right to the Dime Store. And as soon as Mom got off work, we'd meet Dad at the IGA store on Main Street and the three of us would head straight for the frozen-food department. We were on a mission—hurrying to pick out our favorite Swanson TV dinners so we could get home and heat them up before *Rawhide* started.

Mom and Dad ate their dinner on folding trays in the living room with me sitting on the floor between them, balancing my crispy chicken TV dinner on my lap in front of our black-and-white console television. And as soon as the music started and the opening credits started rolling past on the screen, I'd sing along with the theme song:

Keep them doggies rollin', rawhide!

You'd be amazed how often things from my childhood, like *Rawhide*, pop into my head at the weirdest times. A few years ago, when I was in a meeting at a Fortune 500 company, I'd finished my sales presentation and the president wanted to show me a new promotional piece they'd just finished working on. He cued up the video on the big screen and when I heard the accompanying background music, instantly it reminded me of the theme song from *Rawhide*. I couldn't resist telling him about my family's Friday night date with *Rawhide*. It was obvious he was an old *Rawhide* fan—he nodded animatedly as I set the scene. And without giving it a second thought, I started singing the theme song out loud:

Rollin', rollin', rollin' . . .

To my surprise (and I think his, too), after a couple of lines, he started singing right along with me. The other executives sitting around the boardroom were staring at us like we were crazy. But the two of us kept right on singing, and driving those cows home:

Keep them doggies movin', rawhide!

P.S. Yes, I made the sale.

Whenever I go back home to visit Cuba City, one of my favorite things to do is take a walk around town. Last time I invited my husband to come along with me because I wanted to show him some of my favorite places from when I was a kid. But when we were walking the streets and alleys of my hometown, I soon realized my husband was on a different walk than I was.

When we reached my friend Judy's old house, my husband saw paint peeling, duct tape wrapped tightly around an air conditioner in the window, and front porch boards that were rotting. But that's not what the house looked like to me. No peeling paint, no broken shutters in my mind. To me the house that my old friend Judy grew up in—the house that stood before me—was neat as a pin, just the way it looked thirty-five years ago.

The lot down the street is vacant now, but there used to be swings, five in a row, their chains hanging down from tall, steel poles. See the worn spots on the ground underneath the swings? That's where I used to drag my feet. Sometimes I'd go so high in the air it felt like the swing might wrap right around the top of the pole. I'd stretch out my legs, and then pull them back with as much force as a seven-year-old could muster. I was hoping to keep the momentum going just a little bit longer—I was flying. But eventually the swing would start slowing down, and I'd drag the toes of my shoes back and forth on the ground to bring the swing to a final stop.

When my husband and I turned the corner and walked toward Main Street, we saw a commemorative train car for tourists sitting where the train tracks used to run alongside the old post office. I walked those train tracks every day on my way to school. And on the weekends I'd head in the other direction, following the tracks, past the city dump, till I got to the huge mounds of gravel and sand piled high in the middle of nowhere. The perfect place to pretend I was a secret agent.

I worked the Friday Night Fish Fry at the restaurant on the corner of Main Street when I was in junior high. The air conditioner could never keep up with the heat in the kitchen, so we'd always leave the back door open. In between washing dishes, my job was to peel the huge Idaho potatoes and put them, one at a time, in the potato slicer that was bolted on the wall. Then I'd slam the long handle down and freshly cut french fries, with a little bit of peel still left on, would fall into an old white pickle bucket. But one night I miscalculated and my finger got caught in the french-fry cutter and I had to go to the emergency room. That was the bad news. But the owner still paid me for my entire shift, which was the good news, because I was saving to buy my parents a wooden rocking chair for their anniversary. The man at the furniture store on Main Street had it on hold for me.

And walking down another street, the story continues. My husband is admiring the new supermarket, but not me—I'm climbing the old apple tree in Orville Sands's yard instead. Yes, we're walking together hand in hand, but my husband's on Main Street, and me—I'm strolling down Memory Lane.

My Favorite Blueberry Muffins

These won't cost you $3.50 apiece!

I buy fresh blueberries in season and freeze them in a good-quality freezer bag, so I have berries year-round.

Makes 12 muffins

1 cup superfine sugar
½ cup butter
1 cup milk
2 eggs
1⅓ cups all-purpose flour
2 teaspoons baking powder
¾ teaspoon cinnamon
¾ teaspoon nutmeg
½ overflowing teaspoon vanilla extract
¼ teaspoon salt
1 cup fresh blueberries or thawed frozen berries

Preheat oven to 375 degrees.

Using a mixer, cream sugar and butter on low speed until smooth. Add milk, eggs, ⅔ cup of flour, baking powder, cinnamon, nutmeg, vanilla, and salt. Mix just until thoroughly blended. Mix gently, by hand, the remaining ⅔ cup flour and the blueberries. (Batter should still be lumpy.) Fill muffin liners ⅔ full. Muffins will rise one inch. Bake 20 to 30 minutes, until golden brown. Let cool a little bit before serving. (You can double this recipe and it will turn out fine.)

Christmas Eve my parents and I would drive to Grandma and Grandpa Hale's house. Every year Santa would leave new pajamas for me under the tree. My all-time favorite, striped red-and-white jammies with a cap. Yes, I looked ridiculous for a few months, but Grandma believed in growing into things.

For longer than is easy to admit, I walked around with loose wires in my brain. While other teenagers were applying to colleges and planning their futures, I was getting drunk and looking for love in all the wrong places. Some people were quick to blame my parents; instead I used to blame myself. The truth is, Mom and Dad and I were each doing the best we knew how to do. Yes, parents are supposed to know the way, but my parents missed the day they handed out the informational brochure about *How to Love and Raise a Well-Adjusted Child*. (I'm pretty sure *their* parents were absent that day, too.) Mom and Dad didn't intentionally fall down on the job; they simply couldn't give me what they'd never experienced themselves. If they could have freely let go of their love and still survived, I believe they would have.

So where did that leave me? Trying to figure out how to write a successful recipe for my life, a better recipe than the one my parents were using. Common sense told me when you're trying to figure out how to do something better than *before*, you need to take a closer look at *before*. "Learn from your mistakes," advises the old adage, and eventually I did write a new recipe for my life, but it sure was rough going for a while. People seem to be amazed when I find the courage to tell them about the things I did when I was young—young, maybe, but old enough to know better. Some perils are so embarrassing and downright insane, even I shake my head in amazement. What was I thinking?

I don't know for sure, but I am certain I wouldn't go back and change a thing, because even my misguided choices serve me well today. Hopefully the screwed-up scenes in my life help me be less judgmental toward other people. "Why does she stay with that man when he continues to abuse her? How could she make such a stupid choice for her life?" When other folks stand back, roll their eyes and wonder, it's no mystery to me—been there, done that.

By the time I was twenty-two years old I'd already experienced a lot of life, but didn't understand it. I was married when I was sixteen—yeah, I don't know why, either, because when it was time to start walking down the aisle I remember thinking, *I don't want to do this.* But I also knew my folks had paid in advance for the pink and white daisies adorning my bridal bouquet, rented the American Legion Hall (it was a big deal for a small-town wedding), and hired a caterer and a band for the reception, so there was no turning back.

In my mother's eyes when a decision had been made, especially if it involved money, it didn't matter if it didn't quite fit. "You'll grow into it," or "You'll learn to love him," Mom explained the day she informed me I was getting married. End of discussion. My parents would kill me if I didn't go through with the wedding—especially since I was four months pregnant.

In 1971 getting pregnant meant I was asked to leave high school before I was "showing." The father, a boy a year ahead of me, got to stay in school. But not me.

It was traumatic saying good-bye to my teachers, one by one, awkwardly explaining *why*, as if they didn't already know. Of course everyone knew. You were secretly front-page news in the small town of Cuba City if you got pregnant and weren't married.

I remember the first girl who found herself "in trouble" when I was in high school. Her parents sent her away, I'm not sure where, but months later when she returned she wasn't pregnant anymore—and her family still loved her. It seemed to me that her parents must have sent their daughter away because they didn't want her to become the talk of the town any more than she already had. Sending their daughter away for a while felt like a loving thing to do, and when she returned I saw her walking down the street hand in hand with her parents. I was amazed: *How could a girl make such a huge mistake and her parents never stop loving her?*

I still don't know the answer to that question.

My parents never forgave me.

After my daughter was born I went back to finish high school, but not without "a little help from my friends." Frustrated because I couldn't get back into my clothes, a friend assured me, "No problem, try some of these." And she handed me some little white pills. My friend was right. The pounds quickly melted away, and so did the harsh feelings about myself. I was full of energy, finished high school while working part time, and even though my husband and I were young, my speed-induced euphoria convinced me we could make our marriage work, raise our daughter, and live happily ever after. But soon a stack of unpaid bills interrupted the fairy tale and I realized we weren't playing house anymore.

My husband's day job didn't pay enough to make ends meet, so I started working the graveyard shift in a factory. Punched in at 11:00 p.m. and for eight hours stood on a platform, grinding lenses for safety glasses. Eight spools lined up in a row in front of me—put a lens in each spool and take one out—kind of like a juggler spinning plates on top of those skinny poles. It was a mindless job; yet never boring. Because the graveyard shift was really a soap opera—every night a different story line—and considering my *still-wired* condition, I fit right in.

It wasn't unusual for our third-shift manager to offer someone a ride to work, or more truthfully show up at an employee's home and beg them to come to work so he wouldn't have to fire them. Refereeing marital arguments in the break room, hunting down an employee's teenager out carousing in the wee hours, the guy would do anything to make sure production numbers added up in the morning and quotas were met.

Brought up with a strong Protestant work ethic, I certainly did my part to help out. I'd fine-tuned my chemistry by then, so almost every night I met quota two hours before the end of my shift. This was my first grown-up job and from my manager's perspective, I was a shining success. So why did my life still feel so messed up?

Eventually I left the factory job and I left my husband, too. (Mother wasn't right—I didn't learn to love him.) So here I was, a nineteen-year-old single parent not receiving any child support, can't afford child care, it's freezing outside, and the heating-oil tank is empty. I applied for assistance and food stamps. This definitely was *not* a recipe worth keeping, but for a couple more years I kept repeating it anyway, including getting married again.

Of course the second marriage didn't work any better than the first. I'd just turned twenty, and after a few months of wedded bliss discovered my new prince charming was gay—but how could a girl refuse such a romantic proposal?

"Hey, maybe we should get married?"

"Okay, why not," I said, shrugging my shoulders, "it would certainly save money."

As a reader looking in, you must be wondering how this lifestyle affected my daughter. That's what I wish I had been concerned about, too. But I wasn't. I provided for my daughter, but the unfortunate reality is that a child can't raise a child.

Thank heavens, after ending my second marriage, I decided to end another bad habit in my life, too. No big epiphany—the loose wires in my brain didn't suddenly connect, so I made a conscious decision to clean up my life. Addicts don't think rationally. Instead this addict was scared clean. I nearly died a couple of times when I almost overdosed. Finally I had the good sense to send my daughter to stay with my folks, lock myself in my apartment, and not answer the door when certain "friends" knocked. For two weeks I was so sick I prayed for death. Miraculously I stayed clean after those two weeks, but horrible flashbacks haunted me for another year.

Always looking for the positive side in life, the good news about being addicted to drugs was that I qualified for free tuition in a program for recovering addicts at the local technical college. *Okay, so what did I want to be now that I was all grown-up?* Thumbing through the school's catalog, looking at career choices, I decided it might boost my self-confidence if I tried to do something I didn't know anything about. So I enrolled in the two-year auto mechanic program.

It was 1976. I didn't realize it when I signed up, but I was the first woman to ever enroll in the program, which meant I was the only female in a class of twenty-three students. The instructor, a short, stocky, ex–Marine sergeant wearing black-rimmed glasses, navy pants, and a short-sleeved maroon shirt that had his name embroidered above the front pocket, was just what I would have expected.

But I *didn't* expect what happened next. On the first day of class, as soon as the instructor entered the room he headed straight over to my desk, bent down low—his eyes locked on mine—and he announced with an in-my-face delivery, "I DON'T KNOW WHY YOU'RE HERE. I DON'T CARE WHY YOU'RE HERE. I DON'T WANT YOU HERE!" Then he walked back up to the front of the room, did an about-face, smiled, and said, "A fine good morning to the rest of you and welcome to Auto Mechanics."

For a girl who was trying to establish some self-confidence, it was a rocky start. The positive side of this life experience? Mr. Ex–Marine Sergeant's nasty little conniption motivated me to excel, because I knew it would drive him crazy. I definitely had to study more than the other shade-tree mechanics in my class, but I aced every written test and my hands-on work was outstanding, too. You should have seen my first brake job. When I took the car out for a test drive and pressed on the brake pedal—what a smooth stop. *Amazing! I actually did it!* Turned the drums, changed the brake pads, checked the master cylinder—I remember looking at the car and thinking, *This is all right, Suzanne. Maybe you're not such an idiot after all.*

Banged-up knuckles, grease stains on my hands, I was even beginning to *look* like a mechanic. But just because I could learn how to fix cars, was that really what I wanted to do for a living? Searching for guidance, my revelation appeared when the parts cleaner ate the Practically Pink polish off my freshly painted fingernails—it was definitely a sign that this wasn't the right career path for me. The only problem was if I quit before the two-year program was over, my instructor would think he had won. In his eyes I would be a failure, but deep down I knew better.

I signed up for auto mechanics to prove to myself I was a smart girl, and I'd accomplished that and more. Not only did I learn how to do a brake job, the experience made me realize that it didn't matter what anyone else thought about me. What mattered most is how I felt about myself. And ever since auto mechanics class, I've been my *own* biggest and loudest cheerleader. I'm sure when the powers that be tallied up results from the school grant program, my name was listed in the wrong category, because I left before the course was finished. It may have looked like I failed, but I was an overwhelming success. The lessons I learned in auto mechanics inspired me to try to create a new recipe for my life.

WANTED: MANAGER / FULL TIME / CHEESE STORE. BENEFITS INCLUDE HEALTH

INSURANCE, HOLIDAYS AND MEALS. APPLY IN PERSON.

I needed a job, loved cheese, was born and raised in Wisconsin, and every weekend I used to ride along when Dad drove to the cheese factory, five miles outside of Cuba City, to buy Colby Longhorn, Swiss, and Aged Cheddar Cheese—how difficult could it be to manage a cheese store?

No résumé, no experience, just sheer determination. I needed work. So I did a fast talking "sales job" when I answered the ad, persuading the owner that he needed me—and I was ready to start tomorrow.

Excited about my new career I showed up thirty minutes early the next morning, dressed to impress, in managerial attire. After filling out a W-2 and some insurance forms, the bookkeeper announced she would be training me. My first assignment: to clean the huge walk-in cheese cooler.

My new employer also owned the twenty-four-hour truck stop and restaurant adjacent to the cheese store. The bookkeeper—a plain-Jane woman in her early thirties—managed the staff at the restaurant, was smitten with the owner (even though he was married), and until I showed up felt she didn't have any competition. (Was this going to be another on-the-job soap opera?) Like it or not, I'd become part of a love triangle on my first day of work.

Cleaning the walk-in cooler on my hands and knees didn't seem like managerial training to me, but nevertheless I took off my jacket, rolled up my sleeves, and four freezing hours later, the huge walk-in cooler was sparkling clean. My suffering seemed to satisfy the bookkeeper. After that chastening, she left me alone.

Three days of managing the cheese store and it was apparent that my boss was the one who'd done a real "sales job." My impressive "manager" title was a joke, because there weren't any other employees. I was the one-and-only, which meant I was the person who opened the store at 10:00 a.m. and locked the door at 7:00 p.m. six days a week. Clerk, janitor, and soon-to-be illegal truck driver—these were the labels that accurately described my job.

When your boss asks in a hush-hush whisper if you can drive a stick, because he has a little errand for you to do . . . and you'll need to pack a bag because the errand is going to take a few days . . . and "Oh, by the way, here's a map, see the yellow highlighted route? Be sure to follow this route so you avoid weigh stations along the way." It definitely made me nervous.

Yes, I could drive a stick. It was my father's only prerequisite to my getting a driver's license. But what was the mysterious errand?

Apparently in addition to selling retail, my boss had a wholesale cheese business, too. (At least I hope it was cheese that was in the back of the covered pickup truck I drove for two days straight to a warehouse in Iowa.)

Now a rational-thinking person would have questioned, "Why the need to avoid weigh stations?" But not me—there were still too many loose wires floating around in my brain. And if I did get pulled over, "Hey, officer, it's not my *cheese* or my truck. I'm just an employee doing my job." Two long boring days of driving, it turned out to be an uneventful trip, no red lights and sirens. I delivered the "cheese" safely and thankfully my boss never asked me to do "a little errand" for him again.

Customer traffic was steady twenty-four hours a day at the truck stop and restaurant, but there wasn't enough business to keep the cheese store open. After only five months, my boss told me he was closing the store and opening a family-style restaurant in its place.

"I know how to manage a restaurant, too," quickly starting a pitch about how I used to work at my previous in-laws' supper club. (For a change, I was telling the truth.)

My first husband's parents owned a very successful supper club and Fern, my mother-in-law, treated me like a daughter. Hairdresser appointments, new clothes, mini-lectures on manners and style, Fern transformed my look and then offered me a job. Considering my new stylish appearance, it was a real shock when she announced I'd be starting in the supper club's kitchen, doing dishes. But Fern was a skilled mentor, and had a step-by-step plan in mind. After I proved myself as a dishwashing doyen, she promoted me to salads, then personally schooled me in the discriminating details of waiting tables. When those skills became second nature, my name was added to the list of waitstaff allowed to work private parties in the upstairs dining room. (Working private parties meant double the usual amount of tips I'd take home in an evening.) But the ultimate compliment was when Fern asked if I'd like to hostess and fill in for her when she was out of town.

"You could call my ex-mother-in-law for a reference," I suggested to my boss, desperately trying to avoid job hunting again. But he said for a change it sounded like I wasn't padding my credentials, that I actually *did* have restaurant experience. So he agreed I could stay on the payroll helping get the restaurant started, and then I could hostess and manage the waitstaff when it opened.

Opening night at The Farm Kitchen (the new family-style restaurant) was wildly successful—beyond anyone's expectations. "All You Can Eat, Buy One Dinner, Get One Free" was the coupon that brought 'em in. Never in my life have I seen such a turnout. When the doors opened at 5:00 p.m. we were not prepared for the crowd lined up outside, and that long line of people continued right up until closing. Our posted hours were 5:00 p.m. to 10:30 p.m., but we had to close early. We ran out of everything: linens, clean dishes, and food (even after making two trips to the grocery store down the street to supplement supplies).

Business continued to thrive at The Farm Kitchen. I was a natural in my new hostess/management position. Anything I hadn't personally experienced when I was working for Fern, apparently I'd picked up through osmosis from hanging around the supper club. As a hard worker, day and night, most of my time was spent at The Farm Kitchen. Any free time should have been spent with my daughter, but it wasn't. Instead, every night after work, I'd go out to the bar and "have a few." Fern cleaned me up so I looked like a smart girl, auto mechanics proved I was a smart girl, but when it came to my personal life, I was still a mess. No drugs, but vodka and hideous choices in men were just as lethal.

Why do some women gravitate toward bad boys and downright losers? I'm still not sure, but before I met my husband, Bob (we'll be married thirty-two years this December), that was my M.O. Put me in a room filled with men, thirty of them great guys who treat women with kindness and respect because it comes naturally, and instead of going after one of those gems, somehow I'd lock on to the three losers in the room every single time. Even if a loser wasn't interested in me, I'd keep on trying to get his attention. In fact when a man wasn't interested it made him even more desirable.

Fortunately even hooking up with a loser had its perks. Imagine every morning having someone professionally wash and style your hair, including trimming any split ends, so by the time you walk out the door your hair looks picture-perfect. No doubt about it, Alan was a big-time loser who berated me for living in the low-rent district, and for decorating the walls of my townhouse with cheap art (even though he didn't mind living in my abode rent free), but at least he was a hairdresser (unemployed, of course) and I could talk him into styling my hair every morning before I went to work. (If you dig deep enough you can find something positive in the midst of every loser.)

Losers like Alan the hairdresser had been the only guys I'd ever dated until I was introduced to the man who did the best typesetting for miles around.

One of my first assignments before The Farm Kitchen opened was to get the menu printed. My boss handed me a typed list of entrees with prices and I was supposed to figure out the artwork, choose a paper stock, and find a printer. But I didn't know anything about printing and I'd never even heard the word *typesetting* before, so the first thing I had to do was some research. Unfortunately I ended up doing "just enough" research to drive the man at the quick-print shop crazy.

"I'd like it printed on Beckett Cambric paper. The front of the menu should be a drawing of a barn, with a chicken sitting up in the loft and when the barn doors open, the menu is printed inside. Cool, huh?"

But the man just kept shaking his head. "Listen, lady, I'm a quick printer. You're talking a dye-cut and other stuff that I don't do here."

Nevertheless, I kept right on listing the little "extras" I'd like to add. "If we could? Pretty please?"

Totally frustrated, he finally pointed to a display of books on the counter. "See this book? Read it and then go see Bob Beecher, the guy who wrote it. He owns Setype, a typesetting company here in town. Beecher has patience, I'm sure he'll be happy to explain anything you want to know." Then he shooed me out the door.

The printer was right about the book. Even for a novice like me it was an easy read. But before I got around to going to Setype and meeting the owner, I had what might be described as a setback.

My latest loser boyfriend couldn't style my hair every morning, but he did own a Harley. (A Harley qualified as one of those loser perks I told you about.) When we were out for a sunny afternoon spin, even though the traffic light was shining "green-to-go," which meant we had the right of way, a man driving a convertible made an illegal turn in front of my boyfriend's Harley and we—CRASHED! My makeshift seatbelt (arms clasped tightly around my boyfriend's waist) didn't quite do the trick. Immediately following impact, my body became a human projectile. I flew through the air, landed in the front seat of the convertible, hitting the driver so forcefully that my body caused injury to his, and then I ricocheted off the driver's chest and landed on the other side of the road in the middle of the pavement. Instead of my head, the helmet I had snugly snapped in place split in half. I imagine the "Flying Suzanne" was right up there with one of Evil Knievel's early stunts, but I didn't remember any of it—didn't even remember riding in the ambulance. I was out cold.

When I finally came to in the emergency room two hours later, the only thing I could remember, and it was my biggest concern, was where I worked. "I don't know what my name is, but I do remember where I work," I told the doctor who kept asking if I knew what month it was. "Could someone call, describe what I look like, and tell them I won't be in today?"

My dedication to work has never surprised me. When I was a kid, blood would have to be gushing—in a steady stream—before my mother would let me stay home from school. And when I was feeling sick to my stomach on the first day of fourth grade, Mom insisted it was a case of first day nerves. "Tough it out," she preached. "Hopefully someday you'll have a job and you won't be able to call in sick because of every little ache and pain. So get dressed, you're going to school."

But the pain in my side continued to get worse and I kept insisting I couldn't possibly go to school. Furious, eventually my mother delivered an ultimatum: "If you're too sick to go to school, then I'm taking you to the hospital instead. How would you like me to do that?"

"I wish you would," I begged.

The emergency room intern told my mother if she'd waited thirty minutes more, my appendix would have burst.

When I finally did meet Bob the typesetter for the first time, I still looked pretty banged up from the motorcycle crash—bruises, hobbling on crutches, one leg in a cast, the other completely wrapped in an ace bandage, and I was sipping a vodka tonic to help kill the pain. My doctor's prescription had been three weeks bedrest. But The Farm Kitchen was opening soon and if I wanted to keep my job, I needed to get that menu finished.

Not only did Bob Beecher run Setype from an office in the basement of his townhouse, he also owned *Ad City,* a local Madison weekly shopper. Divorced, but granted full-time custody of his two children, Bob worked from home so that he could spend more time with his son and daughter.

Unlike the quick printer, Bob the typesetter was sympathetic to my *impossible* menu concept. He even complimented me on coming up with the idea, especially since I didn't know anything about printing. But he did agree it wasn't a job for a quick printer: "Not to worry," Bob told me. He'd make sure the menu was finished in time for the restaurant opening.

I was impressed—not only was this guy talented, he owned two businesses, took full-time responsibility for his children—and he was a handsome man. Gorgeous, really, but I could only dream. This responsible clean-cut guy was way out of my league.

"But love is blind, and lovers cannot see," wrote Shakespeare, which must account for Bob's impression of me the first day we met: "I was a single parent, working around the clock trying to run two businesses, couldn't remember the last time I'd had a date, or even left my house except to go to the grocery store—and there you were. A goddess walking into my office asking for help. It was love at first sight. You were a smart girl—I knew it right away—and you were hot!"

Hot? A banged-up woman with a crazy idea for a menu, walking on crutches, one leg in a cast, the other completely bandaged, and drinking a vodka tonic in the middle of the day when she was supposed to be working—just what was it that made me so lovable?

Bob may have thought I was hot! But he was a typical guy—he never called.

I was the one who finally called him three months later, but not about a date. I needed advice—business advice. Bob seemed like a successful businessperson and since I was a customer, I thought he might not mind.

"I'm thinking of starting my own restaurant," I told him when I phoned. "All I ever do is work, and if I'm going to work all those hours for my boss at The Farm Kitchen, I might as well be working for myself and get rich! What do you think?"

Bob told me he thought it was a great idea, and said he was really glad I called because he'd been thinking about me. But he went on to say: "I never want to discourage the entrepreneurial spirit, Suzanne. But having said that, just because you'll be working *all those hours* for yourself, it won't necessarily add up to getting rich. Sixty percent of restaurants fail in their first year and most people are undercapitalized. Do you have any money to invest in a business?"

Actually I didn't have any money, which didn't dampen my enthusiasm. Bob's either, because he pointed out a classified he'd seen in yesterday's paper: FOR LEASE: RESTAURANT, FULLY EQUIPPED, GOOD TERMS, PLENTY OF PARKING.

It was the confirmation I'd been looking for.

In my mind, opening a restaurant was merely a $2,000 gamble, the amount I figured I'd need for supplies to open the doors. I'd never asked my parents for anything, including money for college, so I was hoping they'd loan me the money. Or rather Dad would loan me the money; I knew Mom would go along with whatever he decided.

Presentation is everything. You can take a plain $3.95 tuna fish sandwich, add a little dill, and suddenly it's a $7.95 Tuna Dill Delight. And that's the presentation approach I used when I asked my father for a loan. My folks were in town visiting over the weekend. I'd decided to wait until the day before they left to ask Dad if he wanted to take a father/daughter walk through the Arboretum. I realized initially it might seem like a strange request, because Dad wasn't the "strolling" type and we never spent father/daughter time together, but I thought my chances of getting a loan were better pitched in the ambience of nature and the woods than at my kitchen table. And it worked. Dad agreed to a loan and I promised to start making payments, with interest, in four months.

The number of hours I used to work at The Farm Kitchen were nothing compared to the amount of time I spent getting my own restaurant, The Cutting Board, up and running—but at least it was going to be mine. Bob and I talked on the phone daily about my new business venture. He had a lot of good ideas and even offered to typeset my menu at no charge. We weren't dating, but nevertheless he delivered the best pickup line this single mother had ever heard. "You're going to have to put in a lot of hours at your new restaurant and I'm always here with my two kids anyway, so why don't I watch your daughter for you?"

I couldn't believe his kindness. Of course by then I realized he was interested in more than just being a business mentor, but I also knew his offer wasn't contingent on a date.

Out on a limb, the owner of a restaurant, I soon discovered that convincing other people I knew what I was doing was much easier than convincing myself. Even though I'd had plenty of experience working in a restaurant, now that I was the person responsible for everything—it was a bit overwhelming. The only thing I felt totally confident about was the food. I knew how to deliver great food.

Today's Specials: Monte Cristo Sandwich with a cup of fresh fruit; Chicken Salad sandwich with Pesto Mayonnaise and Dried Cranberries; or perhaps you'd like to try our BLT served on crusty whole grain bread, lightly toasted with a cup of Tomato Bisque Soup?

Every sandwich featured at The Cutting Board was served on a wooden cutting board alongside a huge wedge of kosher dill pickle. Real good homemade food, everything made from scratch, including gigantic cinnamon rolls from a recipe we used in my high-school home economics class.

Paying customers loved the food, and so did my employees. They carried it out the back door on a regular basis: cans of green beans, heads of lettuce, racks of ribs, whatever they could get their hands on, including stealing out of the till.

Up at five every morning getting ready for the breakfast crowd, serving lunch until two in the afternoon, washing dishes, scrubbing floors, filling ketchup bottles, adding up receipts, and then cooking tomorrow's specials, I found owning a restaurant an exhausting business. Busy, busy, busy, we were always busy, but after a year the busyness wasn't adding up to enough profit to meet payroll and pay the bills and taxes. The final financial blow came when my landlord, the local bank, blocked off The Cutting Board's entire parking lot so they could install a TYME machine (Take Your Money Everywhere), one of the first ATM machines.

"When parking isn't convenient, people drive on by." I did my best to explain this obvious rule of business to my landlord, but the bankers weren't listening. Two months later when the bank finished installing their fancy ATM machine, my parking lot repaved, including freshly painted white lines for parking spaces, it didn't matter because there weren't any cars. I couldn't recover financially from the drastic two-month drop in business, so I had to shut down The Cutting Board.

Such a sad day. Not only did I feel like a failure, I owed $10,000 to suppliers, and back taxes to the government, and I was broke. Twenty-two years old, deep in debt, I felt like I might as well hang it up, because I'd never recover from this mistake. How was I ever going to pay back so much money?

The worst part about owing so much money was that Bob and I had been married only a couple of months when I closed the restaurant, so now this debt was going to be on his credit record, too. (Obviously Bob and I did manage to find time for that first date along the way. A dinner date at the Red Lobster. We even managed to sneak in a little romance—a first kiss in the parking lot.)

But the amount of money I owed didn't seem to faze Bob; he was more concerned about my sadness. The Cutting Board was "my baby." It felt like someone in the family had died and I needed time to grieve before I could move on. Friends didn't understand, but Bob did. The day Bob found me sitting in the closet crying, with a quilt over my head, he understood and didn't say a word. He just held me tight.

I could find another job, but I was still going to have to settle with suppliers and the government. So I wrote each creditor a letter and included $5 as my first payment, apologizing for the small amount, but emphasizing they would—without fail—receive a payment on the first day of every month until the bill was paid. Five dollars wasn't much, but my intentions were honest, which must have come through in my letter, because not one single supplier charged me interest. In fact, some of them included a personal handwritten "Thanks, Suzanne" on my monthly statement. Not surprisingly, only the government caused me grief.

Instead of looking for a job, Bob and I decided we'd work together in Setype and *Ad City*. Our first executive decision as partners was to rent an office and move the businesses out of our townhouse. Granted, it was less overhead running the businesses from our home, but the downside was customers knew we were "in the office" twenty-four hours a day, seven days a week, so they thought nothing of stopping by and dropping off a typesetting job at nine o'clock at night.

Most people couldn't imagine working with their spouses, but Bob and I loved it—still do—and couldn't imagine life any other way. It's amazing that the two of us hooked up; we were such different people when we first met. Bob says he knew right away, from the minute he saw me, that I was an intelligent and creative woman. The problem was, I hadn't realized it yet. To this day, I joke that he homeschooled me, which may not sound too romantic, but when you're successful in life and you feel good about yourself, everything is better—including the romance. I guess you could say I was the dumbest girl in the room for a while, the last person to recognize the possibilities inside Suzanne.

Suzanne's Cinnamon Rolls

This recipe from my 1968 home economics class is the one I used when I owned The Cutting Board restaurant. Huge cinnamon rolls were one of my trademarks.

It's a cool-rise rapid-mix sweet dough. The neat thing about the recipe is you can start it and leave it in the refrigerator overnight. It has never failed me. Turns out perfect every single time.

5 to 6 cups all-purpose flour
2 packages active dry yeast (quick-rising is what I use)
1 cup sugar
1½ teaspoons salt
½ cup soft butter plus some for spreading
1½ cups very hot tap water
2 eggs, at room temperature
Vegetable oil
2 teaspoons cinnamon

Combine 2 cups flour, yeast, ½ cup sugar, and salt in large bowl. Stir well to blend. Stir in soft butter. Add very hot tap water to ingredients in bowl all at once. Beat with electric mixer at medium speed for 2 minutes, scraping sides of bowl occasionally.

Add eggs and 1 cup more flour. Beat with electric mixer at high speed for 1 minute or until thick and elastic, scraping sides of bowl occasionally. Stir in remaining flour gradually. Use just enough flour to make a soft dough that leaves sides of bowl. Turn out onto floured board. Round into a ball.

Divide dough into two equal portions. Knead each portion of dough 5 to 10 minutes or until dough is smooth and elastic. (I use the dough hook on my mixer, but if you don't have one, you can knead the dough by hand. Your arms will be lookin' great when you're done!) Cover each portion of dough with plastic wrap and then a towel.

Let the dough rest for 15 to 20 minutes on a board. Then punch down.

On a lightly floured surface, roll each portion of the dough into a rectangle. Spread enough softened butter over the dough to cover lightly.

In small bowl combine ½ cup sugar and the cinnamon; blend well and sprinkle over the dough. (I don't use all of the sugar mixture because I like just a taste of sweetness. But use as much as you think you'll like.)

Roll each portion of dough in a jelly-roll fashion. Pinch the edges firmly to seal seams. Cut into 1-inch individual rolls. (I use dental floss to make the cuts.) Place each roll slightly apart in two greased round pans.

Cover the top of each pan with wax or parchment paper and put the pans in the refrigerator for at least 2 hours, but not more than 48. Bake at 375 degrees until golden brown, 25 to 30 minutes.

Frosting for Cinnamon Rolls

¾ cup powdered sugar
1 tablespoon soft butter
1 to 2 tablespoons milk
¼ teaspoon pure vanilla extract

In a small bowl combine all the ingredients. Mix well. After the rolls are baked and slightly cooled, but still warm, drizzle the frosting over the top. These rolls are absolutely worth the extra work! You'll love them.

4. Pretending My Way to Success

When you're an only child like I was, pretending is your best friend. I'd pretend I had a brother and sister to play with, so I could blame it on somebody else when I got carried away with my six-shooters and broke my mother's brand-new lamp.

My husband and I loved working together. Full of great ideas and extremely intelligent, he preferred staying behind the scenes. Me, I was more outgoing, and following through on details is where I excelled. Our skills complemented each other nicely. You might say it was the perfect yin-and-yang business relationship, until we started publishing *In Business*, a regional business magazine. Then suddenly working together became a problem.

Even though my name was listed as publisher on the masthead of *In Business* magazine, when customers walked into our office and wanted to talk to the person in charge, they'd insist on speaking to my husband every single time. Of course I'd assure them I *was* the person in charge, but when you have to *convince* people you're in charge, it doesn't work—and it didn't. The snub got to be really irritating.

I wanted to be righteously angry at someone, and my husband would have been real convenient. But it really wasn't his fault; the poor guy even came to my rescue, suggesting maybe I was sending the wrong cues. Perhaps the solution was as simple as a change of clothes. My desk was the first thing customers saw when they walked into our office, so they probably assumed they were talking to the receptionist, especially since I dressed casually. Might this be causing the problem?

Mind you, this hypothesis was coming from a man who never wore anything except a T-shirt and blue jeans to work. If my husband's theory was correct, then why didn't customers assume he was the janitor? Nevertheless, my husband bought a book supporting his theory and after reading it, I agreed.

"Power dress!" the author proclaimed. "Look like you're in charge and you'll get the respect you deserve!" That's me! That's what I wanted— power and respect! So I filled my closet with new, expensive suits (cheap suits don't project power), and every morning before I headed to the office, I picked out a Dress for Success power statement. I even styled my hair in the recommended middle-of-your-ear Corporate Bob. You know what? The author was right. Black suit, complemented with a white dress shirt, pumps, topped off with a Corporate Bob, no one assumed my husband was in charge anymore. Instead, customers *insisted* on speaking to me.

Every single day for a year I'd suit up, until one morning I started to itch. It was the weirdest thing. I got out of bed, ate breakfast, brushed my teeth, opened my closet to choose the day's power suit and—instant itching. Head to toe, my entire body—scratch, scratch. There wasn't anything visible to itch. Yet day after day, for an entire week, the relentless itching drove me crazy, until finally I got the message—*I didn't want to wear a suit to work anymore.*

The first day I decided to dress *down*, instead of itching, I was worried sick my old problem would reappear. But it never did. People do treat you differently because of how you're dressed; the Dress for Success book was right. But in my case, it wasn't a change in wardrobe that made the difference. I was different. Finally I felt worthy of the title, Publisher of *In Business* magazine, and I didn't need props to prove it—even to myself.

I wish I could report a neat and tidy storybook ending—"Suzanne lived happily ever after, even in blue jeans, never again feeling the need to pretend"—but that wouldn't be true. It's hard to break old habits. The good news is I've decided I don't have to, because pretending is really a very useful skill when you think about it. No need to feel embarrassed or ashamed. The ability to pretend allows me to try new things without feeling so self-conscious in the beginning. When I look back over the careers I've tackled so far in my life, no doubt about it, I've pretended my way into every single one of them. Maybe all that pretending when I was a kid was more than simply child's play?

Secret Agent was one of my favorite television shows when I was growing up. I knew every word of the theme song by heart and I'd sing it out loud as I was zooming through the grocery store's parking lot in my own Secret Agent car. Okay, so my Secret Agent car was really a blue bicycle with two side baskets and a bell on the handlebars, but the bad guys were after me, and I was pedaling for my life.

> *There's a girl who leads a life of danger*
> *To everyone she meets, she stays a stranger.* . . .
> *Secret agent man,*
> *Secret agent man.*

Every week something new and exciting happened in the *Secret Agent* show. An agent needed to create a diversion? Pull the top off a pen and there was a fiery explosion. Pins were cameras, electric razors became transmitters, and the neighborhood Laundromat was really the heart of a counter-espionage operation. And we lived right next door to a Laundromat. (Coincidence? I think not!)

Secret Agent by night, Librarian by day.

My parents weren't big on reading, but Mom bought a lot of books, mainly the classics, because those were the books the grocery store offered every week in a special promotion. If your grocery bill totaled at least $15, then you could buy one of the classics for ninety-nine cents. So every week, when Mom came home from the market, I'd add another book to my library collection.

Can't say I ever really read any of the books—I pretended I did—but I sure was impressed with how they looked. Bound with a gray cover, each book had a brightly colored spine: pink, blue, green, red, and purple, embossed with gold-foil lettering. They made a stunning collection lined up in a row, side by side on my bookshelf. I crafted library card holder pockets out of thick construction paper and taped one in the back of each book. Then I slid one of my mother's recipe cards inside, so people could write their name on it when they checked out a book from "Susan Tindell's Library." (Tindell was my maiden name; my given name is Susan.) An OPEN sign, including library hours, hung overhead at the bottom of the steps that led up to my bedroom in the attic.

Unfortunately, because I was an only child there wasn't anyone else around to check out my library books, but that didn't stop me from recommending books, cataloging new titles, checking out books for patrons, and collecting overdue fines. It was an exhausting yet exciting job. Librarians can only dream about the endless number of people who lined up outside of Susan Tindell's Library every single day. In truth, of course, I was no more a Librarian than I was a Double Secret Agent. But I did use another one of my childhood pretending careers on my résumé later in life, and no kidding, it got me a job doing voice-overs for radio spots.

๑ ๑ ๑

Some people read in the bathroom, but not me. I did commercials. Wedged kitty-corner on the left side of the kitchen near the sink and refrigerator, the one-and-only bathroom in our house must have been an afterthought, because the door, sink, toilet, and tub were squashed so close together when you opened the door, you had to maneuver your body around it to actually get into the bathroom.

You know the phrase "Necessity is the mother of invention"? My mother was too cheap to buy a lock for our bathroom door, so it was a toss-up: Either people out in the kitchen could hear me pitching the "Guaranteed eight-hour fresh scent protection of Secret Roll-On Deodorant," or they'd open the unlocked door (assuming the bathroom was unoccupied) and catch me with my pants down.

So there was only one choice for this kid. Whenever I was sitting on the toilet I'd reach over and rummage through the vanity drawer, pull out a bottle of mouthwash, deodorant, or can of shaving cream, tilt my head to the side—ever so slightly—smile, hold up the product, look into the imaginary camera and (loudly) deliver the advertising copy from the back label using my "commercial voice." Folks in the kitchen, on the other side of the thin bathroom door, smiled and found my commercials quite amusing.

That's the problem with pretending—when you're a kid it's cute, but when you're all grown up, and a housekeeper at a Marriott hotel in Manhattan opens the door when you're not expecting it, things can get a little embarrassing.

I didn't hear her initial knock and the "Housekeeping" shout-out because I was onstage dancing in front of a full-length mirror, my Nano playing with the headset turned up high, a bottle of spring water substituting for a microphone, and in a disco fever I was swinging my hips and singing along out loud with Irene Cara's *Flashdance*.

What a feeling, bein's believin',
What a feeling. I can't have it all, now I'm dancin' for my life.

To this day I'm not certain just how long the housekeeper had stood there watching my performance (another reason to always latch the privacy lock on your hotel room door). But in the middle of my final bow, I realized I had an audience, which might have been only a minor embarrassment (because I'm really a pretty good singer), except I forgot to put the cap back on the water bottle. So as I was gracefully genuflecting, the water ran out of the bottle, down my leg, and puddled on top of the Scotchgarded carpeting. When I looked up the housekeeper was applauding.

Since I wasn't a cute, pretending ten-year-old, what was my explanation? Apparently when you're an adult, you don't need one. I can only imagine what the housekeeper said to her supervisor. "There's a nut-job in room 1412. Clean that room later!"

One of my goals in life is to be approachable. If someone walked into a room filled with strangers, I'd like to be the stranger they felt comfortable enough with to come over and talk to. Don't get the wrong idea. It's not like I'm out to save the world, and I have no desire to solve everyone's problems, but I think it brings people a lot of comfort when they feel like they're not alone. I know it does for me. And that's why I'm not afraid to admit I'm still one of the great pretenders.

I'd just finished giving a speech about "Pretending My Way to Success" to a group of librarians, when a young woman from the audience came up front to speak to me. There were tears in her eyes as she told me how relieved and amazed she felt to hear that I never went to college. "Everyone I work with has graduated from college," she said. "Most have a master's degree, but I've only graduated from high school. I always feel like everyone I work with is smarter and I worry that I'll never fit in."

I smiled and assured the young woman that it wasn't a piece of paper she needed. And then I told her this story. . . .

My husband and I used to live in Madison, Wisconsin. The University of Wisconsin is there and it has a lovely student union terrace that faces out over Lake Mendota. Frequently in the summer, live entertainment was featured on the terrace and my husband would ask if I wanted to go. I loved the idea of spending an evening sitting by the water and listening to music, but every time I went near the university's campus, I started feeling anxious and sick to my stomach.

I never let on how I felt, so my husband and I did go and sit on the terrace a few times and listen to music. But it wasn't ever a pleasant evening for me. I knew he would enjoy it and it had been such a romantic gesture that I didn't want to spoil the evening. But I just couldn't relax. Because when I looked at the people sitting around me, I felt like they were all in a different league.

I didn't have a degree. Instead I spent my college years starting a restaurant and publishing a business magazine. But then one day when a professor from the University of Wisconsin called, asking me to speak to his business class about my magazine, I realized that what I'd been looking for I wasn't going to find in school.

The problem wasn't the piece of paper—the problem was me. It took a long time to find my self-confidence. I always knew it was inside of me. Sometimes I'd come close to spending an afternoon with it, but then someone would say something that seemed to be out of my reach, and I was back to feeling unimportant in the world.

But when the professor called and asked if I would share my business experiences with his class, not only did I give a great lecture, I was finally ready to move on. I "graduated" that day. I told the young woman standing beside me in the library that "today" she'd graduated, too.

My Famous "Almost" Beef with Broccoli

I must have a real knack for pretending, because for twenty-some years I served my Beef with Broccoli recipe to family and friends and no one ever asked, "Where's the beef?" But when I shared the recipe with folks who read my daily column at DearReader.com the emails immediately started pouring in.

"Suzanne, is everything all right? I was reading your Beef with Broccoli recipe in today's column, but there isn't any beef in the recipe. Where's the beef?" So I dug through my recipe file and sure enough I found beef clearly printed at the top of my recipe card *Beef with Broccoli,* but when I read through the recipe, there wasn't any beef—what happened to the beef? And the bigger question, "Where's the beef been all these years?"

Reviewing the recipe I realized that instead of beef, I'd been making the recipe with mushrooms. It's amazing that all those years no one ever asked, "Suzanne, is this Beef with Broccoli, or Mushrooms with Broccoli?" To which I would have replied, "Of course it's Beef with Broccoli. See those mushrooms on your plate? They're a newfangled kind of beef. Vegetarian beef. They came from a cow that had a real thing for mushrooms." So where's the beef? I'm still looking. In the meantime, trust me, this is a fabulous recipe. You can call it what you want, Beef with Broccoli, or "Almost" Beef with Broccoli, and you'll have a fun story to tell at the dinner table.

This recipe serves 6, but I always double it.

1½ pounds broccoli
2 tablespoons cornstarch
2 tablespoons cold water
¼ cup vegetable oil
8 ounces mushrooms, sliced (not too thin)
1 medium onion, sliced thin
2 cloves garlic, crushed or finely chopped
½ teaspoon salt
½ cup chicken broth
2 tablespoons soy sauce

Cut broccoli into bite-sized pieces, about one inch. I don't use the stems, as they are too thick. But if you wanted to use them you could cut them lengthwise.

Mix cornstarch and water together.

Heat oil in skillet or wok until hot. Add mushrooms, onion, and garlic and cook, stirring, until tender. Remove mixture and set aside. Stir-fry broccoli with salt for 3 minutes. Stir in broth and soy sauce. Heat to boiling, then reduce heat. Cover and simmer for 6 minutes, then add the mushroom, garlic, and onion mixture that you'd set aside.

Heat to boiling and stir in cornstarch mixture. Continually stir while cooking until mixture thickens.

5. Failure That Was Good Enough

This "Best Restaurant" award hangs on my kitchen wall. A homeless woman made it for me as a thank-you for my Friday Meals for Madison program.

It's lonely at the top. Especially when you're not really on top, but everyone thinks you are. I'd been publishing *In Business* magazine for eleven years, and since it was such a highly visible company in the community, people thought I was rich and successful, but I wasn't. Far from it.

Every month the magazine was a leap of faith. One month I might make $12,000, but the next I would lose $10,000. It was a slim margin, but just enough to make me believe that by year's end, the magazine would turn a profit. But it never did. Year after year, not only did the magazine lose money, it siphoned away profits from Setype, my husband's typesetting company. But I kept hoping. The magazine was so close to profitability, so very close, that I believed if I threw myself at it, surrendering my heart and soul, how could it fail?

It was easy to fall in love with the magazine. Everything was a new learning experience for me: writing a monthly column, managing sales-people, directing an editorial staff, designing and laying out an entire publication, and enjoying the perk of being well known in the community, so I was invited to all of *the* events—which was fun and made me feel important—for a while. But soon none of those things mattered, because I couldn't pay my bills.

Imagine working Friday night, then all day and night on Saturday, get up and do it again on Sunday, and thank God Monday was a holiday, so I could work all day and night then, too, because the magazine had to go to press on Tuesday. It's more than discouraging to be working 24/7 on a magazine, especially when it's three in the morning and you know you're going to lose thousands of dollars on the issue.

Worrying about money during the day is rough, but let me tell you, it feels even scarier in the middle of the night. Drinking at least three glasses of wine had become an evening ritual. It was the only way I could stop worrying long enough to fall asleep, but not for long. At 2:00 a.m. every morning, like clockwork, I'd wake up and start worrying about money—again. Night after night it was the same routine: terror at 2:00 a.m.

Except for the night when I woke up at 2:00 a.m. and instead of feeling scared to death about how I was going to pay my bills, all I could think about was the number seven. Over and over again, the number seven superseded all of my thoughts. Pretty soon, the brazen number seven was followed by the word *Ecclesiastes*.

Seven, Ecclesiastes, seven, Ecclesiastes—pounding louder and louder. This was getting scary. It had been a long time since I'd opened a Bible, but I remembered from confirmation class that Ecclesiastes was one of the books of the Bible. Every Saturday morning for two months, beginning at 8:00 a.m. sharp, I sat in confirmation class for four hours. One of the prerequisites for being confirmed was memorizing the books of the Bible. For a "handy study aid" the minister had each of us make Books of the

Bible Hands out of construction paper. We traced around our own hands, then cut out several copies of our "hands," stapled them together, and then wrote the name of a book of the Bible on each fingertip. I remember thinking at the time it was a really stupid idea, but apparently it had longevity, because those hands were the first thing I thought about when the word *Ecclesiastes* popped into my mind at two a.m.

Seven, Ecclesiastes, seven Ecclesiastes, taking control of my mind. Maybe this was the beginning of a nervous breakdown? I could see it now—men in white coats carrying me off "for a little rest" as I muttered, "It's on the thumb of my right hand, five hands down in the stack, book number twenty-two, Ecclesiastes. Can I be confirmed now?"

I knew there was a Bible somewhere in our house, but I had no idea where. Instead of turning on a light, I switched on a flashlight. What would I say if I woke my husband up? It would be way too embarrassing. I felt stupid enough on my own rummaging around the house, in the middle of night, looking for a Bible. Obviously I was experiencing some kind of mental episode.

There it was, hidden away on the bottom bookshelf in the living room. Holy Bible Revised Standard Version, with my name engraved in gold on the white front cover. My folks had given me the Bible for a confirmation present.

So this is what stress does to a person? I sat down on the sofa, flashlight in one hand, Bible in the other, nervously looking around the room to make sure no one was watching . . . slowly I opened the Bible. *Thumb on right hand, five hands down, book number 22*, the study aid wasn't gonna help me this time, so I turned to the table of contents and there it was on page 587 in the Old Testament, *Ecclesiastes*. I found Chapter 7, took a deep breath, and started reading.

By the time I finished Chapter 7, I was crying. Nothing I'd read had solved any of my cash-flow problems, in fact I wasn't even sure what a couple of the verses meant. But for some reason I felt at peace—which was something I hadn't experienced for a very long time. I don't know how many times I reread Chapter 7, but eventually I drifted off to sleep.

The strangeness of the night felt even more bizarre in the morning. But it hadn't been a dream, because there was my Bible lying on the floor next to the sofa. I picked it up and started reading Chapter 7 again. Verses 13 and 14 were especially comforting. "Consider the work of God; who can make straight what he has made crooked? In the day of prosperity be joyful, and in the day of adversity consider; God has made the one as well as the other. . . ."

I read the chapter again in the tub when I was getting ready for work, and before I left, I announced to my husband and kids what had happened and I read Chapter 7 aloud. My family was tolerant, yet loving, saying things like "That's great, Mom," and "I'm glad you finally got a good night's sleep, dear."

I took my Bible to the office and went through the entire story again for my secretary. She was tolerant and kind. All right, so no one was as moved as I was about my 2:00 a.m. experience, but that was okay. I needed rescuing, they didn't. And over the next few months I stood on the promises I felt Ecclesiastes Chapter 7 was going to deliver. I thought for sure things would turn around and the magazine would start making money—but nothing changed. The magazine continued to lose money—lots of money—so now I was even more pissed off than before my 2:00 a.m. "experience."

So that's the way it is, huh? The Big Guy comes to my rescue, makes me feel all warm and fuzzy and confident—and for what? More of the same? You've got to be kidding!

Finally, one afternoon, alone in my car, I was yelling, "Just what the heck am I supposed to do here? I've tried everything to make this magazine profitable, I'm juggling money, paying bills on a hope and a prayer, and practically losing my mind. The stress is killing me. I wanted to sell the magazine, but no . . . you made it clear to me that it's not time to sell, that I'm supposed to keep it going. So, Big Talker—do you have any miraculous ideas about how in the hell I'm supposed to make payroll next week?"

No answer.

So I called a meeting for all of the employees from both *In Business* and my husband's typesetting business and explained the dire situation. "We've got to work together to try to solve this problem or we're going to go under." I realized there really wasn't anything more that staff could do to make the magazine profitable. Everyone was working hard. But at least the meeting alleviated a huge amount of stress, because I didn't have to pretend things were okay anymore.

The magazine's financial situation continued to worsen. Sometimes I felt it was rebelling, actually fighting back, because everything I tried to do to cut costs backfired. Printing the monthly magazine was the biggest expense, so I decided to get bids to see if I could find a better price. Line by line, I went through each company's bid comparing it to what I was currently paying, and finally I found a printer who promised to cut my printing bill by $2,000 a month. But after I made the switch to the new printer, my first bill came in $850 more than I used to pay.

How could things go from bad to worse? There wasn't much fight left in me. I pretty much gave up and took the attitude, whatever happens, happens. Two weeks later (eight months from my middle-of-the-night "experience"), I knew in my heart it was time to sell. In my eyes nothing had changed. The magazine wasn't financially any better off than it had been eight months ago, but there was no doubt in my mind, and the Big Guy was giving his stamp of approval—it was time to find a buyer. But how do you sell a magazine that's not making any money?

My CPA assured me people buy companies for all sorts of reasons that have nothing to do with money. A potential buyer would think with their expertise, they'd be able to turn the magazine around and make it profitable. Hearing the CPA's encouraging comments was a bit of a double-edged sword: *Step right up! Be my guest! If you think you can make this magazine profitable, if you think you can do a better job than me, I'd like to see you try. . . . I've poured my heart and soul into this thing . . . it won't hurt my feelings one little bit!*

But please, somebody buy this magazine.

My CPA's instructions were to focus only on the basics. "Show prospective buyers what the magazine grosses before expenses. They can figure out what their costs will be based on the suppliers they decide to use."

In other words, I didn't really have to come right out and say the magazine wasn't profitable. But it didn't seem logical, because the type of businessperson who could pay the huge asking price wasn't going to be an idiot. They'd quickly do the math. And I was right. It didn't take long for interested buyers to figure out the magazine wasn't a break-even venture.

"Yet it only takes one," my savvy CPA reminded me, and she was right. People do indeed buy businesses for all sorts of reasons other than money. The man who ended up buying *In Business* wanted instant recognition in the local business community, and instant recognition was one thing the magazine could indeed deliver.

There's an old saying in the boating industry: "The two best days of owning a boat is the day you buy it and the day you sell it." I'd have to agree those were the two best days of owning a magazine, too. When my husband and I launched *In Business*, it was truly an exciting day, and the day I sold *In Business* for over a quarter of a million dollars—enough to pay off the debt I'd accumulated, and to write a check to the government for its share of my huge windfall, with money left over to buy a house and furnish it from top to bottom—was also a glorious day.

But still it was a melancholy sale. I needed to sell, clearly it was time to let the magazine go and I felt relieved, but it also felt like I was saying good-bye to a friend, and even worse, I left feeling like a failure. In spite of the money I made at the very end, the magazine hadn't been successful. But ironically, success was the topic a businesswomen's group asked me to talk about at one of their upcoming meetings.

I didn't think about it when I agreed to do the speech, but as I was preparing my notes all I could think about was here we go again. The magazine was still misleading people, giving the impression I was rich and successful, when I wasn't. Why did I agree to give a speech about success? This was stupid. What was I going to say to these women?

I began to cry and once again the Lord came to my rescue.

"Suzanne, it makes me feel so sad to see you crying. I'm sorry you don't feel the magazine was successful, because in my eyes, it was a huge success. It did exactly what I needed it to do."

I've never quite figured out what the real agenda for *In Business* was, but I do know if publishing the magazine hadn't been such a stressful time in my life, I probably wouldn't have ever started Meals for Madison, a non-profit free meal program.

Eight of the eleven years I published the magazine, Meals for Madison was my emotional savior. It was the perfect business. (Dare I say a match made in heaven?) I was passionate about the work, there were absolutely no cash-flow worries, and at least 125 customers were lined up every Friday noon waiting patiently for me to open the door. I loved to cook and most of all, I absolutely loved to wait on people—still do. I'd rather be a server at a party than one of the guests. (Though I do admit I love having a reason to buy one of those cute little dresses that makes me think, *I'd look fabulous in that, but where would I wear it?*)

The director of the Neighborhood House Community Center (the oldest community center in Madison, Wisconsin), on South Mills Street, wanted to start serving free noon meals. It wasn't like I had a lot of extra time on my hands, but it felt like there should be something more to life than trying to make the magazine profitable, so I went to an informational meeting.

Representatives from several different local organizations were at the meeting. I've never been a group kind of person (maybe because I was an only child and I'm used to doing things by myself), so when the director announced he was looking for groups to sponsor noon meals, I raised my hand. "Put *me* down for the second Friday of every month."

But when the director asked what group I represented and I told him "Just me," he reiterated what was involved in serving a meal: Cooking, money, people, time, it was a big commitment. How did I plan on pulling it off by myself? I assured him I'd buy the food, do all of the cooking at home in my big sunny kitchen, call friends and ask them to help me serve. If need be, instead of working at the office, I'd have some of my employees help serve the meal. "Don't worry about it. I will absolutely take care of everything one Friday noon a month."

Two months later my initial once-a-month commitment had turned into creating my own nonprofit organization, Meals for Madison, and I started serving a noon meal every single Friday. Friends gladly volunteered to help, but when my employees helped serve one of the meals, seeing how much they enjoyed the experience gave me a new idea. I started offering the Meals for Madison volunteer opportunity to other companies, and soon there was a waiting list.

Sponsoring a meal involved making a cash donation to the program, usually $250, and sending eight to ten employees to help serve the meal. A cross section of the company would show up, from the president on down. I think people were so excited about the opportunity to give, because they could actually see where their money was going and they could get directly involved, without a long-term commitment.

Folks like to roll up their sleeves; there's nothing worse than showing up to volunteer and finding there aren't enough jobs to keep people busy. My volunteers got a real workout—setting up tables and chairs; covering tables with paper tablecloths, salt and pepper shakers, plates, glasses, and silverware; making coffee; organizing the buffet table; driving to pick up catered food donations from restaurants; and making deviled eggs—for most volunteers it was their first time. Oh, they'd eaten quite a few deviled eggs, but they'd never made them before. I grew up on deviled eggs, and to this day whenever I serve a big meal, deviled eggs are on the table in Grandma Hale's deviled egg dish.

The day before our free meal I'd hard-boiled 11 dozen eggs. Three volunteers would be responsible for peeling and cutting the eggs in half, mixing up the filling, thinly slicing green olives for garnish, and then topping off the filled eggs with a light sprinkle of paprika or dill weed. Corporate executives in suits and ties were smiling and giggling like little kids after they finished filling 264 deviled eggs.

One of the jobs for two volunteers was to make the "weekly Friday run." Local restaurant owners like Jim Delaney, one of my biggest supporters, encouraged me to call for a donation every week if needed. Jim would have his chef prepare the main course, another restaurant owner donated tossed salad and dressing for 125 guests, Schoeps Ice Cream company set aside three 5-gallon tubs of ice cream for pickup every Friday, bakeries made fresh dinner rolls (and sent day-old bread for our guests to take home), a paper company donated the plates, cups, silverware, and napkins, and the local dairy donated individual cartons of white and chocolate milk.

Every month I reserved a full page in *In Business* for photos of volunteers and a list of thank-yous to companies who helped sponsor a meal. No one ever refused a request. Whatever I needed for Meals for Madison suddenly appeared. I never ran short of money to buy things like huge Nesco warming pans, coffee pots, and other serving items for the program. I worked very hard, but I had a lot of fun, too. *Why couldn't it have been that way with* In Business *magazine?*

Eventually I got high-school students involved. During the school year, on the fourth Friday of the month, ten high-school students volunteered at the meal site. I'd supply the ingredients ahead of time for the main course and the students would prepare it in their home economics class. A business executive who'd fallen in love with the meal program volunteered to supervise the high-school students. Volunteering at the meal site became the "cool" thing to do. A florist donated red carnations, so every student who volunteered returned to school with a flower. Even the boys loved the flowers, because it signaled they were one of the cool kids who'd gone to the meal site that day.

I recognized the look of pride and accomplishment on volunteers' faces as they were serving the meal. Volunteers left on the same "high" that I experienced every week. One of the neatest things about the meal program was that I wasn't required to do anything except cook and serve the meal. It wasn't my job to judge, to wonder whether this person really needed a free meal or was making good choices in his life. It was my job, and my absolute pleasure, to serve a home-cooked meal and wait on guests as if I'd invited them over to my house for lunch, which, in a way, I had.

I wanted people to feel at home and they must have, because I have a handmade award hanging on my kitchen wall today. A homeless woman who regularly came to the meal made it for me.

She'd cut out words from magazines and newspapers, taped them onto a piece of typing paper, and framed it with red construction paper. "There's a warm welcome waiting for you, Great times, Relaxing Atmosphere, The Toast of Madison, Gifts from the heart, Quality taste, Dine with us and Elegant yet affordable" and with a red colored pencil she'd written the words "Neighborhood House Mills Street, BEST RESTAURANT IN MADISON." There's even a little handle at the top made from red string. At the end of one of the meals, the homeless woman stood up, said a few words of thanks, and with tears in her eyes handed me the award while everyone applauded. The feeling that must have been in that woman's heart as she was making the award is why I love to cook for people.

Hearty Chili

Invite the neighborhood! This recipe is easily doubled, tripled, quadrupled, or decupled for a crowd of 125. I put on disposable kitchen gloves and squish the tomatoes with my hands after I dump them in the pan. If your kids are helping you in the kitchen, let them do this job. They'll love it!

Serves 6

1½ pounds ground beef, browned and drained
1 medium chopped onion
1 (15-ounce) can whole kernel corn (do not drain)
1 (15-ounce) can kidney beans (drained)
2 large (28-ounce) cans whole peeled tomatoes with the juice
1 tablespoon sugar
1½ tablespoons chili powder
2 teaspoons salt
½ cup dry elbow macaroni (cooked and drained)
3 dashes Tabasco sauce

Mix all ingredients together and simmer for at least one hour. Keeps great in the refrigerator for one week, or you can freeze it.

Grandma Hale's Deviled Egg Recipe

"Just mix a little bit of mayonnaise and yellow mustard together, fill the eggs, slice some green olives, garnish each egg with a sliver of olive, and top it off with a sprinkle of paprika or dill weed." I was teaching a cooking class to home-schooled children, and that was the verbal recipe I gave to the young man who was in charge of making the deviled eggs. It was the recipe my Grandma Hale had repeated to me many times when I was helping make deviled eggs in her kitchen.

The recipe always worked for me, but fifteen minutes later when I circled back to check on my cooking student's progress, immediately I could see that something was terribly wrong. I'd never seen such a runny deviled egg filling. It had the consistency of soup. We reviewed the instructions. Yes, he mixed mayonnaise and yellow mustard (to taste) just as I'd instructed, so why was the filling so thin? But then I looked down in the wastebasket and there were twelve egg yolks. In my list of ingredients I'd forgotten to mention egg yolks, so he'd tossed those out in the trash.

I was repeating the instructions I'd heard my Grandma Hale tell me for years. Grandma never wrote her recipe down. "Suzanne, just mix a little mayo and mustard together." And that's exactly what my cooking student did.

Grandma made deviled eggs by "feel." When the filling felt right, it was time to fill the eggs. It's still how I make deviled eggs today, but I'll give you some approximate amounts to start with. There are all kinds of fancy recipe fillings for deviled eggs, but my family loves this simple approach.

12 hard-boiled eggs, cut in half
Mayonnaise
Yellow mustard
Pepper

Scoop the yolks out of the eggs and mash them with a fork. Add 3 heaping tablespoons of mayonnaise, 3 long squirts of yellow mustard, and 2 dashes of pepper.

Mix well, then wash your hands and stick your finger in the mixture. Taste it to determine what it needs—more mayonnaise or mustard, or both. The mixture should be creamy and taste good to you. Wash your hands again, mix some more, and do the finger test again, until it tastes right.

Using a teaspoon, fill each egg. Slice green olives with pimentos and stick one vertically in each egg. Lightly sprinkle paprika on top of some eggs, and dill weed on others.

6. The Boogeyman Just Might Be Under My Bed!

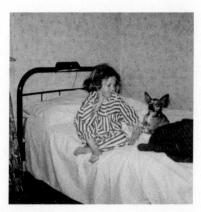

Grandma and Grandpa Hale grew popcorn, so once a year the entire guest bedroom floor would be covered with rows and rows of popcorn cobs drying on top of newspapers, which was pretty exciting for a kid, except at night when I had to tip-toe through the popcorn to get to the bathroom.

Fear comes over me a lot easier than it used to. Maybe it's becase I've been around for a while, been down too many roads, know too much, and experienced too many things—had my mother die in my arms. It changes you.

I never used to give things a second thought. If I got an idea and thought it was worth pursuing, I did. There wasn't any consideration for how it would change my life or that I might not succeed. It might not have been the best approach to take, but it was my style and I was comfortable with it. But lately my style has changed. I seem to be more cautious. Looking in from the outside, you'd think a more cautious attitude might bring me a sense of security—but it hasn't. Instead it's made me more uncomfortable with myself and taken away a lot of my joy.

My husband and I go for a walk every day and as we're strolling through the neighborhood, it's not unusual for us to start brainstorming about new ideas. Back and forth, his idea, my idea—we've done it for years. It's always been "play" for us. But the other day when my husband started talking about a new business idea, I noticed that listening to him was making me uncomfortable—actually quite irritated. I could hardly wait for him to pause so I could blurt out a list of reasons why his idea was dumb and we certainly didn't want to do it. But that's not the way we've always played the brainstorming game. So what was up with me? And in the midst of trying to figure out why I wasn't willing to entertain new ideas, even just for fun, I realized that fear was the problem.

Okay, so what exactly was I afraid of, and why was this fear showing up all of a sudden? I wasn't sure. Maybe I was afraid to entertain any new ideas just in case one of them became a reality. But that never used to stop me; sorting and sifting through different ways of looking at things, it's always been part of the joy in my life.

Thankfully, sometimes recognizing I'm afraid of something, even if I can't figure out *why,* is enough to conquer the fear, and that's what happened this time. When my husband and I went for our morning walk the following day, we both enjoyed playing the brainstorming game again.

I don't know about you, but the boogeyman does in fact hang out underneath my bed, especially at three in the morning. One of my favorite books suggests you should feel the fear and do it anyway, and I'd have to say that's usually the choice I make. But when fear strikes and I'm in the middle of a big "showdown," I'm hyperventilating, curled up in the fetal position, and clinging to my pillow while desperately trying to talk myself out of an anxiety attack.

The problem with fear, at least my kind of fear, is that it's difficult to label. Most of the time there isn't a rational explanation for it. Most of the time my fear is all wrapped up in a lack of self-confidence. People think *I can*, I've told them *I can*, but I'm afraid *I can't. Oh no, what have I done? What was I thinking? If I can't make this happen, I'll be ruined.* Lack of self-confidence has always been my boogeyman and probably always will be.

My first inclination is to joke about my lack of self-confidence and put a lighthearted twist on it. A friend even chided me when I mentioned I was going to write about it. "Talking about a lack of self-esteem—it's old news, Suzanne—been written to death and no one wants to read about it anymore."

I felt hurt. Here I was telling the truth, putting my lack of self-confidence out there for him to see and what does he do? Tells me it's unimportant, I'm being a big baby, and it would be embarrassing to write about such a thing.

Well, I'm here to tell you (and him) the subject is alive and well in my life. Questioning my abilities, talking myself out of feeling like a loser, these are conversations I know by heart—both sides. The boogeyman doesn't even have to actually say anything to taunt me, I do that job myself. *Suzanne, you're not talented, you're a big loser, people think you're strange, crowds of people are snickering behind your back, every other writer is in, but you're out.* The list could go on for hours and, unfortunately, some days it does, until even I have had enough—*for heaven's sake, Suzanne, give it a rest.* I get upset and angry with myself—and that's when the "magic" happens. Because in my weakness I find my strength. Get me angry and I come out fighting. Not fisticuffs, but with just enough feistiness to protect my feelings and in the process, I decide *I'll show 'em I can accomplish great things,* and so I do.

Sun Tzu, in *The Art of War*, said, "If you know the enemy and know yourself you need not fear the results of a hundred battles."

Years ago I decided that if I was going to spend so much time worrying and fearing the worst, I might as well use the boogeyman's visits to my advantage. So I got to know the enemy and here's what I discovered.

Sometimes fear is simply a holding pattern. I know what I need to do, I really want to do it, but I'm still trying to muster up the courage. So even though I feel afraid, I remind myself nothing bad is going to happen, I'm simply circling the airport and killing time, until the clouds clear and it feels safe to land. When I finally decide I can deal with the consequences of my decision—no matter how things turn out—the fear subsides.

Eleven years ago I found myself in one of those holding patterns when I was trying to find the courage to write a letter to my parents. My folks and I never had a loving relationship. Truth is, they never really liked me all that much, and when I got pregnant at sixteen—that was it for them. Embarrassed and ashamed, they couldn't ever bring themselves to forgive me. Even when I was an adult, raising my own children, my father continued to joke about my getting pregnant in high school.

I guess I watched too many episodes of *Leave It to Beaver* because I never gave up on the idea of having a meaningful and caring relationship with my parents. We were all adults now, why couldn't we at least be good friends? It took three years to find the courage to write the letter to my folks and then it took another six months before I found the courage to mail it. When I finally decided to mail the letter, I felt pretty calm and confident about my decision, until I got to the post office and was standing in front of the mailbox. Then reality set in and I fell apart.

Shaking and trying but failing not to cry in public, I stood in front of the mailbox, staring at it—for a very long time. When I finally pulled back the handle so I could drop the letter in the box, I couldn't let go of it. I couldn't release my grip. *Oh my God, if I send this letter, my parents will probably never talk to me again.* But I also couldn't go on with the way things were. Eventually I let go. Sending that letter was the beginning of a new relationship with my parents (even though they quit speaking to me after they read it) because I had conquered my fear.

Fear is one of my loudest emotions. It's one of the best ways to get my attention, sometimes the only way. *Tap, tap, tap, stay with this idea, Suzanne, don't let go of it, even though it seems crazy and makes you feel uncomfortable.*

I'd spent the afternoon at the beach reading the book *Girls in Trouble* by Caroline Leavitt. It's a story about Sara, a sixteen-year-old who's pregnant and decides to give her baby up for adoption. Reading the book was dredging up some pretty powerful emotions that I hadn't felt in a long time. I wanted to stay at the beach and finish the book, but it was getting late, so I packed up and headed home. But I couldn't get Sara out of my mind. I pulled the car over to the side of the road, grabbed the book, and started reading. Pretty soon I was crying and the next thing I knew I had an overwhelming need to call the author.

I didn't really know Caroline Leavitt. We'd been introduced through a friend of a friend and that's why she'd sent me a copy of *Girls in Trouble*. But her phone number was printed on the bottom of the note card she'd tucked inside the book, and the next thing I knew my fingers were dialing and the line was ringing on the other end. Voice mail picked up and after the beep, in between some pretty loud sobbing, I left an emotional message about how I was pregnant at sixteen, how I could relate to Sara's feelings, and that until I'd started reading her book, I didn't realize all of this was still tucked away inside of me. But then immediately after I said good-bye and hung up the phone, fear consumed me.

Are you nuts, Suzanne? What is this woman going to think? You don't even really know her and you leave a crying, blubbering message about how you can relate to Sara, a fictional character in her book. Panicked and embarrassed. The edgy nervous fear that prompted me to call the author in the first place had turned on me. Now it was a scary *You're going to look like a fool* kind of terror.

But thankfully, in the midst of fear, most of the time there's something good waiting for me. Thirty minutes later when Caroline Leavitt phoned back, *she* was crying and thanking me. "Suzanne, your call meant more to me than you'll ever know."

Fear likes to travel, is content to fly coach, and went along with me to St. Louis when I attended a sales seminar. One of my duties when I was publishing *In Business* magazine was to manage the salespeople. The magazine basically had two major areas, editorial and sales. I'd never had any sales training, except for what I'd read in books, so I signed up for a weeklong intensive "how-to-sell" training seminar. It was an expensive seminar, and the sales pitch in the brochure suggested that if you weren't serious about studying and working hard in class, then this wasn't the seminar for you.

The copywriter wasn't kidding. Two days after I signed up, textbooks and a workbook along with my first assignment arrived at my door via FedEx. The next morning the seminar facilitator was on the phone, checking to make sure I received the books and reminding me that even though I wasn't in St. Louis yet, the class was starting now. My first written assignment would be due immediately when I arrived in St. Louis. If I had questions there was a number where I could reach him and he would call at the end of the week to check in and see how I was doing. I was nervous, but excited.

It never dawned on me to ask who the other participants were, or if there would be other people like me in the class who didn't have any sales experience. The thought never even crossed my mind until I arrived at my hotel. Sitting on top of the desk, in my suite, was a welcoming letter from the seminar instructor, another assignment to be completed by morning, and a complete list of seminar attendees, including their company and job title.

Gasp! I thought I was going die. Oh my God, I'd done it again. I'm always crawling out on a limb, trying things I don't know anything about, assuming I can fake it until I learn more about it, but I was in way over my head this time. The list of names included Pepsi, General Motors, Johnson & Johnson, Kraft, Allstate, and Pfizer—every single person was from a

Fortune 500 company except me. And their titles were equally intimidating: National Account Manager, Regional Sales Director, Field Sales Manager, Global Account Manager, Director of Business Development, and then there was me, Suzanne Beecher, owner of *In Business* magazine.

These people all had sales experience—years and years of sales experience. They were here to polish their skills. These were the people who taught other people in their companies how to sell. Me, I was here to learn how to sell something other than lemonade and Girl Scout cookies (even though I was always one of the top two cookie sellers).

Options, what were my options? Keep my bags packed, feign an illness and head back home, or go to class in the morning and if after an hour it became apparent I was the dumbest person in the room, feign an illness, pack my bags, and head back home. I decided to wait and see how I felt in the morning, so I made sure my assignment was finished, just in case.

My wake-up call didn't wake me up; it just reminded me that I was already awake. I'd been up all night worrying and in a state of terror playing out scenarios in my mind of what might happen if I went to class. At the end of every single scene I ended up looking like a fool, but nevertheless I decided to get dressed and give Day One a try.

What do you wear to a training seminar? Do Fortune 500 types wear suits, or khakis and sport shirts? What would the only other woman in the class be wearing? (The only other woman's title was Executive Director of Specialized Sales.) I decided to wear a suit. My theory on clothes is it's better to be overdressed than underdressed. Besides, if I had a suit on I'd feel like someone more important than Suzanne Beecher, owner of *In Business* magazine.

I made sure to arrive exactly five minutes before class was scheduled to start, because I wanted to avoid having to talk to anyone. The plan was to take my seat, smile (try not to throw up), and just listen. People would assume I was the quiet type. But our facilitator had other plans. "Let's get to know each other—we'll go around the room. Tell us your name, what company you're from, what your position is, and what you hope to learn at this seminar. Ms. Beecher, how about if we start with you?"

Suddenly all eyes were on me and my suit. (I was the only one in the room wearing one.) Two distinct dialogues were playing in my head. The louder one, a desperate last-ditch plea: "Please, please, get me through this and I promise I'll never ask for anything again, I'll write a check to charity immediately when I get home, I'll never skip Sunday service again, and I'll never, ever tell another lie." And the other, the one for public viewing, which I managed to adequately deliver: "Hello, I'm Suzanne Beecher, I own a business magazine in Madison, Wisconsin, and I'm here to enhance my sales skills."

After introductions, we discussed our homework assignments. To my surprise I even raised my hand twice to offer comments. An hour into the class when I looked around the room, I realized I had nothing to fear. I didn't have as much experience as the other people in the room, but I was one smart girl and I was going to hold my own just fine.

Just as in St. Louis, the boogeyman doesn't always win the battle, because I've learned a lot about my enemy and the key is preparing ahead of time. Kind of like the fire drills we used to do in school, I need to practice when the building isn't actually on fire. I can't stop my mind from playing a fear-and-worry tape unless I've prepared a plan of attack in advance.

One of my simplest solutions is saying this sentence out loud: "Somebody should have told me about this when I was a kid, but they didn't." The sentence doesn't necessarily have anything to do with what I'm afraid of, but the reason it stops my worrying cycle is because I've rehearsed it ahead of time and assigned it the job of interrupting fearful thinking.

Frankly, somebody *should have* told me about a lot of things when I was a kid—I probably wouldn't be such a nutcase as an adult. But then again, I've never minded being a little strange, because as Leonard Cohen so mindfully wrote in one of his songs, "There's a crack in everything. That's how the light gets in."

It's a quote I keep close to my heart, because it gives me a sense of contentment and always makes me smile. I feel proud of myself every time I think about it. Proud because I'm a little bit strange and I run with it. There are a lot of little wacky, off-balance things in my personality and sometimes I consider chasing them away. I get concerned that someone else might think they're a little too strange. But then Leonard Cohen's words remind me, that even though some people might consider the peculiar parts of Suzanne, "cracks" in my personality, those cracks are how the light gets in. And in my case that light makes me creative, and (I think) a pretty interesting person. So I try not to waste too much time worrying about being different. Instead, I remind myself it's quite all right, because that's how the "good stuff" gets in.

And the good stuff is meant to be shared. Every now and then, I get nervous that maybe I've shared too much with people. Maybe I've stepped over some final line? I guess I really don't know if there are unspoken limits. But I do know that it's easy to cut yourself off before you get to the "good stuff." People do it every day. They stop short before they embrace the words that might make them cry, or give them a reprieve from a burden they've been carrying far too long.

But I've discovered that when the words get stuck in my throat, or bring tears to my eyes, those are the very words—the "good stuff"—that I so desperately need to share and someone else needs to hear. My belief is that folks should talk about what they're afraid of, so I do. Step right up, take a deep breath, and tell somebody what's on your mind and in your heart. You may find yourself thinking, *Oh no, I've let them see the real me. What happens now?*

I don't know for certain what will happen to you, but I assure you nothing bad has happened yet to me. Going through life with things unsaid, or dreams interrupted because of fear, is not the way it was meant to be.

So go ahead. Wrap your arms around the "good stuff."

Suzanne's Beef Stew

Beef stew is good stuff for my tummy. It's one of my comfort foods. A big bowl of stew with crusty bread makes me feel like I'm snuggled underneath a big quilt, there's a fire burning in the fireplace, and all is right with the world.

1½ pounds beef roast, cut into ½-inch pieces or boneless stewing meat (I used to think you had to buy meat the way it was prepackaged at the supermarket, but if you ask, the butcher will cut the meat for you).

1 tablespoon shortening
1½ cups water
1 can condensed beef broth (10½-ounce size)
⅛ teaspoon pepper
Dashes of savory, thyme, and garlic powder
2 large potatoes cut into 1½-inch pieces
3 carrots, 1 medium onion, and 2 stalks celery, each cut into 1-inch pieces
1 teaspoon salt
1 bay leaf
½ cup cold water
2 tablespoons all-purpose flour

Cook beef in shortening in a Dutch oven until brown, 12 to 15 minutes. Add 1½ cups water, the broth, pepper, and other seasonings. Heat to boiling, then reduce heat, cover, and simmer until beef is tender, 2 to 2½ hours.

Add potatoes, carrots, onion, celery, salt, and bay leaf. Heat to boiling, then reduce heat, cover, and simmer until veggies are tender, usually about 30 minutes.

Shake ½ cup cold water and the flour in a tightly covered container, or put in a Ziploc bag, seal tightly. Gradually stir into beef mixture. Heat to boiling, stirring constantly. Boil and stir a couple of minutes until stew is thickened. Remove bay leaf. Serve with crusty bread. This stew keeps great in the refrigerator for one week.

Is it easier to iron clothes when they're frozen? I put my mother's theory to the test and even used some of the same old pillowcases I ironed when I was a kid. Mom was right, it is easier to iron frozen clothes—but I think I'll continue to use the dryer.

Fancy hankies, crocheted pillowcases, photos, and a china cabinet . . . these are some of the mementos I've kept to remind me of my mother and grandmother, now that they're gone. They're nice things, but I've always been a little disappointed that there wasn't some ancestral secret or ritual shared by the women in our family. Grandma would have told my mother, and before she died, my mother would have whispered it to me, and I'd pass it along to my daughter, and my daughter would tell her daughter, and on and on it would travel down through generations.

I realize it's a bit of a fairy-tale longing, but I think about these things when I hear other women describing "women only" family trips to the pyramids, or how every bride in the family carried great-great-great-grandma's hanky when they walked down the aisle, or how the girls get together every year to cook the old family recipes that have been handed down since the days when their ancestors crossed the Rocky Mountains in a covered wagon. (Okay, I may be exaggerating just a bit. But you get the idea.)

Unfortunately my mother never revealed any such profound rituals. Yet after she died I did discover two well-worn 5 x 7 cards in her recipe box that I think were conveying an *unspoken,* passed-down-from-mother-to-daughter tradition.

The cards had almost identical poems written on them. The only difference was that one had Virginia Tindell, my mother's name, inserted in the poetry, and the other had Lillian Hale, my grandmother's name. My Grandma Hale appeared to be the original author of the poem (I recognized her handwriting) and at one time, both my mother and grandmother carried a copy in their purse.

Granted, the poem doesn't rank up there with the sacrosanct family traditions of years gone by, but we've always been a meat 'n' potatoes pass-the-ketchup kind of family anyway. So I'm going to proudly pick up the torch and type up my own copy this afternoon.

Here is the family legacy that Grandma gave my mother and now my mother has passed on posthumously to me:

> Steal not this purse, for fear of shame,
> for ~~Virginia Tindell~~ Suzanne Beecher is not your name.
>
> And when you die, the Lord will say,
> where is that purse you stole that day?
>
> And if you say, I do not know,
> the Lord will say, step down below.

Yes, it's corny, silly humor discovered in my mother's recipe box, but sometimes a little bit of silliness is the recipe I need to get me through the day. The following are some of my favorite "in-a-pickle" (as Grandma Hale used to say) situations. Stories I like to reread on days when life gets too serious and I need to lighten up. I hope you enjoy them. Don't worry about laughing *at* me; I know you're laughing *with* me.

Vanity Checks

I get myself into some bizarre situations, and yesterday was a doozy. I'd eaten a chicken salad sandwich right before I left for an appointment. Thank heavens I decided to do a vanity check in my rearview mirror, because there was a hunk of chicken salad stuck between my front teeth.

The light changed and I had to flow with the traffic, but my mind was on that chicken salad. It's not as if anyone could see it, but I knew it was there, and I'm the best person to drive myself crazy. And I did. I usually have floss in the glove compartment, but there wasn't any. I checked.

So—being the ingenious troubleshooter that I am—I started taking inventory. What did I have close at hand that could flush out this piece of chicken salad? An earring. A pearl chandelier pierced earring . . . now that would do the trick, and I just happened to be wearing a pair.

I know it's not recommended, but I can drive and do other tasks—like putting on lipstick—so taking off one earring and sticking the end of it between my teeth was an easy assignment. The chicken salad problem was quickly remedied. But now I had a different problem. For the life of me, I couldn't get that earring out from between my teeth.

The traffic was getting heavier. I had to keep both hands on the wheel, and now I was driving down the road with an earring hanging between my front teeth. I knew I wouldn't be able to do anything about it until I hit the next long red light. The best I could hope for was that the person in the car next to me would be a teenager—with their own piercings—who'd merely think I was starting a new trend. Thankfully the lights were green all the way.

⑤   ⑤   ⑤

The Dreaded White Smear

Dressed for success, right before I walked into a meeting, I looked down and saw the dreaded "white smear" on the front of my black suit jacket. If you have no idea of what I'm talking about, consider yourself one of the lucky ones and please email me—immediately—and let me know what brand of deodorant you use, because I'm fed up with mine.

The main color in my wardrobe is black, so you can see that I'm not kidding about what a serious problem this has become. I have three different brands of deodorant in my drawer, each claiming "36 Hours of Power—glides on clear, with no white residue." Well, I'd be okay with only eight hours of power before I had to redo my armpits, if they would just get rid of the white residue.

I know the so-called secret to avoiding the white smear and yes, I did put my deodorant on *after* I got dressed. But something still went terribly wrong when I put my suit coat on.

Maybe this white residue thing is actually a marketing plot so I use up my deodorant faster. I fear the white smear on my clothing . . . the thought of it makes me start to sweat . . . I apply more deodorant, but now I start sweating again, worrying about the white stuff . . . so I apply more deodorant . . . I start worrying . . .

Suzanne's Hurricane Checklist

Mother said I should always tell the truth and perhaps today is one of those times when a little white lie would make for more respectable reading material. But I was sick for over two weeks with a horrible virus and truthfully, blowing my nose was the major activity of every day. There's an art to blowing your nose. I've become an expert and I feel a responsibility to pass on to others the things I've learned.

Mother taught me to share, too!

It started out with a sniffle, a dainty event—my grandmother's lace hankie would have sufficed. But midway through the virus, I had to pull out the big artillery—a man-sized tissue in one hand and the other hand firmly braced against a wall, a car, or the person next to me—whatever was handy at the moment, because my nose blowing had now reached wind speeds high enough to be classified as a Category one hurricane, according to the Saffir-Simpson Scale.

Beauford (every hurricane has a name) was scary. The noise was deafening, long and loud hair-raising honks, grab another tissue, and come up for air. It was never ending. How could anyone produce such great quantities? A big blow from Beauford and my three cats and even my husband hid under the bed. When I ventured out to stock up on supplies, children screamed and ran from me in horror, but nevertheless, I needed to be prepared.

Getting ready to tackle Beauford was a lot like getting ready for the "big one" in hurricane season here in Florida, where I live. The two have many things in common.

⑤ Stock up on tissues and chicken soup (I'm not kidding, my doctor wrote on his prescription pad the name of a restaurant that had great take-out chicken soup with matzo balls).

⑤ Blow out gentle puffs, but cover your windows with sturdy ⅝-inch-thick sheets of plywood, so you're ready if the big one comes.

⑤ Keep your mouth slightly open when it's time for the big blow to prevent damage to your eardrums, and store loose items so they won't blow away.

⑤ Secure valuables and remove your jewelry to avoid possible damage and injury.

- ⑤ Take a deep breath (through your mouth) before you blow your nose, so you don't black out.
- ⑤ Put important documents in waterproof containers.
- ⑤ Use tissues—not washable handkerchiefs—and have plenty of big, sturdy trash bags to haul away the man-sized debris.
- ⑤ Have hand tools ready for after the "storm"—screwdrivers, a shovel, and a pickax to loosen any tough clogs.
- ⑤ When you hear the all-clear siren, it's time to clean up—wipe your nose to make sure nothing else is hanging around.

Boastful Behinds

It's always a compliment when someone asks for my business advice. So I was delighted when Mary, an employee of mine, brought her son into the office the other day. He wants to start his own business and she thought it would be helpful if he told me about his idea.

I could tell Mary had "talked me up" as a business expert, someone he should be sure to consult, and I didn't want to disappoint. So I was doing my best to deliver "the goods." I have to admit that this puffed-up, fifty-five-year-old woman was enjoying offering tips and personal experiences. And I think I was pretty impressive, too—until I got up out of my chair.

Do you point out to someone that she has a piece of lettuce clinging to her front tooth? Should you bring it to a gentleman's attention that he may have forgotten to zip up? Toilet paper stuck to your boss's shoe—do you broach the subject or leave it alone? Tricky judgment calls, for sure.

But Mary made the judgment call, and politely pointed out to me, as I was retrieving one of my favorite books to give to her son, that I was carrying unwanted accessories. A lint roller was stuck to my butt. I'm here to tell you, it's pretty tough to impress someone with your wisdom when you have a lint roller attached to your derriere. You tend to lose credibility.

I bring all three of my cats into the office with me, so I keep a lot of lint rollers handy.

Maybe a little too handy?

Misbehaving Appliances

Three weeks ago my husband bought a new microwave—one that has an attitude. Or maybe it just doesn't like short blonde women who like to read. I don't know. I really don't care anymore. I just want to find a way to call a truce. Is it too much to expect that when I hit the START button the microwave will actually turn on?

It works fine for my husband. When he pushes the START button, the microwave does its thing. When I push it, and push it, and push it . . . I can push that START button twenty-five times in a row, and still, nothing happens. I had a hard time convincing my husband that the microwave was refusing to cooperate. But after a few demonstrations, he's now a believer.

I believe there's good in every person and in every home appliance, so when no one was around the other day, I had a heart-to-heart with the new microwave. Understanding is the first step, you know.

"Did you have a troubled childhood? Maybe you come from a big family and got stuck with hand-me-down secondhand parts?"

"Do you have low self-esteem? Parents didn't give you enough attention? How does that make you feel?"

"The box you came in was retaped, did someone return you and now you feel rejected?"

"I'm listening."

"But do you think we could wrap this session up in thirty minutes? I'd really like to warm up my coffee."

⑤　　⑤　　⑤

Whistle While You Work

My toilet whistles at me. It's kind of a sly little "Yoo-hoo! Come hither!" sort of whistle. This is a new thing for me and my toilet. Our past propinquity has been the customary toilet/owner relationship. We keep each other clean and tidy.

Don't get me wrong—I applaud creativity. So at first, a whistling toilet was actually quite amusing. I was even a little boastful, thinking I probably had the most entertaining toilet on the block. Why, my toilet whistles every time I flush! It even puckers up in the middle of the night for no apparent reason. But now this whistling thing is beginning to get a little irritating.

You know how a joke is hilarious the first time out, still funny the second go-around, but after three times, the punch line just doesn't do it for you anymore? Well, my toilet has whistled one too many tunes.

I asked friends if they had any ideas about how to solve the whistling toilet mystery, but they were only amused. "Why does your toilet whistle, Suzanne? Maybe it wants to play 'Name That Tune'? Maybe it thinks you have a cute butt."

Okay, it's time to call a professional.

"Joe's Plumbing. Can I help you? . . . Why does your toilet whistle? . . . Well, maybe it thinks you've got a cute—"

Yeah, yeah, I've heard that one before.

Suzanne's Whoops! Banana Bread

When I was young I spent a lot of time in Grandma Hale's kitchen. Every now and then I'd hear her say, "Hmm, I guess I'm in-a-pickle," which meant Grandma just realized she goofed when she was mixing up a recipe and it was too late to go back and fix her mistake.

Frequently I find myself in-a-pickle when I'm cooking, too. The phone rang and then a FedEx delivery showed up at my door. Even though I'd made my banana bread recipe a hundred times before—"Whoops!"—I put way too much buttermilk and a little too much baking powder in the batter, but there was no turning back now. So I popped the banana bread into the oven. And guess what? I ended up with the best-tasting banana bread I'd ever made. Of course, then the challenge was to try and figure out exactly what I did wrong. After a couple of trial-and-error attempts, I did, and here is the incredibly tasty result. . . . It keeps great in the refrigerator, too!

Makes one loaf

1¼ cups mashed very ripe bananas (the riper or browner the bananas are,
    the better the bread will taste)
2½ cups all-purpose flour
1¼ cups buttermilk
½ cup granulated sugar
½ cup packed brown sugar
¼ cup vegetable shortening
2 eggs
3 teaspoons baking powder
1 teaspoon salt
½ teaspoon baking soda
½ cup (overflowing) chopped walnuts
½ cup chocolate chips

Preheat oven to 350 degrees. Grease bottom only of either a 9 x 5 x 3-inch loaf pan or four small mini pans. Beat all ingredients together, scraping bowl, just until blended. Pour into pan(s). Say "Whoops!" before you pop it in the oven and 50 to 60 minutes later, if you're baking one loaf, or 35 minutes for four smaller loaves, you'll be biting into a tasty, moist slice of banana bread.

Be sure to bake until a wooden toothpick comes out clean when inserted in the center. Immediately remove the bread from the pans after you take them out of the oven. And you really should cool the bread on a wire rack before you slice into it, but that never happens at my house.

8. A Not-So-Perfect Piecrust

Amy's last birthday. My son Brian and I baked a chocolate cake.

Learning how to make a piecrust has been one of my finest accomplishments in life, even though my piecrusts never end up looking like the photo in the cookbook. But that's fine with me, because my not-so-perfect piecrusts have taught me a lot about life. In fact, when I learned how to roll a piecrust, my life was less than perfect. Actually, it was falling apart.

Shortly after I sold *In Business* magazine I was diagnosed with benign essential blepharospasm, a rare disorder that affects your nervous system and makes it practically impossible to keep your eyelids open. Not being able to keep your eyelids open may not sound like a big deal, but if you can't see where you're going, frequently you bump into open doors and walk off front porch stoops. Life got pretty scary when a specialist at the Mayo Clinic handed me a red-and-white cane. "Most people who come to see me are so old they're thrilled when I tell them they won't die from this disorder, but you're only thirty-four."

"No problem," I assured the doctor. "At least I finally know what's wrong with me. I'm tough, been through a lot of difficult stuff in my life already—I can handle this."

Determined to win the war, my *I'm tough* battle cry kept me going strong for a few weeks, but then the conflict intensified. Not only did I have to learn how to get around using a red-and-white cane, the muscles surrounding my eyes were contracting so forcefully the pain became unbearable. Terrified, I hunkered down and switched gears. *Things could be much worse, Suzanne, some people have no arms and no legs. You can do this!*

But then one morning I woke up and realized the truth. I didn't give a crap if some people didn't have arms and legs—too bad for them. This was me and this wasn't fair. I was furious. How could I possibly live this way the rest of my life?

For a while crying was a daily release, but then one day my crying turned to such violent sobbing, I was afraid if I let myself continue I might never stop. Maybe I would step over some line and wouldn't ever be able to bring myself back? Maybe this is what happens right before someone loses their mind?

Day after day, I lay on the sofa in our sunroom listening to books on tape from the Library for the Blind. A mother bluebird building her nest on our back deck kept me company. It felt like such a miserable existence, how was I going to get my life back?

Eventually my husband took charge. "Get dressed, we're going to church." I must have been some kind of mess, because my husband hadn't set foot in a church since college (something about the war and being upset with the Catholic Church). We drove to Sunday service and that's when I noticed the announcement in the church bulletin: "Take communion to shut-ins. Classes starting soon."

Okay, technically I could have been labeled a shut-in myself, but I was sick of lying on the sofa and I thought maybe if I did something for somebody else it might help me feel better. So I signed up for the communion classes and a few weeks later, after my first round of eye injections to help ease the pain and some biofeedback training to relax the muscles around my eyelids, I was ready to try to tackle my first volunteer communion assignment.

Scared to death about maneuvering with my red-and-white cane, nervous about riding in a cab for disabled people, and worried that I might not remember all of the steps for the in-home communion service, I'm sure I looked more in need of a volunteer than ninety-six-year-old Amy did.

"Suzanne, I've been expecting you. Don't you look lovely today." Amy smiled and gave me a big hug, the kind of greeting you'd give to an old friend. "Come on in."

One of the oldest members in our church, Amy never used to miss a Sunday, but now she didn't feel comfortable leaving her house. Her eyesight was failing and she needed a walker to steady herself. Amy missed going to church and saying hello to people, but even more she missed receiving communion, so she'd been one of the first people to sign up.

The bread and wine I used for home communion were the same sacraments that had been distributed in church on Sunday, and there was a brief religious service I was supposed to read out loud. It was a real challenge to keep my eyes open long enough to read, but if I bent my neck way back and held the book up in the air, I could see through the narrow openings in my eyelids.

"Follow the same religious script every week" is what the instructor had preached in my volunteer training, but it wasn't too many Tuesdays before Amy and I broke the rules. After we finished the communion prayer, making sure the "Be Thou's" were in their proper places, Amy and I added our own personal requests: Amy had a doctor's appointment Friday and she was worried about getting down the long flight of steps in the back of her apartment. I was frustrated because I couldn't make a decent piecrust.

Of course, I realized there were more serious things in life than not being able to roll a piecrust, but baking seemed to be good mental therapy while I was waiting to find out if my red-and-white cane was going to be a permanent way of life. So with heads bowed and hands folded, my personal request for divine intervention sounded like this: "How about a little help making a decent piecrust?"

"You want to learn how to roll a piecrust?" Amy asked after the "Amen."

So the following Tuesday after we finished communion, Amy got out her mixing bowl, lard, flour, some ice water, and a rolling pin. "Nothing to it," she assured me.

Amy did make it look simple. Step by step the dough behaved exactly as the recipe promised. Maybe there *was* a secret to rolling a piecrust that Amy could teach me, or maybe the dough just knew better than to argue with a ninety-six-year-old piecrust veteran. After Amy finished her piecrusts, she gave me pointers while I was rolling mine. It was slow going, holding my neck back while trying to keep my eyelids open long enough to see what I was doing. My piecrust didn't look quite as neat as Amy's, but it was the best-looking crust I'd ever made. It felt so good to be able to finally conquer something. I was beaming with pride. We mixed up some sliced apples with a little sugar and flour, put three dabs of butter on top, and slid our pies into the oven.

After sampling Amy's still-warm apple pie (I took mine home to show my family), the two of us decided we really ought to include this new "eating" part in our regular Tuesday get-togethers. So every week after that there was a card table set up in Amy's living room when I arrived: fancy china, linen napkins and tablecloth, cold cuts, bread, potato salad, berries, cheese, and hot tea. I'd bring chocolate-chip cookies for dessert. Twice a month, we'd dine on Arby's roast beef sandwiches—Amy's favorite. The minute we'd finish communion, Amy would call her son to let him know it was time to make the Arby's run. "Two French Dip sandwiches with fries, please, and hurry up—we're hungry!"

Our twenty-minute in-home communion service soon became an all-day visit. Communion, lunch, then baking pies, and when I discovered Amy used to play piano in a swing band when she was younger, we started making music together, too. Amy could barely see the piano keys, but it didn't matter because she'd always played by ear anyway. We added a few hymns at the end of our communion service. I'd start singing a favorite and Amy would pick up the melody from listening to me. Actually, we weren't too bad after a few weeks of practice.

Some people might have thought that my relationship with Amy was one-sided, volunteering to take communion to an elderly woman. It was not. When Amy and I met, it truly was one of those moments when the timing was perfect—Amy needed me and I desperately needed her. A ninety-six-year old woman coming down the home stretch with finesse and grace, teaching a thirty-four-year-old woman how to make a piecrust and how to face the changes in her life.

"Making a pie from scratch is a courageous thing to do," Amy told me the first day we baked together. "The secret to a flaky piecrust isn't in the recipe. There are a lot of different recipes that make a flaky piecrust. But if you don't believe in yourself, if you're not willing to take a chance and ignore what well-meaning friends and family say, 'Don't use too much flour, don't overwork the dough, don't play the piano in a swing band, it's not what a lady should do,' the piecrust will get the better of you and so will life."

We'd been visiting together for over a year when I started noticing it was getting more difficult for Amy to do things. So it wasn't a complete surprise when her son called. "Suzanne, you should come today for your last visit with my mother."

Before I rang the doorbell I stood on the front steps rehearsing my thoughts. This wouldn't be the first time I'd made a final visit. When my Aunt Inez's cancer was no longer in remission, my mother and I traveled to see her before she died. Mom and I talked about it and decided we'd much rather say good-bye to Aunt Inez while she was living, instead of showing up for her funeral. And now, standing on the steps outside of Amy's door, I remembered all too well how difficult and strange it felt saying good-bye for the last time to someone you loved.

"Hello, Amy. I know it's not Tuesday, but I thought I'd break tradition."

Hospice had set up a hospital bed for Amy in her son's living room. Amy motioned for me to pull up a chair and asked her son to let us have some time alone. The minister was planning on coming by later to give Amy communion, but she wanted me to go through our usual communion service anyway, and afterward we sang a couple of verses from "What a Friend We Have in Jesus." Amy and I talked together for a short while, the same kind of chitchat we usually exchanged every Tuesday, and then we both knew it was time to say the Lord's Prayer. The last thing Amy and I did every week before I left was sit on her sofa and say the Lord's Prayer together out loud.

I got up from my chair and sat on the side of Amy's bed. She reached out and took my hand, and together we began, "Our Father who art in Heaven, hallowed be Thy name. Thy Kingdom come, Thy will be done, on earth as it is in Heaven. Give us this day our daily bread. . . ." My chest felt tight, it was difficult to hold back the tears. *This is the last time Amy and I will say the Lord's Prayer together* kept racing through my mind, and I knew the Amen was coming soon. I couldn't bear to say it, because then Amy and I would have to say good-bye.

Amy's son called the following morning—his mother had passed away in the night. He told me how much my visits had meant to his mother. I told him how much Amy's visits had meant to me. When he asked if there was anything in his mother's apartment I would like to have, I asked for the small wooden cross that sat on Amy's table. The cross was crudely made out of leftover wood from a church that Amy's relatives helped build when she was a little girl. It was the cross Amy and I used every Tuesday when we said communion together and it sits on my fireplace mantle today.

I don't know what other folks were thinking about at Amy's funeral, but I could hear her playing the piano in the swing band, I felt the hug she gave me the first day I knocked on her door, and when it came time in her funeral service to say Amen, I asked the Lord to please take good care of Amy, the woman who taught me that life is more interesting when you have the courage to roll a *not-so-perfect* piecrust.

🍥 🍥

Pie Boy

Rolling a piecrust. It's an old-fashioned art that will impress your friends. Even though we're surrounded by high-tech gadgets, it's amazing what a simple wooden rolling pin can create. Take a homemade pie to a family dinner—announce that you rolled the crust from scratch—and your relatives will *ooh* and *ahh*. It's a real self-esteem boost, even for a twelve-year-old boy.

Years ago when I was homeschooling my son, I also taught a cooking class twice a week to eight other homeschooled kids. Our first lesson was how to mix and roll a piecrust. The holidays were just around the corner, so I thought it would be fun if the kids could impress their families by making pies from scratch. Mix and roll the dough, toss out the dough because "oops, somebody goofed," mix up another batch, and finally roll out the finished piecrusts. We cut miniature leaves out of the leftover dough, painted them using food coloring, and circled the edges of our cherry, apple, and pumpkin pies with an assortment of fall leaves.

The kids enjoyed making pies, especially one twelve-year-old boy who got so hooked that he started baking pies every night at home. "We've never seen him so interested in something." His parents sounded a bit bewildered. I think they found their son's interest in baking pies a bit odd, but I was overjoyed. So I didn't mind one little bit when Pie Boy, as I lovingly refer to him now (because over the years I've forgotten his name), called me one evening at ten o'clock. When the phone rang I was in the final stages of tucking myself into bed, just getting ready to pull the covers up, position my pillow, and drift off.

Ring, ring. "Mrs. Beecher, I'm sorry to bother you this late at night. My parents said it was too late to call, but I told them you wouldn't mind. I just finished making two pies, using the recipe from class, but I put peaches in instead of apples. What temperature would I bake them at and for how long?"

Pie Boy had taken it upon himself to experiment, imagine that! I'd never seen a kid have so much fun baking pies. He baked so many pies that by the time we finished our class six weeks later, that boy was a better pie maker than me.

Over the years, I've lost track of my amazing Pie Boy. I wonder what he's doing today. Is he a professional baker? Or maybe he's a Wall Street broker and every year he amazes the relatives on holidays and at family reunions as they watch him make pies from scratch, rolling the dough and even cutting fancy leaf borders. I'm sure his pie-baking skills might have even impressed a date or two along the way. "Hey, how about baking some apple pies tonight?" What woman wouldn't be impressed?

"Where did you ever learn how to bake pies?" someone might ask. And wouldn't it be a magical moment if he told them about the woman who taught a cooking class when he was homeschooled. Who could have imagined . . . a pie-making lesson from Amy, to me, to my Pie Boy.

✑ ✑

Amy's Piecrust

This recipe makes one crust. You'll need to double it, or mix it up twice for a two-crust pie. Don't worry, Amy will be cheerleading for your success every step of the way.

    1 cup sifted all-purpose flour
    ½ teaspoon salt
    ¼ cup cold lard or solid shortening
    2 to 4 tablespoons ice-cold water

Mix flour and salt together. Cut lard into the flour mixture until crumbs are about the size of small peas. Add cold water, a little at a time, mixing with a fork until the dough just holds together. Amy always emphasized using only enough water to hold everything together. Roll out the dough. Line your pie tin. Fill, crimp edges, and bake at the temperature your pie recipe recommends.

Never Fail Piecrust

This recipe makes five crusts. The name says it all; you just can't fail when you're making this piecrust. If you're a beginner, this is the recipe for you.

    4 cups all-purpose flour, lightly spooned into a cup
    2 teaspoons salt
    ½ cup water
    1 tablespoon sugar
    1¾ cups shortening (not lard or butter)
    1 egg
    1 tablespoon apple cider vinegar

Mix all ingredients well and divide into 5 balls. Slightly flatten each like a giant hamburger, cover with plastic wrap, and refrigerate until cold if using right away. Or you can freeze for later use. (To freeze, wrap each one in wax paper and freeze in a freezer bag—you'll always have a piecrust on hand. This dough won't get tough if you re-roll it.)

9. Bull-Puckey, I Can Do This

On the way home from visiting my parents one Easter, I spotted a herd of cows (I love cows) so my husband pulled the car over. It's hard to feel sexy when you're wearing dark wraparound glasses and using a red-and-white cane, but these cows seemed to know I needed a support group. They gathered around and my husband took this photo.

If anyone had told me when I was first diagnosed with benign essential blepharospasm that eventually I wouldn't mind having an eye disorder, in fact I'd even wrap my arms around it with love, I would have felt mightily insulted.

How dare they suggest some Pollyanna make lemonade out of lemons bull-puckey crap? (Bull-puckey. In lieu of cursing, it was one of Grandma Hale's colorful words.) But the reality is that after a period of grieving, I did fall head-over-heels in love with my eye disorder and we're still good buddies today. Don't get me wrong, I'd be in line tomorrow for a cure, but in the meantime I feel like one of the fortunate ones. Because learning to love your disorder, that kind of magic doesn't happen for everyone.

After the sale of *In Business* magazine I'd planned on continuing to run Meals for Madison, my free meal program, but the situation with my eyes was getting worse every day. I couldn't drive any longer; I couldn't even walk down the street by myself because, functionally, I was blind. The disorder had also affected my nervous system, so much that I experienced overload simply going to the market with my husband. It was too stressful to decide what to take off the shelf, and those shopping carts were whizzing by at ridiculous speeds (at least that's what it felt like to me). I ran from the grocery store in horror.

Not only was it a struggle getting used to the limitations of my eye disorder, I was confused about who the heck I was. Four months ago I published a business magazine. Four months and a day later, what was I? A "used-to-be" publisher, walking around with her neck bent way back in hopes of "arm-wrestling" her eyelids slightly open, huge dark glasses wrapped over my regular glasses because lights caused horrific pain, and everywhere I went a red-and-white cane led the way. "Look out, here I come, get out of my way. You can see me, but I probably can't see you."

Benign essential blepharospasm (BEB) is a rare condition, one that is still a mystery to doctors, but I think I know what brought mine on— stress. I believe all of the ingredients for the disorder were tucked away inside me, in kind of a reconstituted state, but instead of adding water to bring the BEB to life, stress was the missing ingredient. Granted, it's my own theory, but my body knows what it needs if I'll only listen. And now I have no choice; my disorder forces me to pay attention.

Since most doctors weren't even aware of BEB, the first round of doctors I saw were quick to dismiss my symptoms, instead suggesting I was the problem. "You're not removing your eye makeup properly, that's why you can't keep your eyelids open," and "You're a nervous woman, Mrs. Beecher. Go home and find a hobby." I realized the translation for those prescriptions was "You're a nutcase who needs a shrink." So after four weeks of scrubbing my eyelids every night and "relaxing" during the day, I went back to the doctor and announced, "Bring on the shrink! Call me a nut-job, whatever you want, but I can't keep my eyelids open—I can't see!"

Finally I was referred to a neurologist who immediately diagnosed my disorder and also told me about Botox, a new drug just recently approved to treat BEB. Only a handful of specialists around the country were trained to give the eye injections, and the neurologist wasn't one of them, but she gave me the name of a specialist who was.

Two weeks before my appointment with the specialist, I realized I didn't really understand anything about the injections I'd be getting. It had been such a relief when I finally found someone who could help that I forgot to ask questions. So I called the doctor and his nurse explained the hows and whys of the injections, which sounded wonderful—finally I'd be cured and I'd be able to see again.

"Oh, these shots won't cure you." The nurse interrupted my rejoicing. "There isn't any cure for what you have. You're going to be this way for the rest of your life."

"What . . . did . . . you . . . say? I must have misunderstood you." But the nurse matter-of-factly repeated that my disorder was a life sentence, and not wanting to leave out any details, she added, "It could possibly even get worse. We really don't know much about it."

I don't know if getting the news from the doctor in his office would have been any less devastating and heartbreaking, but immediately my body and mind went numb. "I'm going to have to hang up now," I told the nurse, "because I think I'm going to start crying."

I sat on the kitchen floor and wept. *"There isn't any cure for what you have. You're going to be this way for the rest of your life."*

I couldn't work and since there wasn't any cure for benign essential blepharospasm I filed for worker's disability, but my claim was denied. The powers-that-be determined I wasn't disabled *enough*, so I was still employable. They could teach me how to put widgets together, so they arranged for widget training at the local Goodwill Center. A transportation service for the disabled picked me up on my first day of training, and by the time I arrived at the training center, there were already twenty-five people sitting at the long worktable. After I found an empty seat, an instructor came over and as she was patting my back, in a very slow and distinct speaking manner she said, "Welcome, Suzanne, it's nice to meet you. I'll be helping you today. Don't worry about a thing. This will be fun."

So this is what I have become. I looked around and realized this was my reality. Four months ago I owned a magazine and ran a nonprofit meal program, and by the end of the day I'd be an employable professional widget assembler. Yeah, boy, this was gonna be fun!

What was wrong with the people at the State? Maybe I couldn't keep my eyelids open and I couldn't be around too much activity, but there wasn't anything wrong with my mind. Or maybe this was the State's style of rehabilitation: *Find a way to work again . . . or it's widgets for you, for the rest of your life!*

I resigned my widget position at the end of the first day and vowed I would overcome this eye disorder.

The Botox injections the doctor gave me wouldn't cure my disorder, but they were supposed to weaken the muscle tissue around my eyes, so I could force my eyelids open enough to see where I was going. Yet it wasn't a guarantee. The Botox didn't work for every patient, but if it was going to work for me, my doctor said I should notice some relief within seven days. And then when the Botox wore off, I'd return for ten more eye injections— forever and ever. (I was still trying to get used to that part.)

Every morning after my first round of injections I woke up with great anticipation, hoping that today would be the day the injections would start working! Today would be the day I could see again! But after five days of being disappointed, I figured I wasn't going to beat the odds, the injections weren't going to work. I gave up hope. It was unimaginable depression.

But then on the afternoon of day seven, when I was riding in the front seat of my friend's car, one minute I couldn't open my eyelids and the next minute they popped wide open. There are no words to explain the glorious gift of suddenly being able to see again. I was jumping up and down in the front seat like a little kid who'd just spied Santa and his reindeer in the sky. "Look at the clouds! Look at the cars! See that sign over there? Oh my God, I can see! The shots are working, they're working!" I was shaking my friend's arm, crying and looking at the world like it was the first time.

Today after I get my monthly eye injections it takes only twenty minutes for my eyelids to jump to attention. They stay wide open and alert for about an hour, and then they settle into what's normal for me—a little more than half-mast.

After a few months of eye injections and some intensive biofeedback training, I finally felt confident enough to leave the house and go on my first outing alone: destination—downtown near the UW campus. I'd decided to take the city bus and spend the afternoon walking around looking in the shops on State Street. I didn't need my red-and-white cane any longer, the Botox injections allowed me to open my eyelids enough to see, but I was still wearing the huge wraparound sunglasses and I felt very self-conscious about them. To me the glasses were beyond ugly and they shrieked "I'm disabled!" But to the college student who stopped me on that warm and sunny afternoon when I was finding my way alone on State Street, they were *cool*. "Where did you get those cool glasses? I want to buy a pair."

I was stunned. As soon as I realized he was serious, I felt a little embarrassed having to admit where I'd bought them. "Well, actually, I have an eye disorder. These glasses are specially tinted and I bought them at the Center for the Blind." My college guy (a cute college guy, I might add) wasn't any less enthused. He still thought my glasses made a "cool" statement. I could have kissed the guy right then and there. It was all I could do to keep myself from sobbing. "You're an angel," I told him. "You'll never know what you've done for me today."

I continued to venture out of the house by myself and eventually the biofeedback techniques taught me how to relax enough so I could start driving again. It had been a year since I'd driven a car and the first time I drove by myself to the supermarket; I felt like a sixteen-year-old who'd just passed her driver's test.

Ever since my widget training, I'd taken the approach that I was going to overcome this disorder. Fight the good fight, be the master of my body, mind over blepharospasm, take charge, and I'd made some progress—but all that *get tough* kind of thinking obviously wasn't a long-term solution. Because declaring war against my disorder had created more stress in my daily life and stress was one of the triggers that made the symptoms of my disorder worse.

Tired of the fight, I woke up one morning and made a courageous decision—I gave up. Giving up is always a last resort for me, I guess because part of me feels like I've failed. But when I gave up that morning, the deep breath came, inhaling, slowly exhaling, my shoulders relaxed, and the pressure was finally off—it felt so good.

My benign essential blepharospasm wasn't the enemy anymore. Instead I wrapped my arms around my disorder (literally gave myself a hug) and whispered, "It's okay, we can work together, we can even learn to love each other." And we have. I still need my eye injections every four weeks, but things are different now, because ever since that morning my eye disorder and I have been friends.

Suzanne's Spaghetti Sauce

Benign essential blepharospasm opened my eyes to a different way of doing everyday things and that included how I approached cooking. Growing up in a small midwestern town, I was a meat, potatoes, and gravy kind of cook. Fresh herbs or edible flowers? Not in Cuba City, at least not in our house. Whenever a recipe offered the option of using fresh herbs instead of dried, there was never any question I'd reach for the store-bought spice bottle in the cupboard.

But benign essential blepharospasm challenged me to look at the world differently. So one afternoon when I was cooking dinner I decided to go fresh. I made a homemade spaghetti sauce with fresh oregano and basil and a tossed salad with edible flowers: violets, pansy petals, and carnations sprinkled on top.

I discovered I'm not a big fan of edible flowers, but since substituting fresh herbs for dried in my spaghetti sauce I can't bring myself to make it any other way. The difference in the taste was amazing—amazingly wonderful!

My spaghetti sauce recipe can even be frozen, so I always make at least a double batch. Enjoy, and don't forget to go fresh!

This recipe is made with a meat sauce, but sometimes I substitute ready-made meatballs from the supermarket.

Serves 6

1 pound ground beef
1 medium onion, chopped
2 15-ounce, or 1 30-ounce, can(s) tomato sauce
2 cloves garlic, minced
1 bay leaf
1 tablespoon minced fresh basil or 1 teaspoon dried
2 teaspoons minced fresh oregano or ¾ teaspoon dried (the fresh herbs will give you a better-tasting sauce)
2 teaspoons sugar
½ teaspoon pepper

Cook ground beef and onion until meat is brown and onion is tender. Add the rest of the ingredients and bring to a boil. Reduce heat, cover, and simmer for at least 1½ hours. Stir occasionally. Serve over spaghetti noodles.

10. Please, Give This Woman a Job!

All dressed up for a job interview, but a little too young to get a work permit.

Once my eye disorder and I called a truce we quickly adapted to each other's wants and needs and settled into a routine. I even started working again, from an office in my home, helping out in my husband's new software company, the Computer Group. Working from home was the perfect place for benign essential blepharospasm and me to get along. I could take a break whenever I needed, and because bright lights caused painful headaches behind my eyes, my husband installed dimmers on all of our light switches. Boy, did it ever feel good to be able to work again. I'd never realized how much of *me* was wrapped up in my job until I couldn't do it anymore.

Some people dream of the day they'll finally retire, but not me. I plan to keep on working right up until my final breath, then take a few vacation days to see who shows up for my funeral, after that get used to my new surroundings (hopefully ocean-front, maintenance-free property), and then I'll be ready to go back to work.

One of my biggest fears about death is I'm afraid I'll be bored. Bored stiff, so to speak! (Couldn't resist!) I know, I know, the sales pitch is strong—satisfaction guaranteed. The streets are paved with gold, you get an automatic face-lift and tummy tuck when you pass through the Pearly Gates, you don't have to share a room, the water's nice and hot the minute you turn on the tap, and you get to see all of your friends and loved ones who have passed on before you. My Grandma Hale and I have made a date for brunch the morning after I check in. Worry is a thing of the past and there's no need to work.

See, it's that last perk—*there's no need to work*—that concerns me.

I like to work, I love to work, and it's satisfying. To me it's playtime. I've seen only a couple of episodes of *Touched by an Angel*, the show where angels were given assignments here on earth, but the idea appeals to me. I'm looking forward to an afterlife career. I'm multitalented, look good in white, and I'm not afraid to fly. I only hope I'm heavenly material. (Since you're reading my book, may I use you as a reference when the time comes?)

My eye disorder and I had become so adept at working together at home that I began wondering: If I didn't tell someone there was something wrong with me, would they even know? And the more important question: Could I function in the real world? What a scary thought. But I needed to find out, so I searched the classified ads looking for a part-time job. It had been fourteen years since I'd had to look for a job, so it felt strange putting together a résumé and trying to figure out what I wanted to do. But then again, maybe the job title wasn't all that important. After all, the real reason I wanted to work outside of my home was to see if I could.

WANTED: PART-TIME VOLUNTEER COORDINATOR FOR NURSING HOME . . .

Compared to publishing *In Business* magazine and running the meal program, I guess most people would have thought that a part-time volunteer coordinator at Sunny Hill Nursing Home was a nothing sort of job. But I wanted this job more than any job I'd ever applied for, or thought about applying for, in my life. This job could be my test and it sounded like fun, too.

When I handed Sunny Hill's activity director a copy of my résumé, she immediately tossed it aside. "I don't need to look at this," she said. "I know you used to publish *In Business* magazine and recently sold it. To be honest, I really called you in for an interview more out of curiosity than anything else. Would you please explain to me why you're interested in this part-time hourly wage job?"

Nothing on the outside suggested my real motives. I intentionally hadn't worn my dark glasses, even though I knew the fluorescent office lighting would cause horrific pain in my eyes, and I'd taken a Valium before the interview so my eyelids wouldn't be blinking nonstop. Stress caused my disorder to be in full bloom and I figured if the activity director knew I was disabled, then I wouldn't get the job. If she didn't ask, I wasn't going to tell. (Okay, so she *sort of* did ask, but I had a second truth waiting in the wings just in case the question came up.)

"Yes, it's true I am plenty qualified for the job," I agreed, "maybe even a little overqualified, but now that I've sold the magazine, I'd like to work part time at something I'm interested in—you know, keep myself busy with something that's fun. And I think setting up a volunteer program for your nursing home would be fun."

My reasons sounded logical and the activity director said the job was mine if I wanted it. But she felt too embarrassed to tell me what the hourly rate was. "Would you give me a few minutes while I speak with the nursing home director about giving you a raise?"

I liked this job already. A raise before I even started! Word must have gotten around that I was a professional widget assembler, too.

My first day at Sunny Hill was routine: filling out forms, learning how to properly punch in and out, studying the rules and regulations book and then signing off that I understood everything I'd read, and finally a tour of the facility. Now that the boring stuff was out of the way, where was I supposed to hang my hat?

Since volunteer coordinator was a brand-new position at Sunny Hill there wasn't any "old" office to occupy, so I'd be sharing. Fine with me. I wasn't expecting anything fancy, which was a good thing, because after the activity director ushered me into my new office, she handed me a vacuum cleaner. "See that stuff over there in the corner? If you push it aside, you should be able to squeeze your desk in there. Go ahead and vacuum the carpet while you're waiting for the maintenance guy to bring a desk up from storage."

The office and desk weren't important. Just give me a phone and some heat! It was freezing in that office! I mean the kind of cold where you leave your coat and gloves on, wear two pairs of socks, and curl your feet up underneath your butt so you can warm them up while you're sitting in your chair. Apparently my new office always had a heating problem—in that it had no heat at all—because there weren't any heating vents in the room. The "office" used to be an elaborate storage closet. The lack of heat didn't bother my new roommate, because she never spent any time in the office. First thing in the morning she'd drop her coat and papers on her desk and then spend the rest of her day on the floor, interacting with residents. It was way too early in my employment to complain, so I made the best of the situation and bundled up.

Okay, so I had a desk, the floor was vacuumed, my paperwork all filled out nice and neat. Now what exactly did a volunteer coordinator do? My job title suggested (pretty definitively, if you ask me) that I'd be coordinating volunteers, but since there weren't any volunteers at Sunny Hill, I assumed the first thing I needed to do was recruit some. But the hows and whys of the job left a lot of room for interpretation, so I asked the activity director if I could have thirty minutes of her time to find out what she wanted me to accomplish in this new position. I asked that question on the first day of my employment and seven days later I was still asking that same question. Day after day, I requested thirty minutes of her time, or "How about if we walk and talk?" But she was always too busy.

"Tomorrow, we'll talk tomorrow."

I liked the activity director and respected her. She was good at her job, I could see that, and she was obviously overworked, but this was crazy. How was I supposed to do this job if I wasn't sure what the company wanted me to do? So after a week of trying to find out what my agenda should be, I decided to create my own. I pretended Sunny Hill was my company, and started making decisions and implementing new programs as if I owned the place. I figured if somebody higher up didn't like what I was doing, by golly then they'd take the time to talk to me. I wasn't angry about the situation, just didn't know what else to do. There was one advantage to being left on my own at Sunny Hill—nobody noticed my eye disorder, which gave me plenty of time to adjust.

The first task on my personally created job description was recruiting some volunteers. Had Sunny Hill ever even had volunteers? Were there any old files, or a list of names somewhere? I still couldn't get thirty minutes with the activity director, but I did get her to answer those questions one day while she was on the run. Twenty minutes later she plopped a brown paper bag on my desk. A crunched-up bag filled with slips of paper, names of people who indicated they were interested in volunteering a while back. Okay, now we were getting somewhere. I dug through the bag and started making phone calls to see if there were still any live ones. I found only one person, but one was a start.

There wasn't an "official" recruiting budget, so I drafted "Wanted—Volunteers!" announcements and mailed them to ministers in the area asking if they'd include a note in their Sunday bulletins. A stack of flyers sat in

Sunny Hill's front lobby and I handed them out to residents' families when they visited. I even finagled some free classified advertising in a couple of shoppers, and I posted flyers in grocery stores and Laundromats, anywhere I could think of, and eventually the phone started ringing. Once I got a system in place for the volunteer program, I decided Sunny Hill needed its own newsletter.

In another walk-and-talk with the activity director, I pitched my idea. Not only would a newsletter bring in more volunteers, but it could be an inviting PR piece for families deciding on a nursing home. "Any objections? And by the way, I'll need some money for paper and postage."

I wanted to mail a copy of the newsletter to each of the residents' family members. Some of their relatives didn't even live in the state, which meant they rarely got to visit. So the newsletter, complete with photos, would be a great way for sons and daughters to know what Mom and Dad were doing every day.

Sunny Hill's monthly newsletter grew to over ten pages, including a column I started called "Aged Advice." Employees and relatives submitted personal problems, and the nursing home residents were the "Ann Landers" of the column, offering solutions. Seniors giving advice seemed like a natural column to me, because when I was a kid I spent a lot of time talking with older folks in nursing homes. My parents would visit Great-Grandpa Shappell, or the neighbor who used to live down the street, but I'd end up poking my head into almost every room. I had some pretty impressive conversations with people in nursing homes. Those old folks might not have been able to walk down the hall without assistance, but they'd been around the block—full of experiences and they loved to talk about them.

In lieu of picnics, movies, or baseball games, visiting someone in a nursing home was pretty much our only family outing. We didn't even take vacations, except for the year Dad put a camper top on the back of a pickup and my folks decided we were going to Expo 67, the World's Fair in Montreal, Canada. I guess I was too young, or too shocked to ask, "Why are we going to the World's Fair?" That vacation is still a mystery to me, because my dad never went anywhere unless there was free beer or old people.

"Aged Advice" gave residents a chance to switch roles with staff. Instead of residents asking for help, suddenly staff needed help from the residents. Employees weren't shy about asking questions, some so personal they were submitted anonymously.

"*Our son wants to dye his hair orange! What should we do?*" Ninety-five-year-old Alice's advice: "*In the grand scheme of things, orange hair isn't a big deal. Your son will grow out of it and if he goes anywhere with you, just make him wear a hat.*"

"*My husband says I pay more attention to our dog than I do to him. I don't agree, but my husband's getting pretty upset about it lately. Don't you think he's being silly?*" —*Mother of a precious Pekingese*

I thought this question called for a man's Aged Advice, so I asked Edward, who'd been happily married twice, but had outlived both of his wives.

"*I don't know if I can help you, but here we go . . . I wasn't ever too good at guessing, so I liked it when my wife told me what she needed. What did she want for her birthday and should I get the blue one or the pink one? I could buy something extra, but I wanted to make sure I made her happy. Both of my wives were kind and loving women and my best friend. A dog can be man's best friend, but you've got a husband who is telling you he wants to be first in your life and then the two of you can love that precious Pekingese together.*"

Still single at ninety years old, Margaret offered unbiased advice for this Sunny Hill employee's yearly family dilemma.

"*Dear Aged Advice, every Christmas we make the rounds, visiting my parents and my husband's parents. This year I want to stay home with my husband and our two children. My husband disagrees and thinks we should go visit our parents. What do you think?"* —Hoping to have a home-cooked meal at my house this year

Dear Hoping, my advice is to find your recipe box and start cooking. Get out some paper right now and send an invitation to the relatives. Invite them to your house this year. Tell them they deserve a break and just to seal the deal, throw in that it's your way of thanking them for cooking all those years. My mama said I should always graciously accept a thank-you. I hope this helps."

"Aged Advice" received local television and newspaper coverage and the corporation who owned Sunny Hill presented the facility with an award, too. I was thrilled that Sunny Hill got press and was recognized by Corporate, but I was even more excited to see employees grabbing a copy of the monthly newsletter the minute I put a stack in the lobby. Eventually my "press run" grew large enough that I was able to sell a few ads to local businesses to help cover production costs.

Since I was making up my own job agenda as I went along, I added a weekly cookie-baking class to my part-time schedule. When I first thought about baking cookies with the nursing home residents, visions of Grandma Hale's kitchen danced merrily in my head. Bowls, measuring spoons, mixers—I had all of the ingredients lined up on kitchen tables for the first day of class. How exciting! Line by line, I'd read the recipe while residents measured and added the ingredients to their own mixing bowls and pretty soon we'd be eating warm-in-your-tummy homemade chocolate-chip cookies, just like Grandma used to bake. But baking with elderly folks in a nursing home who are there because they need a high level of care—what was I thinking? I quickly realized this would never be like Grandma Hale's kitchen.

Ten people sitting around the table, each at a different skill level—what a challenge it was to give everyone the assistance they needed! While I was helping Abby measure one teaspoon of vanilla, Bert opened the package of flour and dumped it on the floor. Eighty-nine-year-old Sarah could use the measuring spoons, but couldn't read the small print—does that say ½ or ¾? Sandy grew impatient with all of us and started eating the chocolate chips right out of the bag. Lillian probably could have mixed up one hundred cookies without any assistance and quickly lost her patience waiting for everyone else to catch up. And then there was Fred, who just wasn't up to doing anything. He needed complete one-on-one assistance. I describe these folks with love. They were each doing the best they could, and I was the one who needed to rethink things and make a change. The purpose of this class wasn't about taking me back to baking in Grandma Hale's kitchen. Instead I wanted to create a "Grandma Hale" memory for each of the residents.

So I asked family members to bring in one of their mom's or dad's favorite cookie recipes, and in addition to baking and eating some mighty good cookies, we'd get to hear a story. "Sarah, can you remember when you used to bake these cookies?"

Baking class started at nine-thirty on Wednesday morning and about an hour later, nursing home employees would just happen to be walking by the kitchen to see if we needed a taste-tester. After a few weeks, the residents and I started getting requests. "What kind of cookies are you baking next week? Can I buy some to take home?"

Soon my baking buddies and I were in the cookie-baking business. Old favorites like peanut butter, snickerdoodles, chocolate chip, and oatmeal raisin were top sellers, but our real moneymaker was the apple-cutout sugar cookies. Selling the cookies at cost meant the baking supplies didn't have to come out of my budget.

I'd been working at Sunny Hill for almost a year, when I realized the job had become routine. Routine in that context meant success. My eye disorder hadn't improved, but I'd learned how to compensate and work around it. I'd passed the test. Yes, indeed, I could successfully work a job outside my home and make a go of it in the real world.

Having been "the boss" most of my life, I realized what a hassle and time-consuming job it was when an employee gave notice: running an ad, interviewing, hiring, training, and waiting for the "newbie" to actually be able to earn their keep. So I gave my boss three months' notice, hoping she'd be able to make a smooth transition. And I let her know if she found someone before three months time, I'd be happy to leave early.

At first she ignored my resignation, which was kind of flattering. When I'd ask about placing an ad or helping to train my replacement, she'd smile. "You're not really leaving, are you? Tomorrow, we'll talk about it tomorrow."

But finally, two months later during one of our familiar walk-and-talks, my boss accepted the idea that I'd really be leaving Sunny Hill. Sad to see me go, she sent me off with not one, but two going-away parties and two serving bowls that I still have today. But the best going-away gift Sunny Hill gave me was the option of continuing my health insurance for eighteen months. I didn't realize it until the eighteen months ran out, but when it did, no company would insure me because of my preexisting condition— good 'ol benign essential blepharospasm.

My husband and I started working together again, but his small group policy had limitations, and my preexisting condition was one of them. The only way I could possibly get health insurance again was if I could get into a large insurance pool, which meant going to work for a big company. I needed health insurance, but my husband and I loved working together and had really missed that closeness during the year I worked at Sunny Hill.

So my little crazy brain went into overdrive and I came up with two possible solutions that would allow me to get health insurance and still continue to work with my husband: get a divorce, become an Avon Lady or a Mary Kay Representative.

"Absolutely not! You're out of your mind!" My husband wouldn't even let me finish explaining why we should get a divorce. But I wasn't kidding. What if something happened to my health? Without insurance I'd drain our savings and we'd both be destitute. This way, if we got divorced, the State would have to provide medical assistance if anything terrible happened to me. I was willing to pay for health insurance, but since no company would sell me a policy . . . the look in my husband's eye suggested the discussion was closed, so on to Plan B.

"Ding, dong, Avon calling."

Every two weeks the Avon Lady stopped by our house when I was a kid. My mother was cheaper than cheap, but every other week she placed an order, which she hid from my dad: bubble bath, lotions, lipstick, eye shadow, wrinkle cream—and the Avon Lady gave free samples, too. My favorites were the little miniature lipsticks in the white tubes. Come to think of it, those miniature lipsticks are probably why I'm so hooked on the miniature shampoos and lotions the fancy hotels give away—blame it on the Avon Lady.

Avon offered health insurance. I wasn't sure about all the details, but I also was afraid to ask right away, because I knew my name had been added to the insurance blacklist pool. (Insurance companies shared their rejection information with one another.) So I decided to become an Avon Lady first and ask questions later. Maybe I could slide into their group insurance pool without being detected. And as backup, just in case Avon rejected me, I became an official Mary Kay representative, too.

I wasn't planning on ringing doorbells and actually trying to sell Avon or Mary Kay products. Instead, my plan was to buy all the products myself. I'd purchase the minimum amount a representative was required to sell, and then eventually when I'd worked for them long enough, I'd try to get in their insurance pool. (Ironically the only makeup I ever used was lipstick, so my friends were well supplied with cosmetics for a few months.) Unfortunately, both brilliant insurance schemes failed. Nobody wanted me and my preexisting condition.

A few months later, none of that mattered because my husband and I decided to move to Florida. What a surprise it was when I discovered that in addition to palm trees and warm ocean breezes, the state of Florida required insurance companies to cover preexisting conditions, even in a small group policy like the one my husband had for his business.

Hallelujah! I finally had health insurance again!

Apple Cutout Sugar Cookies

1½ cups confectioners' sugar
1 cup butter or margarine, softened
1 egg
1½ teaspoons vanilla extract
2¼ cups all-purpose flour
1 teaspoon baking soda
1 teaspoon cream of tartar

Frosting

2 cups confectioners' sugar
¼ cup light corn syrup
2 tablespoons water
Red and green food coloring

In a large mixing bowl, combine the first seven ingredients in order given and mix well. Chill dough for 2 to 3 hours or until easy to handle. Roll out on a lightly floured surface to ¼-inch thickness. Cut with an apple-shaped cookie cutter dipped in flour. Place on greased baking sheets. Bake at 375 degrees for 7 to 8 minutes or until lightly browned. Cool on wire racks.

For frosting, combine sugar, corn syrup, and water in a small bowl. Transfer three-fourths of the frosting into another bowl; add red food coloring for apples. Add green food coloring to remaining frosting for stems. Frost cookies. Allow to sit overnight for frosting to harden.

11. He Loves Me, He Loves Me a Lot

My husband, Bob, and I are best friends and still crazy in love, even after thirty-two years. Photo by John Allaman.

My husband says he was put here on earth to take care of me. Now how could a woman possibly argue with that kind of logic?

Our marriage must be for keeps because every day it just keeps getting better and better, even after being married for thirty-two years and working together every single day. But working together harmoniously wasn't something that came about naturally. Shortly after we were married, we went several times to see a therapist so we could learn how to work together. "Learning" required *several* sessions because it took me a while to recognize and to finally 'fess up to the fact that I tend to think my way of doing things is the right way. (And just between you and me—most of the time it is! I'm smiling, just kidding.)

Seriously, my husband and I learned a lot about each other in those "shrink" sessions, and over the years, we've developed a Recipe for our Marriage. . . .

My husband gives me a foot rub every night, I bake chocolate cakes from
    scratch—they're his favorite.

I wash and dry, he folds and puts away.

He takes care of the trash, I do the gardening.

He kills any misplaced bugs, I leave the room while he's hunting them down.

He encourages me in whatever new thing I want to try, I reciprocate.

And when I ask, "Honey, do I look fat in these pants?" my husband reassures
    me I don't. "The older you get, the sexier you look, dear."

We're both committed to making our marriage work, but more impor-
tantly, my husband and I are best friends. We enjoy being downright silly
and strange sometimes, like when we lived in Wisconsin and we used to eat
lunch in the hospital cafeteria.

The hospital's food tasted great, I'm not kidding. And the price was
right, too, especially when I was wearing a black suit, because the cashier
would automatically assume I was a doctor and she'd give my husband and
me the employee discount. The first couple of times we thought it was a
fluke, and didn't even realize we'd been given a discount until later, when
we were looking at our receipt. So to test our "black suit" hypothesis, we
conducted our own clothing-discount experiment and after pitting pastel-
colored suits up against black suits, we did indeed discover that our theory
was correct. Only my black suit was discount worthy. When I wore pastel
we paid full price.

Most people would shake their heads and wonder, *Why would anyone
want to eat in the hospital cafeteria?* But those lunches are delightful, funny
memories for my husband and me—a wonderful recipe from our life.

Yes, my husband and I are best friends, but unfortunately he never
gets very excited about extending our circle of friends. Every time I suggest the idea of getting to know our neighbors—"How about inviting
some people over for dinner?"—he changes the subject. So it was a real

surprise when out of the blue my husband came in the house one day and announced he'd just met John, a neighbor who lived down the street, and we were going to a dinner party Friday night at John and his wife Dianna's house.

How did we get an instant dinner invitation from neighbors we'd never heard of before?

Some people can walk right up to a stranger, say hello, introduce themselves, and strike up a lengthy conversation. They're a natural and the desire is built in. That's not my husband's style, but that's exactly what John (who was now my husband's new best friend) did when he was walking by our house. John and my husband ended up talking for an hour and now we were going to John and Dianna's house Friday night and I was supposed to bring my famous Skunk Beans. Dinner was at seven-thirty.

First-time party invite, first-time opportunity to make an impression on new friends. I wore a stunning white linen summer skirt with a halter top, and my husband—he got locked in the bathroom.

It wasn't the bathroom on the first floor, the one that other party guests were using, the bathroom where people would've heard him pounding on the door for help. No, my husband wandered upstairs to the second-floor bathroom, pushed the door closed, and as he was getting down to business, he noticed the bathroom doorknob sitting on the top of the toilet tank. Strange place for a doorknob, but not to worry, my husband thought he'd merely slide the handle in the bathroom door when it was time to leave, and he did just that. But the door didn't open.

"There's that moment," my husband said later when he was telling the story at the party, "there's that moment when it hits you. I'm locked in the bathroom. It's pretty quiet up here, pretty noisy downstairs—there's a party going on, no one knows I'm up here, and I don't have my cell phone.

"HELP! HELP!"

But none of us heard him.

You'd think a wife would miss her husband, but I'd struck up a conversation with a man from South Africa, so I had no idea my husband was locked away in the loo.

Push, heave-ho, my husband tried to open the window, but our new friends' home was historical and the bathroom window had been painted shut. It wouldn't budge. But then my husband looked down and noticed three people walking by on the street below, and thankfully they looked up and spotted him swaying back and forth in a game of bathroom charades. Holding the doorknob in one hand and turning his other hand back and forth with an imaginary key, finally the people in the street below guessed the right answer. Soon three strangers knocked on our friends' front door, and informed them that a man appeared to be locked in their second-floor bathroom.

Yes, some people, like my husband's new friend John, are a natural. They can walk right up to a stranger and strike up a conversation. But I think it takes more talent to get three strangers walking by on the street to play a game of charades. Don't you?

My husband is definitely a very talented guy and he's also a down-to-earth, romantic, rational man—rational except for one weird phobia. He worries that we might run out of ketchup and toilet paper. It's a real mystery to me, because it's not like we've ever had to knock on our neighbor's door to ask if we could borrow a cup of ketchup, or beg for a few squares of Charmin.

I admit I lovingly tease my husband about his ketchup and toilet-paper phobia, but after staying with some relatives for a few days, I realize it could be much worse. Believe it or not, there are other people in the world who are even more obsessed about keeping track of their toilet paper inventory than my dear husband.

It was the third day of our visit, my husband and I were sitting down to breakfast, and after our hostess asked us how we wanted our eggs cooked, she casually commented, "Boy, we seem to be going through a lot more toilet paper since you guys came to visit. What are you doing with it?"

Initially I was speechless and then I assumed she must be kidding. But from the look on her face I realized she wasn't. "I don't know," I finally managed to reply, "I guess we use toilet paper for the same things most people do."

Thankfully our hostess didn't continue her toilet-paper inquisition. And since worrying about toilet paper and worrying about ketchup go hand-in-hand in my husband's mind, I refrained from asking for ketchup for my scrambled eggs.

My husband does most of our grocery shopping, and in addition to keeping us well-stocked with toilet paper and ketchup, he finds the most incredible, almost unbelievable bargains—including free stuff. Not those wimpy, teeny-tiny sample-product sizes. My husband brings home the "real deal." The other day he came back with a free half-gallon of ice cream. "It's a brand-new product and a nice little old lady was handing out free samples." My husband was beaming.

"That's wonderful, dear, and it's chocolate, too. Your favorite flavor!" My first thought had been to remind him that his doctor suggested cutting down on ice cream, but since it was free and he was so excited, how could I possibly spoil his fun?

I didn't think anything more about my husband's knack for finding free stuff, until three days later when he came back from another trip to the supermarket. He plopped two grocery bags on the counter and while he was unpacking them, he gave me a play-by-play. "Bought a pizza, it was on sale, and I got milk, apples, and peanut butter—the crunchy kind that you like."

And then he pulled out a big bag of Doritos and gave me one of those kid-caught-with-his-hand-in-the-cookie-jar looks. "Oh, these Doritos? That nice little old lady was giving out free full-sized samples again. Aren't I lucky?"

Hmm, free ice cream, and now Doritos? He *is* one lucky guy! That little old lady sure stays busy. Who does he think he's kidding? Maybe I should rethink *my* shopping approach. That cute pink cashmere sweater I saw the other day, "Wrap it up!" And when my husband asks, I'll just say, "Oh, this sweater? I got it for free. I was the ten thousandth blonde customer who writes for a living to walk through the door, and this was my prize.

"And these new shoes? They were free, too, part of a market survey. All I had to do was agree to wear them to lunch at the Columbia Café and then out to dinner at that new restaurant on Dalton Street. And after I complete a customer survey card, I'll automatically be entered in a drawing for a free housekeeper for six months—and *dear,* I'm feeling lucky!"

Yes, my husband is lucky at the market, lucky in love (he's got me!), but not so lucky in the U-turn lane.

My husband never gets up before me, but one morning when I walked into the kitchen to make coffee, he was already sitting at his desk studying something on his computer screen. Apparently he'd been up for over an hour working on a strategy to defend himself against the traffic ticket he got, when the two of us were out picking up trash in Sarasota. (Keep Sarasota Beautiful—we try to do our part.)

We were driving on an unfamiliar road, spotted some trash, turned onto a side road, drove a little ways, and then did a U-turn to head back in the direction we needed to go. But almost immediately after the U-turn, my husband saw flashing red lights in his rearview mirror.

"License and registration, please."

My husband handed the officer his driver's license while I was digging through the glove box for our car registration. "I'm sure it's in here somewhere, officer." Plastic fork and spoon, extra napkins from the deli, anti-itch cream, baby wipes, a disposable camera, two little packets of ketchup (what, no toilet paper?), and three insurance cards all from different carriers.

Clearly the officer was getting impatient. "If the car is registered to you, I can look it up on my computer." And away he went.

And then we waited—a very long time. I knew what the wait meant, especially when I looked in the rearview mirror and saw the officer filling out a piece of paper. Once they start writing the ticket, there's no turning back. (I know this from experience.)

Ever since the officer handed that citation to my husband, it's been his one and only topic of conversation. All night long mumbling (out loud) about the injustice of it, and now when I desperately needed to brew that first morning cup of coffee, my kitchen counter had been transformed into the scene of the crime. Complete with the CVS Store on the left (a bag of flour), a gas station on the right (a can of string beans), the NO U-TURN sign (handcrafted with a straw and construction paper), the painted lines in the road (represented by a line of white candy sprinkles that I use on top of cupcakes), and our Blue Toyota (creatively represented by our grandson's little red triangle block). My husband had several sheets of paper in his hand—the county government's rules about deciding where a U-turn sign is needed.

"Let me guess, dear, you've decided to go to court and fight the ticket?"

And my husband began to present his case.

"Yes, dear, I'm dying to know how you're going to explain that you're not guilty when there was a no U-turn sign posted in the road, but right now I need to make my morning coffee. Judge Suzanne can't listen to any testimony until after she's had her caffeine. And by the way, you might get rid of the sarcasm when you tell your story before a real judge."

I wasn't buying his story. For one thing the red block was heading in the wrong direction and my recollection of what was where and how it all happened was totally different. Upset that I didn't find him "not guilty," my husband grabbed his camera and headed back to the scene of the possible U-turn crime.

"Great idea. You go take pictures and I'll drink my coffee, and remember, no U-turns."

It's been proven that eyewitness testimony is unreliable and my husband proved it again. There wasn't any gas station, the driving lanes were positioned differently from the white cupcake sprinkles on my kitchen counter, the bag of flour was actually on the opposite side of the street, and in addition to "our" no U-turn sign, there were five other signs lining the road.

My husband is sitting in front of his computer signing up for traffic school.

"He loves me, He loves me not."

Reading a book of love poems the other day made me think about my husband. No, he doesn't write poetry, but my husband romances me every day with little things and they feel like poetry to me.

Whenever he hands me a bottle of water, he always loosens the cap first.

If I wake up at three-thirty in the morning, he rolls over and says, "Suzanne, I recorded one of your favorite shows. It's on the television in the kitchen."

When my husband knows I'm planning on taking a bath, he offers to fill the tub for me and he even puts a hand towel on the back of our old-fashioned claw-foot tub, so my back doesn't lean up against the cold porcelain.

When he fixes me an ice cream cone, sometimes there's a surprise in the bottom of the cone. Two scoops of strawberry and he'll add one small dollop of chocolate at the very bottom with a splash of chocolate sauce, for the last surprise bite.

If I have a morning appointment and the car is near empty, or it got caught in the irrigation water the night before, my husband makes an early morning run to the gas station—fills it up and washes off the windows.

And my husband always seems to know before I do when I'm going to be tired. Because when I head for the bedroom, I discover he's been there first. My pillows are propped up against the headboard, the corner of the sheet on my side of the bed is neatly pulled back in a triangle, and the lamp is turned on low.

It's my husband's way of bringing poetry to life. I'm one lucky woman. *"Ah . . . He loves me—he loves me a lot."*

Every woman in the hair salon was staring at the mysterious man who walked through the door, and so was I. He looked incredibly sexy in his black suit, white shirt, and dark tie. His shoes were polished, there was a black chauffeur's hat on his head, and dark shades were covering his eyes.

"Is Suzanne Beecher just about finished?" the handsome man (who sounded like my husband) asked the receptionist. And when the receptionist said it would be another ten minutes, the handsome man (who also looked like my husband) thanked her and replied, "Would you please let Suzanne know that her driver is waiting outside?" And out the door he went.

I was in shock. Within seconds every woman in the salon, including me, was pressed up against the salon's front window. We were all staring at my husband, who was standing alongside a stunning old-fashioned MG Roadster sports car.

It was my birthday and my husband had rented an MG Roadster for the weekend. He was in character, playing the part of my personal chauffeur, and for the rest of the day he drove me around town, stopping at all of my favorite boutiques and galleries. At each stop my *driver* would hurry to open my door, and then he'd escort me to the front entrance of the store.

My personal chauffeur never went inside the store with me—that would have been a driver's indiscretion. Instead my "guy" waited at his "post"— legs stretched out, chauffeur's hat tipped ever so slightly, leaning up against the side of the MG Roadster. Everyone inside the store and outside in the parking lot was dying to know: "Who was this woman with the fancy car and driver?" It was a Cinderella birthday, complete with my very own prince charming.

"Ah, yes . . . He loves me—he loves me a lot."

Thirty-two years ago my husband and I were married by a justice of the peace.

Nothing fancy.

"Do you take this good-looking guy to be your husband?"

"Do you take this crazy woman to be your wife?"

(Remember, Mr. Beecher, this is for better or for worse.)

"I do."

"I do."

And we were married.

Nobody showered us with rice, but when you're married by the justice of the peace in Dubuque, Iowa, after "You may now kiss the bride," they hand you a two-foot-long plastic bag filled with product samples instead. At least they used to thirty-two years ago. Miniature laundry soaps, shampoo, mouthwash, toothpaste, tissue, aspirin, potato chips, and a trial-sized can of pork and beans. It's a bizarre wedding gift, but it's been a memorable one. Every year when my husband and I celebrate our anniversary, we reminisce about the "recipes from our life together" and it's always the two-foot-long bag of samples that we remember first.

And now we move to our eighth anniversary—the year we decided to dress up for dinner instead of going casual. A suit and tie for my husband and a long, flowing evening dress with strappy heels and a stunning shoulder wrap for me. All dressed up by five, but no place to go. It was way too early for dinner. So my husband and I decided to take a drive—and I have no idea how it happened—but eventually we ended up at the mall.

Yes, we looked a little strange all gussied up, walking down the aisles of Payless Shoes, but we looked even more out of place later that evening, when we ended up dining at Wendy's.

That year's anniversary plan was to keep the evening spontaneous, so we hadn't made a dinner reservation. But by the time we'd cruised around town and spent time window-shopping at the mall, it was eight-thirty, we were starved, and every restaurant we stopped at had a long waiting list—except Wendy's!

So what the heck—"Table for two, please!" And we dined on two singles with cheese, two fries, and we even ordered ice cream Frosties—after all, it was our anniversary!

"He loves me, he loves me a lot!"

Cooking with My Husband— Our Favorite Recipes

It was a long Labor Day weekend, so I challenged my husband to a Bread Bake-Off Contest. The only rule was that the bread recipes we used had to include yeast. My husband found a Hearty Wheat Bread recipe on the back of a package of gourmet flour. And I decided to make two entries: a Northern Maine Oatmeal Bread (a recipe I'd never tried before) and a Daisy Braid from an old, reliable, sweet dough recipe.

One of the first steps in my husband's Hearty Wheat Bread recipe instructed him to warm up the mixing bowl, so of course he got out the hair dryer, turned it on full blast, and aimed it at the inside of the bowl (everyone interprets a recipe a little differently). Okay, I admit it worked. The hair dryer did warm up the bowl, but maybe he should have used the low setting on the dryer, because his bread didn't rise—at all. Yeast can be tricky. If the water you add is too hot, it kills the yeast, and if it's too cold, nothing happens.

After the first bite of my Oatmeal Bread and Daisy Braid rolls, my husband awarded me the Bread Bake-Off Blue Ribbon and suggested it would be better if I didn't even taste-test his bread. The poor guy's Hearty Wheat Bread turned out so hearty that in his words, "If we ever decide to build that addition to our house, we can make the bricks out of this dough."

Northern Maine Oatmeal Bread

Years ago I found this recipe in an old cookbook. It looked good, but I never tried it until our Bread Bake-Off Contest. I couldn't get the loaves to rise as high as they should have, but the bread was still fantastic. Next time I'm going to put the pans on top of my dryer to rise, cover them with a dish towel, and then turn the dryer on high. (Another dryer tip from my husband, but this one actually works.)

Makes 2 loaves

2 cups boiling water
1 tablespoon butter
1 cup rolled oats
1 package active dry yeast
½ cup warm water (110 degrees)
½ cup molasses
2 teaspoons salt
5 to 6 cups all-purpose flour
Melted butter

Combine boiling water, butter, and rolled oats in a bowl and let stand for one hour (or 30 minutes if you're using "quick" oats).

Dissolve yeast in warm water. Add yeast mixture, molasses, salt, and as much flour as you can stir into oat mixture. Mix thoroughly. (I use my KitchenAid counter mixer on low.)

On a lightly floured surface knead dough for 6 to 8 minutes, adding more flour if necessary to form moderately stiff dough. (I use the dough hook on my mixer to knead the dough.)

Place dough in a greased bowl and turn the dough over once to grease the surface. Cover with a damp cloth and let rise in a warm place until doubled in size, about 45 minutes. If it's a warm, sunny day put your bread pans in the car. The dough will rise and your car will smell like freshly baked bread. Or do some laundry and set your pans on top of the dryer while you're drying clothes.

Punch dough down. Divide dough in half. Cover and let rest for 10 minutes.

Shape each portion into a loaf and place in a greased loaf bread pan, seam side down, and let rise again until almost doubled in size, 30 to 40 minutes.

Preheat oven to 375 degrees. Bake for 30 to 40 minutes or until bread tests done. (I tap the top of my bread—if it makes a hollow sound, it's done.) Remove loaves from the pans and brush the tops with melted butter to soften the crusts. Cool on wire racks.

Hot 'n' Sour Soup

Hot 'n' Sour Soup, an easy recipe, is my husband's favorite. Even though I'd been making it for him ever since we were married, I never actually tried the soup myself until a couple of years ago when Bill, a friend from Oregon, came to visit. Bill's favorite soup is also Hot 'n' Sour, so to look polite at the table, I ate some of my own creation. It was delicious! All those years I was afraid to try this strange-looking soup. Now I double this recipe because it keeps great all week long in the refrigerator.

Serves 6

3 dried wood ears or 4 dried mushrooms

20 dried lily buds, optional

1 boneless, skinless chicken breast half

1 tablespoon dry cooking sherry

4 cups chicken broth

½ cup sliced bamboo shoots (half an 8-ounce can), drained and cut into matchstick pieces

4 ounces bean curd, drained and cut into ½-inch cubes

3 tablespoons distilled white vinegar

1 tablespoon soy sauce

½ teaspoon ground white pepper

2 tablespoons cornstarch

3 tablespoons water

1 egg, lightly beaten

1 teaspoon sesame oil

2 green onions, cut into 1½-inch slivers

Place wood ears and lily buds (if using) in separate bowls. Cover with hot water. Let stand for 30 minutes. Drain and squeeze out excess water. Pinch out hard knobs from center of wood ears and discard. Cut wood ears into thin strips. (If using mushrooms, cut off and discard stems; cut caps into thin slices.) Cut off and discard hard tips from lily buds.

Cut chicken crosswise into thin slices; sprinkle with sherry. Let stand for 15 minutes.

Bring chicken broth to a boil in 3-quart saucepan. Add wood ears, lily buds, chicken, and bamboo shoots. Reduce heat and simmer, uncovered, for 3 minutes. Add bean curd, vinegar, soy sauce, and white pepper. Cook for 3 minutes more.

Blend cornstarch and water in a small cup; stir into soup. Cook, stirring, until slightly thickened. Turn off heat. Stirring constantly, slowly pour egg into soup. Stir in sesame oil and onions.

Potstickers

On my thirtieth birthday my husband planned a surprise birthday party for me. Not only was I totally surprised, he even managed to have me unknowingly do all the cooking—except for baking the birthday cake. Every other week a girlfriend and I were in a routine of cooking together for fun, and my husband overheard us making plans to cook several Chinese dishes the next time we got together. Our next cooking date just happened to be May 25th, the day before my birthday.

"Surprise Birthday Party" May 25th, at 6:30 p.m. The menu was all of the Chinese dishes my girlfriend and I had made earlier in the day, including Potstickers and Braised Shrimp with Vegetables.

This recipe takes a little work, so I double or triple it. But don't let the directions scare you off. Just follow them step by step. Actually, filling the wontons is a fun thing to do together as a family or with a group of people at a dinner party. These potstickers are delicious. The frozen ones you can buy in the store are no comparison.

You can prepare the potstickers and then cook them much later. After you've filled the wonton skins, put the potstickers on a baking sheet, or anything flat, and cover with foil or plastic wrap. Refrigerate overnight or you can freeze them. Once the potstickers are frozen, put them in a bag. Take out a few at a time and follow the cooking instructions.

Makes 36 potstickers

1 tablespoon cornstarch
2 tablespoons dry white wine
1 tablespoon vegetable oil
½ pound lean uncooked pork (I ask the butcher to send it through the grinder two extra times. The butcher may tell you it's not necessary, but smile and ask if it could be done anyway.)
2 green onions, minced
1 cup minced Chinese cabbage
1 tablespoon soy sauce
1 tablespoon brown sugar
¼ teaspoon salt
⅛ teaspoon pepper
36 round or square wonton skins
½ cup chicken broth

Dissolve cornstarch in wine and set aside. In a skillet, heat 1 tablespoon vegetable oil. Add pork and cook, stirring, until meat is no longer pink. Stir in green onions, cabbage, soy sauce, brown sugar, salt, and pepper. Stir cornstarch mixture then stir into pork mixture. Constantly stirring, cook pork mixture over medium heat until translucent. Let cool slightly.

If using square wonton skins, cut square wonton skins into 3-inch-diameter rounds. I use a glass to do this. Put the glass on top of the square wonton and cut around it with a knife. You do need to keep the wonton skins covered with a damp paper towel so they don't dry out. Now you make the wontons, one at a time. Spoon about 2 teaspoons of the pork mixture on one half of the round wonton skin. Don't overdo it. You don't want the filling seeping out of the skin when you seal it. Moisten the edges of the wonton skin with water. Run your dampened finger around the edges and bring one side up. Bring the other side up. You should now have a semicircle. Pinch the edges together, then seal with three or four tucks along the sealed edge. Don't be afraid when you get to this part. Just figure that the first few are a trial run. You can take them apart and start over if they don't turn out.

After you've "tucked" the edges of the wonton skin, place the potsticker, tucked edge up, on a flat surface. Press down lightly until it sits flat. Repeat the steps until the pork mixture is all used up.

To cook potstickers, pour 2 tablespoons oil into skillet. Put 6 potstickers in the skillet, flat surface down. Do not let the potstickers touch while they're cooking. Cook uncovered until the bottoms are golden brown, then remove them from the frying pan. Repeat with remaining potstickers, 6 at a time.

Return the browned potstickers to the frying pan. Pour the chicken broth over them. Cover and cook over low heat for 10 minutes or until the potstickers are translucent. And they're finished!

Potsticker Sauce

I like to drizzle this sauce over the potstickers.

1 tablespoon soy sauce
2 teaspoons balsamic vinegar
¼ teaspoon minced fresh ginger
¼ teaspoon Chinese oil or ⅛ to ¼ teaspoon hot chili oil

Mix these ingredients together.

Braised Shrimp with Vegetables

Makes 4 servings (I always double this recipe.)

1 tablespoon vegetable oil
1 pound raw medium to large shrimp, shelled
8 ounces fresh broccoli, cut into small pieces
8 ounces mushrooms, sliced (not too thin) or canned whole button
    mushrooms
1 can (8 ounces) thinly sliced bamboo shoots
½ cup chicken broth
1 teaspoon cornstarch
1 teaspoon oyster sauce
¼ teaspoon sugar
½ teaspoon minced fresh ginger
⅛ teaspoon pepper

Heat oil in wok or large skillet over high heat. Add shrimp and stir-fry until shrimp turns pink. Add broccoli and stir-fry for one minute. Add mushrooms and bamboo shoots and stir-fry one minute more. Combine remaining ingredients in small bowl and mix. Pour over shrimp and vegetable mixture. Cook and stir until sauce boils and thickens.

12. Somebody Should Have Told Me About This!

My son and daughter-in-law filled my lawn with pink flamingos one year for my birthday. I loved them so much that after the rental company came to take them away, I bought two dozen pink flamingos of my own.

Up until the moment my husband and I landed at the small St. Petersburg, Florida, airport, this Wisconsin girl had kept pretty close to home. But now the Florida sun was shining on my face, a light warm breeze was blowing through my hair, and palm tree branches were swaying high up in the sky just like in the movies—surely I must be in heaven.

I realize that my moment in the sun may sound somewhat insignificant, but keep in mind that my husband and I had never traveled anywhere warm when it was freezing cold in Wisconsin.

"SOMEBODY SHOULD HAVE TOLD ME ABOUT THIS!" I shouted, arms raised high over my head, hands waving frantically in the air as I descended the ramp onto the tarmac. No doubt every passenger on board heard my proclamation, but I didn't care. Truly I was amazed! Earlier that morning snowplows had been working hard to clear the six feet of snow that had accumulated overnight in Madison, and because I didn't want to have to lug my winter coat along, I practically froze to death running from the airport parking garage to the terminal. But four hours later, here I was in a little bit of paradise.

The only reason my husband and I had even thought about vacationing in Florida was because friends of ours had recently moved and they extended an invitation: "Come on down, it's eighty degrees in January," and they insisted we stay at their house.

I didn't need to do anything fancy on our Florida vacation—just waking up to the warm sun every morning was vacation enough for me. After three days in paradise, I suggested to my husband that next winter we should vacation in Florida again—only instead of two weeks, "Let's make it three, dear." Two days later I was pitching four weeks, three days after that five weeks sounded reasonable to me, and by the time we were ready to head back home, no doubt about it, next year's winter visit shouldn't be anything less than two months. Then again, on second thought, what the heck, let's just move to Florida and visit Wisconsin in the summer.

Initially, my husband's enthusiasm about the idea of moving to Florida lagged way behind mine, until I mentioned the word *boat*, and then the tipping point came quickly. In fact, by the time our plane landed in Madison, my husband had tipped so far over, he pictured us living on a 52-foot Irwin sailboat. "We could rent an office for our business and live on a boat in a fancy marina. The big marinas have laundry facilities, stores within walking distance, cable television, bathrooms, showers, and even a pool!"

Yeah, boy, what more could a girl want? It wasn't exactly the picture I'd had in mind when I mentioned the benefit of year-round boating in Florida. But then again, I do think it's every man's dream to own a boat. Owning a boat is a grown-up boy's version of a tree house, only on the water. Fix it up, tinker a bit. Invite your friends over to trim the sails, cleat the jib sheet, and just hang out, because as "real" boaters know, you can accomplish all of these things without ever leaving the dock—and most boaters never do.

I was hoping my husband wouldn't, but he finally popped the question. "Suzanne, could you imagine living on a boat for a year? How about it?"

Well, I was speechless. After all, it's not every day a girl gets an invitation to live on a boat (thank heavens). How would I fit all of my clothes in those little, itty-bitty boat compartments? And where would I put my treadmill? My husband had that *won't-you-please-pretty-please* look in his eyes, I just couldn't say no—but I emphasized it would be only for one year. So on our flight back home, excited yet nervous, we drew a line down the middle of a piece of paper and wrote down the pros and cons of moving to Florida. What did we have to lose?

Wisconsin's fall season (my favorite time of year) had practically become nonexistent, winters were freezing cold, and weren't we still shoveling snow last Easter? Our software company was virtual and since all of our employees worked from their homes, it really didn't matter where our business was located. If we didn't like living in sunny Florida we could always move back to Wisconsin.

So ten months later my husband and I packed up a U-Haul truck and headed south on I-90. The entire first year after our big move, this girl was on a Florida high, but thankfully *not* on the high seas. In the process of buying our 52-foot Irwin "home," negotiations fell apart. The seller pulled some strange last-minute maneuvers, which made my husband so disgusted with the entire transaction that he passed on buying the sailboat. Instead, we rented a house on the water near the marina. Lucky me, to this day I get brownie points for agreeing to live on a boat for a year, even though I never actually had to do the deed. (It's a great story and whenever my husband tells it, he beams with pride in front of the other men in the room!)

We may not have ended up living on a boat, but my husband did go a little boat crazy. The marina became our second home and guess what card we never left home without?

Sea Tow!

Sea Tow is a "road assistance" type card for boaters. You pay $95 a year, and if your boat breaks down, or if you run out of gas, Sea Tow will come to your rescue—no charge. It was a real deal for us, because the first few years we were in Florida, Sea Tow had to come to our assistance so many times I thought my husband and I would be their first customers to ever be refused a renewal membership. At the very least, I expected Sea Tow to add a "Bob and Suzanne Beecher–only" clause, stipulating that we were required to give them advance warning before we left the dock so they could have a Sea Tow boat and crew on standby.

Our Sea Tow adventures all started when my husband bought a new-used boat and the man who sold it to him failed to mention the faulty gas gauge. The selling-a-used-boat code of ethics seems to be, "If they don't ask, then don't tell 'em." And of course my husband never inquired, because he'd already fallen in love with the boat, sight unseen. He'd fallen head over heels the very first day he read the classified ad—even slept with it under his pillow that night. Nope, he didn't feel comfortable asking too many questions when we finally got our first look at the boat, because in my husband's eyes "she" was already a member of the family.

Wood rot, leaky motor, mildew, these were just some of the problems I noticed, but my husband assured me they were all minor repairs. How could we possibly turn our back on little *Solitude*? (Yes, he'd already named our new arrival.) So we trailered our little bundle of joy home.

A couple of weeks later, when we left the dock on our maiden voyage, I noticed *Solitude*'s gas gauge read half-full. Later in the day, even though we'd been cruising on the water all afternoon, the gas tank was still at the half-full mark. But when I voiced my concerns to my husband he started bragging about how great the gas mileage was in his new boat. Minutes later, we heard the sputtering sound of an engine desperately trying to suck up its last few drops of life from the gas tank. That was our first—but certainly not our last—call to Sea Tow.

My husband replaced the gas gauge, but *Solitude* continued to be a rebellious child, breaking down each and every single time we went out on the water. And, of course, each and every time we had to call Sea Tow. Neither my husband nor I wanted to be the one to make the call. It had become very embarrassing, because by now the guys at Sea Tow recognized our voices.

After a few years my husband finally gave up the ship—literally. But it's hard to break old habits.

What's the card I never leave home without?

Sea Tow! Just in case!

Marinated Flank Steak
A Recipe to Make While You're Waiting for Sea Tow

Our boat had a handy grill attached to a railing on deck. My favorite recipe to make was Marinated Flank Steak. Marinate it at home the night before and simply throw it on the grill. It's fabulous! And if you save a helping for the guys at Sea Tow, they give you a discount (at least that's been my experience).

Flank steak, any size
1 teaspoon tenderizer
Your favorite seasoned mustard (I use Grey Poupon)
3 tablespoons Worcestershire sauce

Score meat crisscross on both sides. Do not cut all the way through. Sprinkle approximately ½ teaspoon tenderizer on both sides of steak. Lightly and evenly cover each side of meat with your favorite mustard. Place meat in a shallow pan and pour 3 tablespoons Worcestershire sauce over it. Turn the meat, cover with plastic, and put it in the refrigerator overnight (8 to 10 hours), turning occasionally. Grill each side for 6 to 8 minutes. Slice thinly and enjoy!

13. Muffins and Mayhem

The two people who brought love into my life when I was growing up, Grandpa and Grandma Hale—and that's me in the middle.

"Warm and sunny, warm and sunny." It's a Florida meteorologist's mantra (in between an occasional hurricane). So it was easy to adjust to the weather when my husband and I moved from Madison, Wisconsin, to Sarasota, Florida. We bid farewell to the snow and cold, but that also meant saying good-bye to cold-weather treasures like tulips and daffodils. They're my favorite spring flowers.

Tulips and daffodils won't bloom in Florida because there's no resting period for the bulbs. Nevertheless, they show up in my yard every spring, because when I was young I learned a gardening secret from my Grandma Hale.

Even though the ground was still covered with a light dusting of snow, Grandma Hale always had the first spring flowers blooming in her yard—because she cheated. Just like seat-fillers at the Oscars, Grandma would carefully line up artificial but realistic-looking tulips and daffodils along the front of her house, until the real "stars" appeared. No one ever doubted that the flowers were real, because Grandma had such a green-thumb reputation.

But it wasn't just the flowers that were a real eye-opener when I first moved to Florida. The animals were pretty strange, too—especially since they tend to show up in places you wouldn't expect to see them. An alligator taking a dip in my neighbor's swimming pool, lizards scurrying back and forth across the sidewalk when I'm out for a relaxing walk, invisible biting flies—appropriately called no-see-ums—and twice a year it's mating season for love bugs. Thousands of females emerge from their larvae looking for an acceptable male suitor and when they find one, they latch on to each other in midair, but instead of rolling over and going to sleep afterward, the two lovers fall to the ground in the heat of passion. Frequently they fall into the path of a moving vehicle. Splat, splat. (What a price to pay for love.) My windshield, everybody else's windshield, and sometimes the entire front end of every single car in Sarasota is covered with a sticky adhesive-like love-bug mess. Superglue should be so strong. And the worst part is, if the aftermath doesn't get cleaned off immediately, the love-bug leftovers will eat right through the paint on your car.

And then there are the roaches. When I moved to the south I was prepared to see an occasional roach—on the floor—but the first time a three-and-a-half-inch cockroach flew across the room (Palmetto cockroaches do indeed fly) and landed on top of the cookbook I was reading, I seriously considered moving back to a cold-weather climate.

Palmetto bugs flying through the air, little black bugs tunneling through my flour—oh, did I forget to mention flour weevils? Well, let me tell you: "Buy-one-get-one-free" isn't really a sale in Florida if it's for flour or cereal—not unless you're going to use a lot of it soon—real soon. I never had a pantry pest problem when I lived in Wisconsin, but if wheat products sit around in Florida for too long—even if they're in a Ziploc bag or a plastic container sealed tightly with a lid—little itty-bitty black bugs hitchhike their way in and set up shop. Bran flakes with raisins seem to be one of their favorites, at least at my house. I suppose even bugs have heard about the benefits of eating bran and staying "regular."

Bran flakes are a staple in my husband's diet, too. He eats about four bowls a day and he doesn't like the idea of sharing his bran flakes with insects. So our solution was to buy smaller quantities and it worked—at least for a few months. But guess who showed up the other day?

I was in the middle of making my Dolly Madison Muffins, had already measured the sugar, eggs, cinnamon, flour, and buttermilk, and had stirred in the rest of the ingredients—including the bran flake cereal. A couple of final swirls with the spoon and the batter would be finished, and that's when I saw it—a bug—scurrying along the counter beside my mixing bowl. Oh no! There was another one, and another one, and when I looked down to survey the situation, there were bugs crawling up out of my muffin batter. Gross!

The bugs were frantic—running for their lives. It was a flour weevil 911 alert! The black critters were panicked, desperately trying to scale the inside wall of my mixing bowl, stopping periodically to shake the muffin batter off their legs—that buttermilk is sticky stuff.

But the batter was like quicksand. The weevils were putting up an organized fight, linking their little legs together like a safety chain, from deep in the middle of the bowl. Some of them had even broken out the emergency landing equipment, their nose plugs and swim caps keeping them dry, while they backstroked to safety. Surely I was in the middle of a horror novel.

Before the batter went into the trash, I must admit a couple of other options did run through my frazzled mind: The little critters are going to get baked at 400 degrees and don't people regularly eat bugs on reality television shows?

I may be a northern transplant, but I think I'm starting to think like a real Floridian. When I told my born-and-raised-in-Florida neighbor my gruesome little black-bug story, he smiled and shared this recipe for "How to Tell When You've Become a Real Floridian"—and it appears that I'm almost there.

> Bugs in your flour?
> A first-year northern transplant throws the flour out with the bath water, so to speak—anything and everything that's touched the flour goes in the trash.
> The second year—where are the tweezers?
> Third year—little black bugs—hey, they're protein!
> Bon appétit!

Actually most Florida critters and bugs are manageable once you learn how to avoid or head off their visits. And there's always a funny story behind the first time you meet up with them. Here are some of my favorites.

Run-ins with Critters from my Recipe File

Knock, Knock. Who's There?

I was flying back home and was in the middle of the most interesting conversation I've ever had at 28,000 feet in the air, or anywhere for that matter.

The woman sitting next to me was a faithful daughter, about my age, who told me that every year right before summer officially begins in Florida, she battens down the hatches on her eighty-year-old father's waterfront condo. The first year the loving daughter did the deed, everything looked secure, so she closed the door and they headed back to Indianapolis. But when she brought her dad back in the fall, it was apparent that someone had sublet their condo without permission.

"It was all new to me," the woman sitting next to me on the plane said, "but since you live in Florida, you probably know all about sewer rats, don't you?"

No, couldn't say that I'd ever had the privilege of meeting one, but I had the feeling I was going to hear all about them. Apparently sewer rats aren't content with their underground décor. And why should they be, when in the summer there are perfectly good Florida condos going to waste? So they pack their bags and move in.

"Knock, knock."

"Who's there?"

It's a sewer rat knocking on your toilet seat.

Yep, rats swim up through the sewer pipes, lift the lid on your toilet seat, walk right into your vacant condo, and make themselves at home for the summer—first one out gets dibs on the master bedroom!

Sewer rats are no fools. While most of us are spending the six weeks before summer trying to get into shape so we look good in our swimsuits, sewer rats are working out with a personal trainer, building up their biceps for the big push—on your toilet seat.

Actually, when you think about it, sewer rats are performing a kind of public service. No need to pay a house sitter to watch your place over the summer, sewer rats will gladly house-sit your condo for free.

Heck, they'll even water your plants if you leave your cable TV hooked up. And a little suggestion: It would be a nice gesture if you left some cheese as a thank-you gift. Everybody likes to be appreciated—even sewer rats.

"But I fixed those sewer rats good the second year," my seatmate continued. "I researched the problem on the Internet. You fill up your toilet with antifreeze, strap duct tape around the rim of your toilet seat, and then top it off with something heavy like bricks."

I could see it now—a kind of hot fudge sundae challenge for the rat. If a sewer rat can hold his breath long enough to swim through the antifreeze, rip through the duct tape with those razor-sharp incisors, and heave-ho, push that lid open, it's paradise for the summer.

And I'd have to say if a sewer rat could make it through all that, I think he's earned his keep, don't you?

Squirrel Psychology

I used to think the little skinny Florida squirrels in my yard were cute. But now we're at war. I didn't start it. Okay, I'm sure if you asked them they'd put the blame on me—but you know how squirrels are.

Last week when I was planting flowers and mulching in my garden, there was a squirrel that seemed to be keeping a pretty careful eye on me. Every time I'd put my spade into the ground, he started squeaking and jumping up and down on the tree limb above me. He was more than persistent, so I assumed he'd buried his food stash in my garden, and I was making him nervous.

I didn't think anything more about it until I sat down to take a break and something hit me hard on the top of my head. When I looked up, I saw the squirrel had found a partner in crime, and they each pitched another acorn at me. Amused, but rubbing the top of my head because those acorns smart, I asked the squirrels nicely to stop. They didn't. In fact, they kept running through the maze of tree limbs, following me around the yard all day long, and they wouldn't quit throwing stuff at me.

I was no longer amused.

I could understand the need for a squirrel to be concerned about his winter food supply, but these squirrels are Floridians. Yeah, yeah, it's been passed down through the generations to store up food for the winter months and these squirrels could be Wisconsin transplants, like me, and they just can't help themselves, blah, blah, blah. My husband has explained all the possibilities to me, but he's sympathetic to those warriors only because they haven't thrown a single thing at him. As far as I'm concerned those squirrels need therapy.

I checked the yellow pages, but there seems to be a shortage of Squirrel Psychoanalysts, so I decided to try my own brand of squirrel psychology. Just how complicated could a squirrel's mind be?

My plan was to convince those yeahoots that there wasn't a shortage of nuts, and then we could call a truce. So before I went to bed, I set a pan of assorted in-the-shell nuts underneath the tree. The next morning the pan was empty. Even so, I have the feeling I'm not going to prevail in this conflict, because when I was walking back toward my house, one of those squirrels *whacked* me with my own peace offering.

Even Mama Snake Needs a Night Out

I don't mind sharing my space with wild Floridian creatures, because I realize they're probably thinking *they're* the ones who are tolerating *me*. But the big black snake—the *bigger around than a garden hose* snake—the one that's been hanging around my house lately, we need to come to some sort of an agreement, because he's scaring the bejeebers out of me.

As far as I know, black snakes are harmless. (Usually I love to hear from readers, but if you know something to the contrary, please don't write and tell me I'm wrong—I think I'd rather be in the dark about what this snake likes to eat.)

Black snakes, at least the one that likes to sun himself on my porch, are docile. Mine doesn't rattle and he doesn't rise up and hiss at me. We haven't discussed it, but I get the impression that I make him just as nervous as he makes me. There's plenty of sun to go around in Florida, so I don't understand why all of a sudden this snake wants to sunbathe on my back porch.

Let me tell you, once you nearly step on a snake, everything that moves seems to slither. But after a couple of days with no snake on the steps, I forgot about him—until today, when I went out the back door, and my foot landed right beside his head. There we were, side by side on the same step, then he side-winded off, insulted that I'd almost tromped on him—and I was screaming.

There's always a reason for everything, and since I've seen some little baby black snakes around lately, maybe this is really a mother snake in desperate need of a few minutes away from her demanding children.

Maybe she's searching for a day at the spa—a little sun and a little snake cocktail, topped off with one of those fancy paper umbrellas.

Maybe I need to be more tolerant and understanding. I've raised children, heaven knows I can relate.

Slither On up to the Bar

I was planting geraniums in front of my house the other day, feeling all calm and relaxed, when it started to drizzle and the drizzle turned into a pretty good rain. But I kept on working anyway until all of a sudden, in the middle of the downpour, I was surrounded—they were everywhere. Snails! Slimy, disgusting, huge—I'm talking Texas-sized snails crawling all over the very plants I'd just been lovingly tending to.

I've never been squeamish about garden creatures before. Bugs, grubs, they've never bothered me. Big, fat night crawlers—no fear—I bait my own hook and I even talk to them when I'm gardening. "Keep up the good work, guys. Thanks for hanging out in my dirt."

But apparently I've met my match, because when I saw an army of snails crawling all over my geraniums, I freaked! No exaggeration. *What to do, what to do?* I picked a bunch of snails off the geraniums, but when I saw them crawling on my gardening glove, my primal instincts took over. I SCREAMED and flung them into the street. The people in the cars passing by thought I was a nut. "What is this woman throwing at us?" But I couldn't help myself.

"Help!"

I threw my gardening gloves on the ground and went running into the house, yelling for my husband. "You've got to come out and get rid of these snails!"

The snail affront ended my gardening for the day, and the day after that, and the day after that. I was worried I'd never be able to garden again, so I decided to find out how to get rid of snails.

Every relevant website I visited on the Internet had a photo of a snail, but I couldn't even stand to look at one, so I started visiting websites for children. "Meet Mr. Snail!" Yeah, Mr. Snail is supposed to look like a cute little cartoon character, with his smiley face and his little wiggly tentacles, but I knew the truth. Those smiley little slithering things would invade your garden and hunt you down.

Unfortunately I discovered that the best way to get rid of snails is to pick them off the plants, put them in a sealed bag and, well you know. . . . But since I'd already attempted that method and failed, I decided to get the snails drunk. Yes, option number two for exterminating snails is to sink a jar into the ground so the rim is flush with the dirt, fill the jar almost to the top with beer, and watch those snails conga line right up to the bar, fall in, and party to the end.

It's been a couple of weeks since I've seen any snails. My all-you-can-drink beer party was a big hit, but when I walked by my neighbor's house the other day I noticed they'd added a new yard ornament—a ceramic snail. I know it's supposed to be cute, but I still don't like it.

So I think tonight I'm going to have to get it drunk.

The All-You-Can-Drink Lunch Buffet

I'm trying my best to get my work done today, but welts—actually big pink mosquito bites—are bubbling up, especially around my ankles, and it's really getting difficult to concentrate on anything except this itching.

It's driving me crazy. I can't stand it and I shouldn't be itching, because I followed the rules. Life isn't fair.

I preplanned and sprayed myself with a bottle of advanced insect repellent before I went outside to pot some flowers. So instead of my body parts smelling like a lunch buffet—two legs, two ankles, an arm, and even a big toe—the mosquitoes should've been pinching their noses in disgust. "Phew, that woman stinks."

Yes, when that hungry swarm of skeeters buzzed near me they should have been repulsed, because the spray is supposed to trick them into thinking that my blood bank is tainted. Maybe I need to get a refund, because they seem to love the stuff. I swear I saw a swarm of six mosquitoes flying around with straws in their mouths. The little buggers congregated, battle plans were formed, and I heard a loud, humming war chant right before they attacked. I'm so tasty, they even came back for seconds—good to the last drop.

Again, I stress that life isn't fair, because I didn't buy the cheap stuff. I bought the top of the line: "Guaranteed to repel mosquitoes, chiggers, biting flies, no-see-ums, gnats and fleas." But apparently these mosquitoes, now filled with my fresh red blood, don't read labels.

Then again, apparently I don't either. My husband handed me a tube of hydrocortisone cream. "Put a layer of this on and the itching will stop." So I followed his advice, layered it on my arms and was spreading it real thick on my legs, topping off my big toe, when my husband ran back into the room. "Wait! Stop! I gave you the wrong tube. That's the special toothpaste the dentist gave me last week."

So I'm still itching, but at least I smell minty-fresh and my legs are tartar free.

Dolly Madison Muffins

Mix together in a large bowl:

4 eggs, beaten
2½ cups sugar
1 cup vegetable oil
1 tablespoon cinnamon
5 teaspoons baking soda

Then add these two ingredients alternately:

5 cups all-purpose flour
1 quart buttermilk

Next add 6 cups raisin bran (the cheapest is okay).

Mix well by hand. Cover, and let the batter stand in the refrigerator for at least 24 hours before baking.

Fill liners in a cupcake pan with batter. Bake for 20 minutes in a preheated 400-degree oven. (Sometimes I add fresh blueberries right before baking.)

Batter keeps four weeks in refrigerator with or without the little black bugs! Use the batter as you need it. Make three or four muffins every morning.

14. May I Please Have This Dance?

My husband and I dressed in our rented 50s attire, ready to rock at the big dance.

Me, myself, and I. We can be a bit strange sometimes. A good friend called the other day and we made a date for dinner, but ever since then part of me has been trying to come up with reasons why I should call her back and cancel. It's a very weird thing. Whenever I accept an invitation, initially my adrenaline gets a little push and it feels good thinking about doing something fun and different. There's no doubt I'll have a great time. I'm looking forward to the date, and even enjoying thinking about what I'll wear. But the closer it gets to the day of the event, the more uncertain I feel, and that uncertainty continues right up to the time I'm getting dressed to leave. Even then I'm wishing more than ever that I hadn't accepted the invitation. "Why did I say I'd do this? I wish I could just put on my pajamas and stay home."

Moan and groan—regrets about accepting the invitation overwhelm me. But by then it's too late to cancel and it's a good thing, too. Because as soon as I meet my friend and we sit down to dinner my feelings change. And that's when the mystery gets even more bizarre, because in the middle of our dinner it'll dawn on me how much fun I'm having and I'll be chastising myself: *Suzanne, you really ought to get out and do this more often.*

Me, myself, and I. Yes, we can be a strange bunch. Thank heavens people overlook our little bit of strangeness and invite us out anyway. And thank heavens we accept their invitations, or I would have missed two "recipes" in my life that turned out to be unexpected, precious moments.

The first was an invitation from one of the biggest advertising agency executives in town: "Live Band—Dress in 50s Attire." My husband and I moseyed on down to the costume shop. He picked out a white jacket, black pants, bow tie, and white shoes. I found a strapless flowered cotton dress and a pink sweater with an antique sweater clip, and I completed the look with white canvas tennies, ankle socks, a bouffant hairdo with a pink scarf tied in the back, and a single strand of pearls. My husband wore a pink carnation boutonniere on his lapel and I had a fresh flower corsage on my wrist. We definitely looked the part and were ready to rock at the 50s dance.

Well, ready to rock might be exaggerating just a bit. My husband and I had plenty of enthusiasm and desire to rock, but we really weren't very good dancers. When disco was in, we took dance lessons at Arthur Murray, so we figured if we stood on the dance floor at least twelve inches apart and each of us did our own disco-dancing thing, we'd probably look respectable. But, if at any point during the night we were required to actually touch each other and slow dance, we were in big trouble.

I suggested to my husband that we practice slow dancing before going to the party, and he thought it was a good idea. So in our living room, two hours before the big dance, Tony Bennett was in the background leaving his heart in San Francisco, and my husband and I were doing our best to two-step, three-step, box-step—anything that looked remotely close to dancing. But soon (too soon) it was time to go.

It was an impressive-looking party. The band sounded great, people were already dancing when we arrived, and waiters circled the floor holding trays of fancy hors d'oeuvres high up in the air. At first my husband and I felt a little awkward on the dance floor, but it was crowded, so no one noticed us. We were actually starting to have a lot of fun when suddenly the music stopped. Our hostess took the microphone and said that she had planned on having everyone vote for a King and Queen of the dance, but after seeing one couple's outfits, there was no doubt as to who should be crowned.

"Suzanne and Bob Beecher, would you please take the dance floor and dance the first slow dance as reigning King and Queen?"

This can't be happening. Were those our names I heard? People were clapping and looking at us, waiting for my husband and me to take the dance floor. A slow dance? The two of us slow dancing with everyone at the party watching? I'd always dreamed of being Prom Queen . . . but this felt like a nightmare.

We had no choice. The music started, my husband put his arm around me, our feet started to shuffle, and somehow we were moving around the floor. Well, we were barely moving, but at least we weren't stepping on each other's feet. I'm sure people watching thought we were playing up the part, as we gazed into each other's eyes, but really it was panic. I whispered to my husband, "Thank heavens we practiced. Do you realize how stupid we'd look if we hadn't?"

It was the longest song I'd ever heard. Halfway through I invited the other guests to join us on the dance floor. Finally my husband and I could go back to our two-step shuffling in the midst of the crowd.

Most of us wish for a happy ending to every story, and in the end, the 50s dance (our solo slow dance included), turned out to be a dream come true. My prince charming held me in his shaking arms and in the midst of our slow shuffle around the floor, he whispered in my ear, "Suzanne, you're my dream come true and I love you."

The second invitation was two months after my father died, when I was home visiting my mom. Some of her friends stopped by and invited us out to dinner. They were going to the Elmo Club, and afterward they were heading to the big senior dance in Platteville to listen to the Busch's Swing Band.

My mother immediately declined, insisting it was too soon for her to be seen out in public. But I knew that the alternative was the two of us sitting in the living room watching television and sharing a liverwurst sandwich. So I coaxed Mom along, reminding her how much I loved to go to the Elmo Club. My parents used to take me there when I was a kid and my dad always ordered a kiddy cocktail for me.

"Couldn't we just go for an early dinner, Mom, and then come right home?"

She finally agreed.

I knew all of the women sitting around the table because most of them were moms of the kids I used to play with, and if I didn't show up on time for dinner, my mother would call looking for me. The seventy-eight-year-old woman sitting across from me was one of my high-school teachers. So it did feel a little strange at first switching roles, but there we were having dinner together, all talking on the same level as if it had always been that way.

The Elmo Club didn't disappoint me. The food was just as good as I remembered it being thirty-some years ago, though I didn't order my usual kiddy cocktail. Yes, it was a great idea going out to dinner. Mom looked a lot more relaxed, until someone mentioned the dance again. But before my mother could refuse, there was kind of a group intervention. All of Mom's friends were widowed, too, and they knew she needed a real night out. So after more coaxing we were all on our way to the dance.

The parking lot was full and buses were dropping off seniors near the front door. It was a huge dance hall, decorated with crepe paper and balloons. A sign on the way in read: GET YOUR NAME TAG AND SIGN UP FOR DOOR PRIZES! We were lucky; we found a big round table near the front. The band had already started playing, but no one was dancing. I was thinking, *This is pretty much like the beginning of every dance I've ever gone to. Who is going to be the first couple on the dance floor?*

Two songs later, when the slow beat changed to a swing, the first couple, two women who must have been in their late seventies, braved the dance floor. Hands clasped together, not the least bit concerned—all eyes were on them—they held the dance floor alone, and when the song finished they stayed put, anticipating the next number. But when the music started again, couples (mostly women dancing with women) flooded the dance floor. "If you want to dance," one of my mother's friends advised, "you'd better not wait around for a man to ask, because there aren't enough of them to go around."

I noticed my mother tapping her foot and there was a remnant of a smile on her face when she leaned over and whispered to me, "May I please have this dance?"

Now it was a very strange thing to be dancing with my mother. At first I just stood on the dance floor staring at the five-foot-tall woman, my dancing partner, my mother—whom I'd never, ever seen dance before. I was shocked. Who was this woman? Her hips swaying side to side, shoulders loose, keeping time to the music. Just when did my mother learn how to do this? I had no idea how to do these dance moves, but it didn't matter. The next thing I knew, my mother took me by the hand and I was twirling around the dance floor. I could have sworn her dark brown hair was pulled back in a ponytail, and she was sporting white bobby socks and saddle shoes.

Breathless and a bit stunned, I started walking back to our table when the song was over, but instantly the music started again and so did my mother. We danced another dance, and another dance, and another dance.

After that—it was all kind of a blur, and finally when the music moseyed its way into a slow song, I was so thankful, thinking I'd finally get to sit one out.

But my mother stood her ground, grabbing my elbows and then gently looking into my eyes, letting me know that for whatever reason, she had to keep dancing. Then she slid her arm around my back, our hands came together, my mother closed her eyes, and some of her sadness melted into a smile as we glided around the floor.

It was the most memorable dance of my life. Slow dancing with my mother.

Recipes Me, Myself, and I Dared to Try— AND We're So Glad We Did!

I've never been a big fan of zucchini (too many bad zucchini memories from my childhood). I have a lot of great memories about growing up in a small town, but zucchini season is not one of them. Every year when the first homegrown zucchini was spotted, word spread quickly and the friendly community where I lived suddenly became a ghost town. The small-town dwellers locked their doors, pulled the drapes, and hid in fear until the zucchini plague had passed over.

Gardens are plentiful in a small town and so is their bounty—especially zucchini. Each zucchini seed packet contains about forty seeds and no respectable gardener can seem to resist planting each and every one of them. If it were any other vegetable you could count on casualties, so things would even themselves out, but not with zucchini.

Zucchini have got the vegetable procreation thing down pat. Plant those forty seeds in lousy soil, ignore them, deprive them of fertilizer, but as long as the sun shines and it rains, they'll grow . . . and grow . . . and grow. And that's the problem. Zucchini bread and cake, stuffed zucchini, grilled zucchini pizza, chocolate zucchini slices, zucchini and cream cheese sandwiches. Enough already.

So when my friend Linda cooked a birthday lunch for me and the first course was Zucchini Bisque, I ate it only to be polite. But to my surprise the bisque was fantastic—actually, now I rave it's the best soup I've ever tasted. I think you'll like it, too.

Zucchini Bisque

Serves 4

2 tablespoons butter
1 medium onion, coarsely chopped
1 cup chopped carrots
4 cups coarsely chopped zucchini
1 can chicken broth (or one bouillon cube dissolved in 1 cup boiling water)
¼ teaspoon marjoram
¼ teaspoon sugar, optional
¼ cup cream or milk, optional
For garnish: nutmeg, fresh parsley

Melt butter in a large saucepan over medium heat and add vegetables. Cook until onions are limp. Stir in broth, marjoram, and sugar (if using). Simmer for 20 minutes until vegetables are tender.

Cool slightly, then mix into a pulp till smooth. Add ¼ cup cream or milk, if using, and return to heat till warm. Serve garnished with nutmeg and parsley.

You can freeze the bisque before adding cream or milk. I freeze portions in sandwich bags.

The soup is great served cold, but I like it warm.

Company Fare Pork Chops

This is a recipe that I found in my Grandma Hale's old recipe box. It's written out on a 3 x 5 recipe card in her handwriting, and there's a note she added before the recipe: "Don't shy away from this recipe, absolutely delicious! Can be prepared in advance just as well as not."

Grandma's last note: "Don't plan on serving six people with this recipe. It is too good—people will want more than a second helping."

  6 thick pork chops
  12 small white onions
  5 tart apples, peeled and quartered
  ½ cup raisins, parboiled until plump
  1 tablespoon brown sugar
  1 cup beef consommé
  Salt, pepper, nutmeg, clove, bay leaf, parsley (no notation of how much, I
    just sprinkle some over the top)

Brown pork chops on both sides and then place in a small roaster or a deep casserole.

Arrange onions and apples over them, and then add raisins and sprinkle with brown sugar.

Add consommé (not diluted), salt, and pepper, and then sprinkle the other spices over the entire thing. Cover tightly and cook at 350 degrees for 1½ hours.

Chicken Crepes

They are divine!

This recipe sounds like a big deal to make, but it's not. The first time I tried it I was afraid because of the crepes. I'd never made any and figured it would be too difficult. The first few crepes I made were too big, but then I quickly got the hang of it and you will, too. People will think you were in the kitchen cooking all day long when you make this!

Serves 6 or 7

12 crepes (see page 156)
2 (10-ounce) packages broccoli spears frozen in butter sauce
¼ cup flour
1½ cups water
1 tablespoon instant chicken bouillon
1 cup shredded Cheddar cheese
2 tablespoons sour cream
2 tablespoons sherry
1 tablespoon minced fresh parsley
Dash onion salt
Dash pepper
1½ cups cubed cooked chicken or turkey
2½-ounce jar sliced mushrooms, drained, or fresh mushrooms
¼ cup grated Parmesan cheese

First make the crepes and set aside. Cook broccoli according to package directions. Snip corner of pouches and drain butter sauce into medium saucepan. Stir in flour until smooth. Add water and bouillon and heat, stirring constantly, until thickened and smooth. Stir in ½ cup Cheddar cheese, the sour cream, sherry, parsley, and onion salt and pepper; heat until cheese is melted. Add chicken and mushrooms.

Preheat oven to 350 degrees.

Place a broccoli spear on each crepe. Top with 1 to 2 tablespoons of chicken sauce. Fold crepes and place seam side up in 13 x 9-inch baking dish. Pour remaining sauce over crepes. Sprinkle with remaining ½ cup Cheddar cheese and Parmesan cheese. Bake for 20 minutes.

Basic Crepes

4 eggs
¼ teaspoon salt
2 cups all-purpose flour
2⅓ cups milk
¼ cup oil

In large bowl, beat eggs and salt until foamy. Lightly spoon flour into measuring cup and level off. Add flour and milk to the eggs and beat well. Add oil and beat until well blended.

Heat small 7- or 8-inch skillet over medium-high heat. A few drops of water sprinkled on the pan will sizzle and bounce when heat is just right. Grease pan lightly with oil. Pour about 3 tablespoons of batter into pan, tilting pan to spread evenly. When crepe is light brown and set, turn to brown other side. Remove from pan. Adding oil as necessary, repeat with remaining batter. Stack cooked crepes, putting wax paper or parchment paper in between. You can freeze any extra crepes.

15. I Miss My Mother

My mother and I were clowns in the annual Cuba City parade, and we even won a prize two years in a row.

Love isn't always a guarantee between a mother and a daughter, at least it wasn't for my mother and me. We cared for each other, but I think it was more out of a sense of duty. So it was very difficult, twice a year, when I found myself standing in front of rows of greeting cards, agonizing over which birthday or Mother's Day card to buy.

I couldn't bring myself to give my mother a card thanking her for her love and affection, or for how special she made me feel. But I also didn't want to send a generic "Happy Day" card that might suggest how I really felt about our relationship. I guess a daughter always holds out hope—who knows, maybe it was that way for my mother, too.

Was I the only daughter who felt this way? When I asked my friend Linda, she was sympathetic but didn't offer any advice on how to change my relationship with my mother, or about which card to buy. But she did tell me, "Suzanne, even though my mother's been dead for quite some time now, I still think of her every single day." Linda's eyes were misting over.

"You must have had a wonderful relationship with your mother," I told her.

"No, not at all," she replied.

And then Linda told me a story that left me in tears—a story that made me want to hold my friend in my arms and console her, even though this terrible thing had happened to her a long time ago.

When Linda was a teenager, she got pregnant and her parents made her leave home. "Don't ever come back," they told her. And this wasn't the kind of leaving where your mother and father arranged for you to stay somewhere until after the baby's born. No, her parents just opened the front door of their home and told their daughter to get out. A pregnant, scared young girl who had no job, no place to live, and now no family to love her, Linda left home and was never invited back.

I was stunned. "Don't you hate your mother? How could you possibly miss your mother and still think of her every day after she did that to you?"

Holding back her tears, Linda assured me that every single day, if only for a moment, she still misses her mother.

"Well, that may be how *you* feel," I told my friend, "but that will never happen to me. When my mother dies, I'm sure I'll feel sad, but we've never had a close relationship, so how could I possibly miss something I never had?"

"It's a very strange thing indeed," Linda said, "but yes, Suzanne, you'll miss your mother every day after she's gone."

My friend Linda was right.

I miss my mother.

The boxes came today. The ones my husband and I packed up after my mother's funeral. Deciding what to keep and what to toss or give away was a slow and difficult process. What looked like junk to most people was actually full of precious memories.

Sorting through someone else's possessions, even my mother's, made me feel uneasy. The things left behind expose a person after they're gone, and that person's not around to explain why they kept something for all those years. So I could only guess why my mother had hung on to a tall, decorative, gold glass bottle with a pointed top. The bottles were popular when I was growing up, and ours used to sit in the corner of the living room. It didn't do anything except sit there and collect dust.

Looking at it now, I can't for the life of me understand why my mother found it attractive. It's one of the ugliest bottles I've ever seen. Nevertheless, it went into my "save" pile of things. How could I say no to a bottle that I'd dusted throughout my entire childhood?

And that's how my sorting-things task went for most of the day. After four hours my save pile was overflowing and the toss pile had only six items in it. I finally asked my husband to help me make decisions. Thank God he was patient. The two of us started over again, from the beginning. I'd pick up an item, tell him a story about it, and then he'd help me make a less sentimental decision about whether or not to keep it. By the end of the weekend, we'd filled twelve huge boxes with things I was shipping to our home in Florida.

I immediately opened a couple of those boxes today when they arrived, but I think I'm going to have to leave most of them taped up for a while. It took a lot out of me to pack up those memories, and I don't think I'm ready to start unpacking them quite yet.

I miss my mother.

After my mother's death I couldn't shake the feeling that I was left alone in the world. My father had died four years earlier, I was an only child, and my grandparents were gone, too. And I guess that's the thing that started haunting me—everyone was gone. I realized my "all alone" feeling wasn't rational, because I had a wonderful, loving husband, two grown children, three grandchildren, and friends who cared about me. But the little girl inside of me felt like she'd been abandoned.

How was I going to get through this? I could hardly function; the sadness and confusion of grief consumed me, and none of it made any sense. It wasn't like I'd relied on my parents for anything, especially emotional support. Besides, in my mind I'd already grieved both of their deaths, while they were still alive.

A few years before my father died I'd sent my parents a letter, hoping it would mend our relationship, especially my relationship with my father. But the letter made things worse. After reading it my father disowned me and expected my mother to do the same. And that's when I worked my way through mourning the loss of my parents, and finally accepting that some things never change. The reality was that my father was an alcoholic and my mother covered for him, even when it meant shortchanging herself and her daughter.

It had been five years since I'd sent the letter, so when I got the call— "Your father's dying"—I had to decide . . . should I go or not? Five years of silence was a long time. It would feel like a lie to show up after such a lengthy separation. But if I didn't go and regretted it afterward—this was *the end*. I wouldn't get a second chance.

When I arrived at the hospital, there was a very awkward moment when my mother and I figured out how to greet each other. We didn't hug. Dad was unconscious and the doctors didn't expect him to wake up. One of my father's sisters was also there and I suggested that she take Mom home to get some rest. Thankfully they decided to leave. It gave me a chance to adjust and be alone with Dad. I pulled a chair over by the side of his bed and bent down, so I could be close to him. He looked so much older than I'd remembered, but I guess I'd always seen my dad through the eyes of a little girl.

My father and I got along when I was growing up, especially when he was drunk. Dad wasn't a mean drunk, quite the opposite. If he'd been drinking, he'd tell me how much he loved me and how proud he was of me. But of course those words meant nothing. When Dad was sober, I tried to stay out of his way because he was unkind and ornery. I actually liked my father the best when he was drunk. So tagging along when he went to the corner bar was one of my favorite things to do, especially on Sundays.

Every week Mom would drag Dad to church with us on Sunday morning. After church was over, I went to Sunday school for an hour and then Dad would pick me up and we'd drive to the bar—"To have a few before lunch, while your mother's home cooking." It was our father-daughter outing, sit in the pew on Sunday morning and sit on the bar stool Sunday afternoon.

I loved riding in the car with Dad. I thought my daddy was the best driver in the world when I was a little girl. Riding in the car with my dad behind the wheel was the only time I felt safe and cared for by him.

Years later when I was living on my own, I went back home to visit my parents, and Dad invited me to go to the bar with him just like old times. But when we walked out of the bar and I reached to open the car door on the passenger side, I realized that if I got in, I'd be riding home with a drunk. And the truth was that I'd *always* been riding home with a drunk, and that reality compelled me to write the letter.

Now here I sat staring at a "stranger" who hadn't talked to me for five years. This was my dad—the person I wanted so desperately to have a relationship with, but it was too late.

It was so quiet in his room. I started softly singing "The Old Rugged Cross," because I knew it was Dad's favorite hymn. I had no idea if he could hear me, but in the middle of the second verse my father woke up, looked at me, and smiled. Then he raised his hand, brushed it against my cheek, and with tears in his eyes he said, "I never thought it would come to this. I'm so sorry for everything."

I'd pictured an ending similar to this many times before—my dad wanting to make amends at the last minute—and so I was prepared. *No way, forget it, it's too late,* were the words I'd rehearsed. But instead, I took my dad's hand and told him we both did the best we could, and that I loved him.

My father died the following night.

The End, how it all wraps up, is a choice. My father may not have had much to give to me when I was a little girl. But when he died, he took the anger and sadness that I felt along with him—and it is still the greatest gift I've ever received.

After my father died I was hopeful that the relationship between my mother and me would change. Finally there wouldn't be anything standing in the way. But you can't instantly have a relationship with someone without a little practice, and it had been too many years. My mother never learned how to feel and show love, so she didn't have a clue how to begin—until she met Ron.

Some people find love early and it grows along the way, but some have to wait. My mother had to wait a very long time, but two years before she died, she met Ron, the love of her life.

I remember the day they met. My phone rang and a "girl" who just got asked to the "prom" was on the other end of the line. It was my mother. "I met this man." I could hear my mother's smile through the phone. "I think he likes me. His name is Ron and he wants to take me out for a ride in the country and then have dinner."

Mom was giggling like a schoolgirl who couldn't wait to call and tell her friend the news. What should she wear, what should she say? She was worried she'd forgotten how to go on a date. But from the very beginning it was a sweet, tender love, and it became the kind of marriage that neither of them had experienced, or even dreamed possible.

I remember early one morning I was visiting my mother, sitting in the living room reading a book, when I heard her in the hallway outside her bedroom. She was walking toward me and right behind her was Ron—a big brute of a man, a man who can be so brusque at times you wonder where he hides his gentleness. He was crawling down the hallway on his hands and knees and when his eyes caught mine, he put his finger up to his lips to silently shush me. Then he reached out and gently touched the back of my mother's leg, and with the silliness of a child playing tag, he called out, "I love you!" It was a game they played every morning to see who could say the words first.

Ron gave my mother a second chance at finding true love, but he also gave Mom and me an opportunity to work on our relationship.

When it got cold in Wisconsin, Ron and Mom headed to Florida, rented a house near my home in Sarasota, and officially became Florida snow-birds—and garage-sale junkies. I don't think either of them ever went to a garage sale when they were in Wisconsin, but every afternoon around three o'clock Mom and Ron would pull into my driveway, open the back of their van, and holler for me to come out and see their "finds" for the day.

"How much do you think we paid for this?" They were so excited, like two little kids, and they could hardly wait for me to guess.

A fair estimate would probably have been in the twenty-five cents to $3 range, but I didn't want to spoil their fun, so I'd always guess high.

It had become their morning ritual. Ron would buy a copy of the local newspaper, circle the garage-sale ads, and plan out their route. Then they'd hit the road very early, partly because they assured me that the "early bird" garage-saler does indeed get the best stuff, and partly because they'd get lost—a lot.

"See that," Ron's pointing to a blue cooler sitting way in the back of their van, "your mom and I were looking around at a garage sale in Venice and when the woman asked if I saw anything I was interested in, I spotted this cooler sitting in her garage. It didn't look like it was with the garage-sale items, so I asked if it was for sale."

At first the woman told Ron it wasn't, but then suddenly even she got caught up in the garage-sale fervor. "What would you give me for it?"

"Five bucks!"

"Sold! And it's even filled with my husband's beer"—the woman was smiling—"you can take that along with you, too."

What a deal! Ron and my mother were both beaming with pride as they showed me their $5 cooler filled with ice and beer. It wasn't that Mom and Ron needed any more stuff—they already had three coolers—but the story behind the stuff was a recipe in their new life together. And it quickly became one of their favorites, because between the two of them, they must have told four slightly different versions of the "cooler" story before they left my house later that evening.

At the end of the winter, I waved good-bye and Mom and Ron drove back home to Wisconsin. Two months later, I got the call and flew home to be with my mother.

It's a very strange thing talking with someone about their death. You're sitting there, having a fine conversation with them, but you both know that in two or three days they'll be gone. And so you begin making preparations because as unreal as it all seems, death is on the way.

I'm great at making lists and getting things done—I got it from my mother. She had already made arrangements with the funeral home director, and three days before she died, when Mom and I were sitting in her living room, she was handing me scraps of paper—notes she'd written recently about what she wanted her funeral service at the church to be like—suggested readings, songs, and scriptures. "My funeral service needs to reflect love," she told me. "It's important that people attending the funeral realize that love is the most important thing in life. I'll leave the rest of the details up to you, Suzanne."

Mom's only absolute was "no ham sandwiches," and I knew why. After my father died, my mother and I met with the woman from church who was in charge of preparing the lunch after Dad's funeral service. The woman was outlining the menu for us—potato salad, baked beans, Jell-O salad, turkey and ham sandwiches—and that's when my mother interrupted her and practically screamed, "We're not serving ham! I hate ham!"

I was as stunned as the poor church woman! "Mom, I never knew you didn't like ham. You used to serve ham every Easter dinner."

"I only made it because your father wanted it, but I hate ham—and I'm never serving ham again!"

As strange as it sounds, I think my mother's "No ham!" proclamation was a kind of coming out, a debut. Even though Mom was the real breadwinner in our family, she put up with my father's drinking and went along with whatever he decided.

"No ham, Mother. I promise no ham sandwiches at your funeral luncheon."

Except for her bald head, the night before my mother died no one would have suspected anything was wrong. Mom was sitting on the sofa, eating some fresh fish the neighbor had brought over, and she was asking for seconds. "I can't remember the last time I had such tasty fish. Can I have some more?"

Fresh fish had always been Mom's favorite. She was asking for seconds, just like she used to do when I was a kid, and she looked better than I'd seen her in days.

But the next morning, my mother is talking about death again, and as the day moves forward, I realize we've stepped over the line. My mother hasn't died yet, but I am looking at the other side of life—too late for a conversation, too late for one final good-bye. I don't know where my mother is now, so all I can do is try to make sure she isn't in pain. The hospice nurse is on the way to help us make it through the night.

My mother's breathing is shallow now and at times she's gasping for a breath. I think this will be her final breath, but it's not. Mom keeps going—not ready to leave—and as the night wears on, my patience runs out. I'm tired, my emotions are battered, and my mother keeps hanging on. I feel like a horrible daughter. I wish my mother would die. I wish she would let go. I can't take this much more, but I remind myself that this is my mother's death, to be lived any way she sees fit. The final scene on this earth belongs to each of us alone.

Two hours later, my mother slips away.

"Is there anything I can do for you?"

People have been asking me that question a lot since my mother passed away. Asking if they can help may seem like a simple gesture, but it's such a comfort to me. I was never quite sure how I could help someone when a person close to them died, but now I realize it's the little things that make all the difference.

Friends and neighbors are great at the little things. They stop by your house with casseroles, cakes, and salads. They offer to dog-sit your mother's poodle. They show up and mow the lawn because it needs it; they drop off your black suit at the dry cleaners and pick it up for you so you have it in time for the funeral. When they hear that you woke up with horrible neck pain (because they're chiropractors, husband and wife, and they live two doors down), they meet you at their office early in the morning two days in a row, and don't charge you a thing either time. "It's the least we can do," they tell you.

Cards, emails, flowers, and people sharing stories, saying, "I remember when your mother did such and such . . . she was so funny . . . she was such a wonderful woman." These simple words help ease my pain. And letting me talk about my mother—sometimes listening to me tell the same stories over and over again, until I don't feel the need to repeat them anymore—what a gift that can be!

"Is there anything I can do for you?"

That simple question brought tears to my eyes and comfort to my heart.

Several months had passed since my mother's death and I wished things would get back to normal, the way they were *before*. But then I'd think of the things I'd learned about myself since my mother died, and how her passing had changed me. I look at the world differently now, I'm a better writer, and I've changed some of the priorities in my life. I consider these "gifts" my mother left for me.

Yet every time I sat down to work, the first sentence I needed to write before I could move on was *"I miss my mother."* I rationalized that it was time to move on and most days I was able to go about my normal routine—but then out of the blue the sadness was overwhelming again.

I'd accepted that grieving takes time and a lot of hard work, but for some reason I thought I should do it alone. Whenever I felt the urge to say out loud "I miss my mother," a list of questions flooded my mind: How long can I grieve? Are my friends tired of hearing about my mother? Will I be stuck here in this emotional place forever? Some days it seemed like everywhere I went, something reminded me of my mother.

I arrived early for my hair appointment and while I was waiting, I noticed her from across the room. She was a short woman with a round face, her cheeks had a natural blush when she smiled, and a whitish tint covered her head. She was getting her hair colored, but it was her smile that first caught my attention.

I stared—couldn't help myself. For a moment I could hardly breathe and I tried to hide my trembling hands. I thought it was her. She looked just like my mother. But of course it couldn't be my mother. My headphones, where are my headphones? I turned the music on loud and then louder, thinking maybe I could transport myself somewhere else. It was all too much for me.

Every Wednesday I have an appointment with my hairdresser. I don't even own a bottle of shampoo, and my mother's to blame. Yes, my mother who washed out every container: "Throw nothing away, buy nothing unless it's on sale, buy the wrong size and make it fit, if it's a good price." Oh, how many times did I hear those words? Yet Mom had a standing weekly appointment at the hairdresser. In fact, I don't ever remember seeing my mother wash and dry her own hair—not even once.

The small-town price of a weekly wash and blow-dry, and a monthly tint, was somehow justifiable in Mom's self-imposed budget. Maybe it was because she always worked a full-time job, or maybe my mother was like me—I can't blow-dry my hair into anything that looks even remotely respectable.

The first year Mom and Ron came to winter in Florida, my mother gasped when I took her along to my weekly hair appointment. Thirty dollars for a wash and blow-dry, fifty dollars for a haircut. My mother was beside herself, but it was one of the few times in her life she decided to take a chance.

"Go ahead and cut my hair," Mom told my hairdresser. "Make me look beautiful."

An hour later I barely recognized my mother. She became a different woman that day and she had a special smile—it was the same smile I was looking at now across the room. Oh, how I wish the woman with the tint on her hair was my mother, even for a minute—just a hug, an embrace, just to feel my mother's arms around me again.

But all I could do was stare. I walked away until the woman was out of sight, thinking maybe I was imagining things. But when I returned, she was still there and so was that smile. A smile from across the room—a smile meant just for me, to tuck away in my heart.

I miss my mother.

After my mother died, a close friend of mine gave me permission to grieve for as long as it took. She knew I needed to hear those words because I was frightened—afraid that I'd never find my way back. But one morning, almost a year and a half later, when I woke up things were different. I missed my mother, but now when I said those words, I was at peace and I felt different. The pain was gone.

Grieving had been a long journey. I realized that it didn't end that day, that it would never end, but the road before me had changed. I could see the lights; I could see a new wonderment in the world. Now when I looked at other people smiling, I didn't wonder anymore *What's wrong with them, don't they know how sad life is? Don't they know the world has come to an end because I miss my mother?*

The days and months, when would this pain end? How could it ever go away? Stories about my mother—I used to think about them over and over again, but they only made me miss her even more; the last words we said to each other; the day my mother pulled a magazine off the rack in the supermarket, opened it, and proudly announced to everyone, "That's my daughter on page thirteen." The afternoon my mother sat beside me on the sofa and told me she was going to have to leave, but she knew I'd be all right. I was a good girl and she loved me. Those stories used to bring me to my knees, but now they comforted me.

Yes, things were different now. The grip on my heart was now an embrace. I could breathe. I felt joy. My mother was right. I will be okay.

But still . . . *I miss my mother.*

My Mother's Oatmeal Chocolate-Chip Cookies

Baking chocolate-chip cookies and giving them away is something I do for fun. Friends, neighbors, and even business associates refer to me as "the Cookie Woman." I used to think giving away cookies was my own idea, but apparently it's in my genes.

My mother never enjoyed cooking. So I was really surprised when I was standing in the receiving line at her wake, and after people offered their sympathies, they said they'd never forget my mother because she was always baking cookies and giving them away. I was amazed. All those years, I guess my mother and I had more in common than we realized.

Mom's specialty was Oatmeal Chocolate-Chip cookies. Here's a copy of her recipe I found when I was digging through her old recipe box.

1½ cups all-purpose flour
1 teaspoon baking soda
1 teaspoon salt
1 cup butter
1 cup granulated sugar
1 cup light brown sugar
2 eggs
1 teaspoon pure vanilla extract
3 cups oatmeal
chocolate chips (my mother never indicated how many, but I use 1 to 2 cups)

Preheat oven to 375 degrees.

Mix the flour, baking soda, and salt together. Mix remaining ingredients together with the flour mixture and then add the chocolate chips.

Bake for 10 to 12 minutes until cookies are light brown. (Cool and then give them away to friends, neighbors, and strangers.)

Ron's Goulash

My mother didn't like to cook, but Ron did. In fact, he's a great cook. Ron's shy about his cooking talents, because he says "there's nothing to my recipes." They may be simple to make, but they sure do taste good. Here's one of his favorites and mine, too.

2 pounds hamburger
1 medium onion, chopped
8 ounces elbow macaroni
1 (15-ounce can) Hunt's tomato sauce
1 can cut green beans, optional
Salt and pepper to taste
Clove garlic, crushed, optional

Brown the hamburger and onion together. Meanwhile, cook macaroni per directions on package. Mix rest of ingredients together with hamburger and macaroni and simmer until it smells good enough to eat.

16. Still In-a-Pickle and It's _Not_ What Miss Manners Would Do

Rolling my own dough and baking pies is a messy job, but it's so relaxing.

"SHHH!! It's a Surprise Party! For Kiki on May 6th at 7 p.m."

The party invitation addressed to me included an address and a phone number, so I could RSVP, but the invite didn't say who was throwing the party for Kiki—not that it mattered—because I had a much bigger problem . . . WHO THE HECK IS KIKI?

Obviously a good friend of Kiki's sent me the invitation, because she thinks I'm also a good friend of Kiki's. But now I feel like I'm really losing my mind, because I'm supposed to be good friends with two people I don't know: the party giver and the party girl. Why else would I get an invitation, but . . . WHO THE HECK IS KIKI?

It was amusing for a while, receiving an invitation to a party where I didn't recognize any names or the address, and when I drove by the house I was certain I'd never seen it before in my life. To save my sanity, I started questioning my friends (friends I was absolutely certain I knew) to see if they knew a friend, or if we know a friend, or if anyone knows a friend of a friend—could anyone help me? But they all just wanted to know "WHO THE HECK IS KIKI?"

"Pick up the phone and just ask," my real friends suggested. But how do I call an unknown *someone* who invited me to a party for *our* dear friend Kiki, and casually inquire, "Who are you and . . . WHO THE HECK IS KIKI?"

It would be very embarrassing if the reply was "What's wrong with you, Suzanne? Of course you know Kiki! We all had lunch together last week. Don't you remember you ordered the chicken salad?"

So I asked my daughter-in-law to make the call instead. Her story (well, the lie we made up, because if there was ever a time to lie this was it) was that the postman had delivered the invitation to her by mistake, and she thought she'd better call to let someone know it went to the wrong address. And of course, then she'd get the chance to ask that ever burning question, "WHO THE HECK IS KIKI?" and the mystery would be solved.

But that's not what happened. Instead, things took a nasty turn.

The woman curtly interrupted my daughter-in-law. "Why are you bothering me? You shouldn't have opened the invitation. If you don't know who Kiki is, the invitation obviously wasn't meant for you, and I'd certainly never invite anyone like you to the party."

"WHO THE HECK IS KIKI?"

Nobody really cares anymore.

But my daughter-in-law and I are dying to meet Kiki's pretentious friend. What was the date and time of that party?

Kiki's getting two new friends for her birthday.

(Don't worry, the name and date in this recipe from my life was changed to protect the smarty-pants! I ended up not going to the party because I came down with a bad cold, and I figured even Kiki didn't deserve that for her birthday.)

Door-to-Door Etiquette

Dark suit, white shirt, dark tie, and a book and pamphlets tucked underneath his arm. I knew right away who he was, and what he wanted the minute I spotted the "tools" of his trade. So after he delivered his opening line, I butted in and suggested we just cut right to the chase.

I explained that normally he'd want to show me "the way" and then I'd try to tell him that I was already taken care of in that department, but nevertheless, he'd still keep right on talking, because he doesn't like "my way" and eventually I'd politely shut the door in the middle of his sentence.

"So here's the thing," I told him, "my writing muse is on vacation and it's been kind of tough going today. You see, when I get to a certain point in a column, I usually call my writing muse and she listens to me talk. And since I'm without someone to listen to me today, and you're here, and you want to talk and hang around my front porch anyway, how about if you listen to me talk about my column and then it will be your turn to talk, and I'll listen. Have we got a deal?"

And before he could realize what he'd agreed to, I pulled up a lawn chair and told him to sit down and put his feet up. "Do you want a glass of lemonade? I think we might be here awhile. I can't quite decide on a lead."

Line by line, I delivered my column and he even laughed in the places I was hoping for at least a giggle. But when I got near the end and I was starting to stumble, because I still needed to do some rewriting, he started getting impatient. He looked down at his watch and when I heard him clear his throat, I was afraid that Persuader Man was going to try to slide in one of his "this is the way" lines. So I just kept right on going at the end of my sentence, rolling right over the period, not even stopping to take a breath. Then I slid right into the next sentence, and when my substitute muse's attention started to wane even more, I reminded him that we had an agreement.

"Doesn't it say something in that 'persuasion' book you're totin' around about keeping your side of a bargain?"

I give him credit. Persuader Man sat back down, and he was a pretty good listener—he didn't have too many creative suggestions, but then again that wasn't part of our deal. And soon it was his turn. But by then, the sweat was running down his face (it was 98 degrees even in the shade), and in all fairness, he'd probably forgotten his lines because I'd interrupted his usual presentation flow.

"Not to worry," I told him. "My muse takes two vacations a year. Give me your card and the next time she leaves town, I'll call you."

All You Can Eat . . . If All You Can Eat is One Bite

Every invention comes from necessity, and whoever invented the garbage disposal must have been inspired by a mother and 125 miniature white Styrofoam containers from a senior meal site.

When my mother died three years ago, it was very difficult to pack up her things and find a home for them. However, it was not difficult to haul 125 Styrofoam containers out to the curb for Tuesday's trash pickup.

Mom didn't enjoy cooking, so after Dad passed away she started having lunch at the senior meal site in the small town where she lived. It was the perfect cooking solution. Not only did Mom get a hot lunch every day, but because she started volunteering, she got to take home leftovers—food that would have been thrown out anyway. In theory, this all sounded wonderful. The problem was when I'd visit Mom, she'd never let me take her out to dinner.

"Why waste food?" Mom would reply when I'd extend an invitation. "There's roast beef, turkey pot pie, scalloped potatoes, coleslaw, corn, fruit salad, and cherry cobbler in the refrigerator for dinner."

I admit, it sounded like a smorgasbord; she must have been cooking like crazy anticipating my visit. So I started setting the dining room table for a fancy feast, but my mother started lining up fifteen little miniature Styrofoam containers on the kitchen counter. Taking the lids off the containers one by one, Mom took my order for the evening's fare: "What would you like? How about a little of everything?"

Yeah, boy, that's what it was going to have to be. Because there was one bite of roast beef in one container, maybe three bites of turkey pie in another, six kernels of corn in yet another, and five miniature containers with dabs of cherry cobbler—enough to actually make one dessert. But whose dinners were all of these miniature containers left over from? I could only hope they were my mother's. Bon appétit!

My mother grew up in the "waste not . . ." era. So I knew the only way to get rid of the Styrofoam leftovers was either to eat them or get up early before she did, switch on the radio to drown out the sound, and then turn on the garbage disposal. "Mom, I ate the rest of the leftovers for breakfast, so we'll have to go out to dinner this evening."

I used to feel a bit guilty about tossing out my mother's Styrofoam collection after she passed away, but I'm pretty certain there's no use for Styrofoam in heaven. It's true you can't take it with you—but if you're like my mother—you'll drag it along as far as the front door of the Pearly Gates, and then you have to lay your bag of Styrofoam containers down.

And when you lay it down, I like to think that it's someone like my mother who is in charge of finding a good home for all those little containers. After all, you never know when you'll need a pint-size Styrofoam container that used to have a single serving of baked beans in it.

Even Miss Manners Would Lie

I was in the tub, the telephone rang, and the next thing I knew my husband was handing the phone to me. "Who is it?" I whispered.

My husband shook his head and mouthed, "I don't know." My dear husband is very uncomfortable lying to people, so he gets flustered when the phone rings and the caller asks for me. What's he to say? "Suzanne can't come to the phone, she's in the tub," or "Suzanne told me to tell anyone who calls that she's not here." The phone becomes a game of Hot Potato, my husband quickly handing it off and hoping it doesn't circle back around to him.

The woman on the other end of the line said, "Hello, this is Christine and I'm calling from the church. I'd like to know if you want to get your picture taken for the directory."

"No. Thank you very kindly, but I'll pass," I told her.

"Well, are you still a member?" she asked.

"Yes, I am."

"It doesn't cost anything to get your picture taken."

"I appreciate that, but I would really rather not. My life is kind of complicated right now."

"Well, okay, thanks anyway. Good-bye."

After I hung up the phone my first thought was *What have things come to? Why did I say that? I wonder what that woman is thinking now.* If I asked someone to do something and they told me, "No thank you, my life is kind of complicated right now," I would assume something awful—somebody died, someone was ill, or they were in the early stages of a nervous breakdown. But everything's A-OK in my life, so what's up? Before I could further analyze my mysterious reply, another thought popped into my head, one that was even more disturbing.

I started thinking about my old high-school yearbook, and then I got to worrying about what they'd print in the church directory. I can't remember exactly what the yearbook staff said the year Danny Coohn's picture was missing, but it went something like: "Danny's picture isn't here because he was expelled from school for two weeks, so he couldn't come on school grounds to get his picture taken."

Oh no! I can see it now: "Suzanne Beecher is not listed in this year's church directory because she was taking a bath when we called, and she told us her life was too complicated. We're all praying that her bath is successful and that her life uncomplicates very soon."

Gotta, Have-to, Even in the Pew

The minister was in the middle of his Sunday sermon and when he mentioned "Robert's Rules of Order"—well, that did it. Words started popping into my mind, coming at me fast and furiously. One after another, I couldn't stop them. Pretty soon the words were forming sentences, and the sentences were lining up like jets on the tarmac waiting their turn for takeoff. I had to get this stuff out of my mind. I didn't have any choice. I had to write a column then and there.

I always carry a notebook with me, but I was nervous about getting it out because my son and daughter-in-law, who are usually sitting in the pew next to me, said that the last time I received so-called divine writing inspiration, I was oblivious to the commotion I created. You see, sometimes when I write, the ideas come so quickly and I'm so completely engrossed in the words that I'm unaware what's going on around me. Apparently, the single sheet of paper and the stubby pencil that I was using that particular day were crinkling so loudly that people were turning around and staring at me. I do remember my son giving me the evil eye to stop, but I thought he was just passing judgment on whether or not I should be writing a column in the midst of a church service.

So this time I gently and quietly (*shhh . . .*) pulled my notebook out of my purse, softly clicked the end of the pen, and when I started writing, I listened—spot-checking for sound effects—heard nothing, and it was my turn for takeoff.

By the time the minister finished his story, I'd finished mine, too, and

I discreetly put away my tools. But in the middle of the following prayer, two more thoughts that were the perfect finishing touch for my story were begging to be written down—I couldn't resist. I mean, who would know? Every dutiful praying person should have his eyes closed and head bowed, right? Anyone who didn't—and could see me writing—well, it was kind of like getting caught doing something you shouldn't, by someone else who was doing the same thing. So you're both in deep doo-doo and neither one of you will fess up. And we didn't.

Chicken Scratches

I was on the phone talking with an author about his book and hurriedly jotting down every word he said. But when I tried to read his quotes back to him, I was stumbling over the words in front of me. I couldn't read my own handwriting, or as my friend Hilda would call it, "chicken scratches."

Hilda is ninety-five-plus years old. She's a friend of mine, and when I went to the market the other day, she came along. When she pulled out her shopping list, I noticed it looked like it had been drafted in the middle of an earthquake. We were both laughing about it and simply decided that things can get a little shaky with age.

I told Hilda not to worry or feel one little bit embarrassed about her handwriting, because it happens to me, too. Sometimes when I have an idea for a column, especially if I'm on the run, I grab whatever I can and quickly jot my thoughts down. It's always a relief to know that my idea is safely written down, so I let it wander out of my mind. But unfortunately, the next day when I try to type up my notes, it's all a mystery to me. I can read only about every third word. And some sentences are totally lost in translation, because my writing is as cryptic as Hilda's shopping list. Assuming each line on the shopping list was a separate item, Hilda and I decided there were twenty words we needed to decode, so we started at the top.

"Okay, Hilda, this looks kind of like a *p*, doesn't it? And it appears to be a long word, so let's see, what do you think?"

"Pepper? Potatoes?" (No, her neighbor brought six potatoes over yesterday morning.)

"Popcorn? Hilda, do you think it's popcorn?"

Yes! That was it! One down! (Hilda remembered she ran out of popcorn Thursday night while she was watching her favorite TV show.)

And with the skill of two veteran *Wheel of Fortune* players, down the list we went, letter by letter, item by item. By the third entry on our list, the shoppers around us must have thought we'd both lost our minds. Practically yelling back and forth—Hilda's a little hard of hearing—we'd be exchanging guesses.

"This one looks like it's eggs, Hilda, but it starts with a *d*."

"Do you want to buy a vowel?"

"Gimme an *e* for $250, Pat. Spin that wheel for us, Vanna."

A *d* and an *e*. Eggo waffles? No, I bet it's a dozen eggs.

"Do you need a dozen eggs, Hilda?"

I do believe it was the most entertaining shopping trip either of us had been on in a long time. Now, if I could just decipher the chicken scratches in front of me. What did that author say again? It looks like it starts with a *g*, but it could be a *p* . . . maybe I need to buy a vowel, or call Hilda?

Hurry, Wrap It Up So I Can Write

I should never, ever go to the market when I'm hungry. It can be disastrous. Everything looks so inviting to a hungry woman. When I walk into the market (my stomach growling), the first place I head for is the deli counter, where they slice the meat and cheese to order. I take a number and wait patiently, but I don't mind because I'll be rewarded with the first slice.

"Is this thin enough for you, ma'am?" The clerk gently raises the corner of the sliced ham for my inspection and then the question my stomach's been waiting to hear, "Would you like to try a slice?"

It's a repeat performance when he slices my cheese and other deli requests. By the time I move on to another department, I've pretty much curbed my appetite and I can shop without fear of any hunger-induced impulse buys.

Another thing I should never, ever do is go to the market without my notebook and pen. While I was waiting for my deli order to be filled, I felt the urge to start writing a column. But I didn't have anything to write on, except the butcher paper wrapped around my thinly sliced Baby Swiss. No complaints, though, it was the perfect palette, quite inspiring really—a big wide open white space to write on. But when I went to check out and handed over the Baby Swiss package to be scanned, I realized from the cashier's look that I'd better give her an explanation, and fast!

"Don't worry, it's not a stickup note," I said, trying to smile and hold my hands where she could clearly see them. "I'm just a writer who forgot to bring her notebook and this is tomorrow's column."

Ron and Virginia's Bread-and-Butter Pickles

My mother canned pickles when I was a kid, but my mother's pickles weren't edible until she met Ron. Mom's pickles tasted like kerosene. But I never had the courage to tell her, because she proudly served her homemade pickles with every meal. I got real good at hiding them in a napkin and tossing them in the trash.

But when my mother married Ron, not only did she discover the love of her life, he came with a tasty pickle recipe, too. These are fabulous Bread-and-Butter Pickles.

1 gallon cucumbers
8 small white onions
2 green peppers, shredded, if you want
½ cup canning salt
1 quart cracked ice

Pickling Syrup

5 cups sugar
1½ teaspoons turmeric
½ teaspoon ground cloves
2 tablespoons mustard seed
1 teaspoon celery seed
5 cups white vinegar

Select crisp fresh cucumbers and wash but do not peel them. Slice crosswise in paper-thin slices. Slice the onions thin and cut the pepper, if using, into fine shreds. Mix the salt with the vegetables and bury pieces of cracked ice in the mixture. Cover with weighted lid and let stand for 3 hours. Then drain very thoroughly.

Make pickling syrup. Mix the sugar, turmeric, and cloves together, add the mustard, celery seed, and vinegar, then pour over the sliced pickles. Cook over low heat and heat the mixture to scalding, stirring occasionally with a wooden spoon, but do not boil. Pour into hot sterilized jars and seal.

Two wooden Christmas trees, two snowmen, an Indian and a Pilgrim sit on the shelf of my china closet, but every year on Thanksgiving and Christmas I take them down and put them in the center of my table and I retell the story of the boy who made them for me.

My Grandma Hale's china cabinet was delivered yesterday. It traveled all the way from Wisconsin to my home in Florida. Grandma left the china cabinet to my mother after she died, and now my mother had passed it on to me.

When I was a kid, every Sunday my parents and I would drive from Cuba City to Lancaster (thirty-two miles one way) to eat noon dinner at Grandma and Grandpa Hale's house. I say noon dinner, because in the Midwest where I grew up, the noon meal was lunch and the evening meal was supper. In our house the term *dinner* was reserved for special occasions and holidays. Grandma wasn't a gourmet cook, but going to her house for Sunday dinner always felt like a special occasion to me.

Her recipe box was filled with make-you-feel-good dishes—and boy did they make me feel good. Tummy-warming soups, hamburger casseroles, cookies, Grandma's signature poppy-seed cake (three layers with filling in between), raspberry pie (the berries were from her berry patch in the back-yard), and roast beef with homemade gravy. And Grandma never minded a bit when I soaked up the leftover gravy on my plate with a slice of her crusty homemade bread.

It was my job to set the dining room table every Sunday with Grandma's very best dishes—the dishes in her china cabinet. I guess you could say it was a tradition. No one ever talked about traditions when I was a kid, but I recognized them anyway, and setting the dining room table became my own personal Sunday ritual. I knew every dish by heart in that china cabinet, so it was a real surprise after it was delivered to me in Florida and I discovered a mirror behind the top shelf. All those years when I was setting the table and I never knew it was there. I guess I was just too short to see it (things look dif-ferent when you're a kid). My favorite pieces are still the red and green ivy Christmas glasses that used to sit on the bottom shelf, but there are only two of those left now. Unfortunately there isn't a full set of anything in Grand-ma's china cabinet anymore, but when I open the door and look inside, the memory of those Sunday dinners is still there to comfort me.

Having Grandma's china cabinet in my own dining room inspired me to try to re-create her Sunday tradition. But then I quickly realized there wasn't any way I'd ever be able to get my family to show up every Sunday for dinner, and frankly I'd probably protest if they did. So I started a new tradition of my own—eat-and-run dinners.

Normally *eat-and-run* would be a grievous faux pas, but not at my house. I encourage it! If I find a great-looking roast at the market and it happens to be Tuesday (eat-and-run dinners don't have to actually be on Sunday), I pick up the phone. "Would you like to come over for a roast beef dinner tonight? It's an eat-and-run affair. Dinner will be ready at six p.m., enjoy the food, and when you're finished eating you can simply leave. No need to help with the dishes, no sitting around making small talk, eat that second piece of chocolate cake (or wrap it up and take it with you), and out the door you go."

I admit when I first thought of the eat-and-run dinner idea it made me cringe, because it goes against all social graces and it's not the way I was raised. Eat-and-run after one of Grandma's Sunday dinners? It would have been unthinkable! My parents and I spent the rest of the afternoon at my grandparents' house and we didn't leave until Grandma served leftovers for supper. But things are different today. The truth is everyone is busy, and if coming to my house for dinner wasn't such a big production, then maybe my family would accept my invitations more often. When you come to dinner at my house, it's fine to eat-and-run, but not on holidays, or the three times a year I cook a big turkey dinner even when it's not Thanksgiving. That's a different kind of invitation.

I love everything on my Thanksgiving dinner menu and so do my friends and family. A few years ago when people were complimenting me and saying things like "Wouldn't it be great if we could eat Thanksgiving dinner more often?" I agreed. Why not cook the big dinner three or four times a year? So now I do just that, and I even serve dinner on the same china turkey plates that I use on Thanksgiving. Cooking a turkey is easy. Wash the bird, stuff it, pop it in the oven, and don't worry about a thing until the thermometer reads 180 degrees. Granted it takes time to make all of the side dishes that I serve along with my 23-pound bird: stuffing, mashed potatoes with gravy, sweet potato casserole, fresh cooked cranberries, skunk beans, shrimp salad, coleslaw, fresh green beans, deviled eggs, pumpkin and cherry pies, and dinner rolls, but the leftovers are definitely worth the effort. Makes me hungry just writing about it. In fact, leftovers are the best part of a Thanksgiving meal, and I'm not the only person who feels that way.

My father-in-law lives in his own apartment in a retirement center, and most of the people there are single. So one year I suggested he invite two or three of his neighbors to our Thanksgiving dinner. Two extra people at the table—that was okay with him. Three? No way. He was concerned that inviting that extra third person might mean no leftovers for him.

People do indeed get serious about leftovers and if it looks like there might not be any, they take matters into their own hands. Mom loved my shrimp salad and every year when she'd come to my house for Thanksgiving dinner, she'd gobble up at least three helpings right away. Then she'd spend the rest of the meal keeping tabs on anyone who headed back to the kitchen for seconds. Following close behind, Mom would do her best to encourage them to eat more turkey, mashed potatoes, or coleslaw—anything other than the shrimp salad because she wanted to take home the leftovers. However when my husband and I went to my mother's house for Thanksgiving dinner—no leftovers for us. And here's the reason why.

The first year Grandma Hale passed the Thanksgiving dinner rite of passage preparation on to my mother, she fixed a pretty tasty meal. But then Mom started dieting and the menu got down to basics—basically our dinner now involved my mother opening a can of peas and a box of mashed potatoes, putting a glob of cranberry sauce on a plate (still in the shape of the can it slid out of), and opening a package of white dinner rolls. The only thing that wasn't out of the can or the box was the bird.

I didn't want to complain about the food and hurt Mom's feelings, and in her defense, she really didn't enjoy cooking. So the following year, after the first instant out-of-the-box Thanksgiving, my husband and I offered to help her cook. We went to my mother's house the day before Thanksgiving, did almost all of the cooking ourselves, and then spent the night. We had a wonderful Thanksgiving meal, and my mother even commented on how good everything tasted. Before my husband and I headed back home, I asked Mom if we could take some leftovers with us and she matter-of-factly said "No."

I was shocked—no further explanation and no leftovers for us that Thanksgiving.

So the following year I suggested that perhaps it was time for Mom to pass the Thanksgiving dinner on to me. Thank heavens she agreed, so I took the bird and ran with it—not only would we be guaranteed a tasty Thanksgiving meal, but for sure we'd get leftovers. And just to make real sure there was plenty of food left over, my husband and I made two of everything that year: two turkeys, two batches of potatoes, gravy, vegetables, shrimp salad, double the number of deviled eggs, and we bought fourteen loaves of bread at the bakery. Everyone who came to our house for Thanksgiving dinner took home a leftover dinner, complete with a piece of homemade pie and their own loaf of bread.

The year of the leftovers left such an impression that I've considered extending the Thanksgiving celebration to two days. On Thursday everybody gets formally dressed for dinner (including the turkey) and then on Friday we all gather together again for a leftover dinner. Sitting at the Thanksgiving table in pantyhose and a form-fitting dress, I can't really do the original twenty-course holiday meal justice. But slide me into some stretchy, elastic-waisted pants on Leftover Day, slip on my flip-flops, twist my hair up and stick it under a baseball cap, and I could probably even go back for thirds on pumpkin pie topped with whipped cream.

When my husband and I moved from Wisconsin to Florida, we wanted to start a new Thanksgiving tradition to remind us of the first holiday we celebrated in the new chapter of our life. So the day before Thanksgiving we furiously shopped all of the antique stores in Sarasota looking for something for our Thanksgiving table. It was a quarter to five, the local shops were getting ready to close, and we'd pretty much given up hope of finding something. But the very last antique store we hurried into, there they were—antique Thanksgiving plates for our dinner table. "His Majesty's china plates Made in England." The rim of each plate hosted a cornucopia of fall vegetables and in the center there was a proud colorful turkey in a country setting. Mixing old and new traditions, I set the Thanksgiving table in our new historical home with Grandma Hale's pink water glasses, our new china turkey plates, and the wooden figurines from the year I taught a cooking class to homeschooled children.

Eight sixth-grade students enrolled in my cooking class, including Max. It was obvious that Max didn't want to be in my kitchen. He was tough looking, the kind of kid that would make you cross over to the other side of the street if you were out for a leisurely stroll. Ragged hair that always looked like it needed to be washed, baggy clothes, and oversized, steel-toed curb-stomping boots. In his mind, I'm sure Max thought he was lookin' cool.

He had been kicked out of every public and private school he'd been enrolled in and homeschooling was a last resort for his parents. I'm sure his folks were jumping for joy and would have gladly paid double the price when they saw my announcement—Six-Week Cooking Class for Home-schoolers—because it would give them a three-hour break during the day.

On the first day when we did introductions, I asked each student to tell me what they hoped to learn. Tough kid's response: "My parents made me come here. Sounds stupid to me."

Okay, I could work with that. Maybe.

But Max would never give an inch. It would have been giving in to the establishment to actually enjoy himself, even when he was eating a cream puff. "Well, what do you think? Do you like them?" I was hoping the fluffy white filling might force one crummy smile from him, but no . . . he was one tough cookie. Nevertheless, I genuinely liked the kid. I respected his pigheadedness. It reminded me of myself when I was his age.

Each student had kitchen assignments, but I never pressed Max to do much of anything, except I did enforce a "no smoking" rule during the three-hour class period. However, I'd still catch him smoking outside when we'd take a break. I spoke to his parents about it, but they just shrugged their shoulders: "What can you do?"

Max wasn't disrupting the class and the other kids accepted his behavior for what it was, so I figured no real harm done. Tough boy would try to follow a recipe every now and then, but he moved so slowly—to emphasize his disgust in being there—that by the time he'd get some cookie batter mixed up we were out of time.

The finale of the six-week cooking class was to prepare a holiday buffet for the kids' parents. Thanksgiving was only a couple of weeks away, so we decided to do a half-Thanksgiving, half-Christmas theme with the table decorations. All of the kids showed up for class early on the big day, including Max, which surprised me, because I wasn't sure he was going to show up at all. That's why I hadn't given him an assignment.

"Here, these are for the table," Max said, his eyes looking away from me. "I made them last night." And he handed me two wooden snowmen, two Christmas trees, and a Pilgrim and an Indian.

I was stunned—they were adorable. He'd hand-carved and painted them on all sides, so no matter where they sat on the buffet table you'd be able to see the detail of his work. You never know about people. I thought I was going to cry, but I could tell Max didn't want me to make too big of a deal about it. His parents were as shocked as I'd been when I pointed out what their son had made.

Two wooden Christmas trees, two snowmen, an Indian, and a Pilgrim sit on the shelf of my china closet, but every year on Thanksgiving and Christmas I take them down and put them in the center of my table, and of course I retell the story of the boy who made them for me.

Remembering Max's story has become a cherished holiday tradition, and when my husband is carving the turkey, we remember the year Mom attempted to solve the turkey-leg dilemma.

Some people want the white meat, some will only eat the dark, and for years our family used to argue over who was going to get a turkey drumstick. Every year it was the same routine. Mom would ring her china bell, "Dinner is ready. Come to the table." And we'd all start calling dibs on a turkey leg. When there are only two turkey legs, but ten people want one . . . it used to be a huge problem, until the year my mother made her now-famous Turkey Drumstick Thanksgiving Dinner. It looked like one of my mother's usual Thanksgiving meals until she announced, "I've got a surprise. No one will be disappointed this year. Everybody gets a drumstick, because that's all I cooked. Dig in!" And then she plopped down a serving platter piled high with twenty turkey legs in the middle of the table.

This felt more than a little strange—everyone was shocked! "What, no bird this year? Only drumsticks?"

Mom was beaming, so proud because she'd finally found a solution for the annual turkey-leg squabble. Apparently she began working on this year's Thanksgiving surprise the day after last year's turkey-leg spat. For the past year, whenever she went to the market she kept her eyes open for a turkey-leg sale. It all sounded okay in theory, but either Mom didn't wrap the legs in freezer paper, or the turkey legs were on sale because the date on the package had expired, or it was just a bad year for turkeys, because when we tried to stick our forks into our drumsticks, we couldn't!

I'm not exaggerating here; the turkey legs were nowhere near fork-tender. The tines of our forks actually bounced off the drumsticks when we tried to pierce them. A table knife wouldn't even saw through the sinewy—who knows how old—freezer-burnt turkey legs. My son suggested we fire up the chainsaw.

Mom was right, none of us fought over who would get a drumstick that year. Instead we ended up dueling with them—those were some tough birds.

Every year when our family sits together at the Thanksgiving table and it's time to give thanks, we take hold of the hand of the person sitting next to us and one by one around the table, each of us shares what we're thankful for.

People normally give thanks for things like family or good health, but one year when it was my turn, in the solace of the moment, I bowed my head and with a giggle and a smile I announced that I was thankful I'd finally found a new faucet for my bathtub. It might have sounded a little misplaced, but it was the truth, I really felt blessed.

It's the little irritations in life that drive me nuts, and before I found a new faucet, a simple thing like taking a bath had become a big production. If I wanted to take a bath I had to make plans at least one hour in advance. Because when I turned on the faucet to fill the tub, water would only trickle out of it. The plumber was as bewildered as I was. He'd taken the faucet apart, blew on this and that hoping to dislodge something, he even tried re-piping a little section, but finally on his third and last visit my plumber gently placed his hand on top of the worn-out faucet and proclaimed, "May it rest in peace."

I couldn't believe it was finally "The End" and I was very worried. The old claw-foot bathtub and faucet came with the house, so I didn't know how much the faucet would cost to replace. But from the looks of the impressive, fancy faucet with pipes leading up to an old-fashioned shower head, surrounded by a white curtain on a golden rod, I was sure it was going to cost a fortune—that is if I was even lucky enough to find another one like it.

Afraid to even look for a replacement, two months later I was still limping along with the "deceased" hoping for a miracle. But when the water wouldn't even trickle out of the faucet and I had to boil pots of water on top of the stove if I wanted to take a bath, I knew I had no choice. It was time to buy a new faucet, but by then I'd created a monster in my mind.

I could see it now . . . I'd spend weeks searching for a new antique-looking faucet and when I finally found it, I wouldn't be able to afford it. So after spending all that time and energy looking, I'd have to end up settling for something I didn't even like. Yes, the faucet monster had already won, but in reality I hadn't even started looking.

When I finally did face my faucet fear, it took only ten minutes of searching on the Internet and there it was—the exact same faucet I had right now, reasonably priced and the seller would send it to me overnight.

The plumber hooked up my new faucet and at last I was able to turn the knob and fill up my tub any time I wanted to take a long hot bath—and believe me, that's something to be thankful for. . . . *Amen.*

Crock Pot Dressing

Whenever I stuff my turkey, even my 23-pound bird, I have dressing left over, but I don't have any room in my oven for an extra casserole dish. So I make my dressing in the crock pot. This recipe has never failed me.

1 cup butter or margarine, melted (I use a little less, though)
2 cups chopped onion
2 cups chopped celery
¼ cup parsley (fresh or dried)
2 cups sliced fresh mushrooms, or canned mushrooms, drained
2 eggs, beaten
3½ to 4½ cups chicken broth, or enough to moisten well
13 cups dry bread cubes
1½ teaspoons poultry seasoning
2 teaspoons salt
2 teaspoons sage
1 teaspoon thyme
1 teaspoon pepper
½ teaspoon marjoram

Melt butter or margarine in large frying pan and sauté onion and celery until soft. Mix with remaining ingredients and toss well. Pack in large crock pot. Cover. Cook on high for 45 minutes, then turn to low and continue cooking for 6 to 8 hours.

It's great and never dry.

Grandma Hale's Stuffing for a Fifteen-Pound Turkey

My recipe box is filled with Grandma Hale's recipes, written out in her own handwriting. She wrote everything down on recipe cards—household tips, birthdays, anniversaries, and, to my surprise, even jokes. I discovered this Thanksgiving stuffing recipe in Grandma Hale's old recipe box.

   1 loaf bread
   2 teaspoons sage
   3 eggs
   1 cup water
   1½ teaspoons salt
   1 cup popcorn

Stuff turkey. Bake at 450 degrees. Stuffing is done when corn starts to pop and blows the turkey's ass clear out of the oven.

Shrimp Salad

This dish needs to be made ahead of time and gets better if it's chilled for several hours, preferably overnight. My mother loved this recipe and it's my daughter's favorite, too. Whenever my daughter comes to visit, I make a double batch, because she covets the bowl, marking it as her own personal shrimp salad.

   1 (7-ounce) box macaroni shells (about 2 cups) cooked and drained
   17-ounce can small early peas, drained
   ½ to ¾ pound medium or large shrimp, cooked, peeled, deveined, and cut
      into halves (if medium) or thirds (if large)
   2½-ounce jar sliced mushrooms, drained
   1 cup finely chopped celery
   2 tablespoons diced pimiento
   1⅓ cups mayonnaise
   ½ cup cocktail sauce

¼ cup milk
½ teaspoon salt
¼ teaspoon onion salt
¼ teaspoon pepper
⅛ teaspoon celery salt
I add horseradish, to taste

In large bowl, gently combine shells, peas, shrimp, mushrooms, celery, and pimiento. In small bowl, combine remaining ingredients for dressing. Gently stir dressing mixture into macaroni mixture. Cover and chill for at least 2 hours before serving.

Skunk Beans

8 bacon strips, cooked till very crisp and broken into pieces
1 chopped onion, sautéed
½ cup cider vinegar
1 cup brown sugar
¼ teaspoon dry mustard
Dash garlic salt
½ cup ketchup
½ teaspoon salt
1 (15-ounce) can kidney beans, drained
1 (15-ounce) can lima beans, drained
1 (20-ounce) can pork and beans, drained

Mix all ingredients together in a Dutch oven or casserole dish.

Cover and bake at 350 degrees for one hour. Uncover and bake for another 30 minutes.

surrounded by Christmas figurines. The mobile had four miniature candles on the bottom, and when the candles were lit, the golden angels above them twirled around in the circle. A Christmas tree covered with bubbling lights sat in front of the big picture window, and potted poinsettias were scattered on the floor and end tables. Grandma's huge Christmas cactus was displayed on a wooden pedestal next to the television. I don't know how she did it, but that Christmas cactus was always blooming by December 25th.

When Grandma was too frail to have Christmas at her house, the tradition of the big holiday celebration was passed on to my mother. Years later when my mother died, I realized that someone older than me had always been in charge of creating holiday memories. But now that *someone* was me. It felt like a huge responsibility—none of Grandma's holiday traditions would continue unless I made sure they did. Deep down I knew it was an exaggerated way of thinking and when I shared with my daughter-in-law that I was worried I might not be up to the task of keeping family traditions alive, she looked at me and smiled. "Suzanne, don't you think you've already been doing that? I'm coming to your house for Christmas dinner and I know exactly what the menu will be and how the table will be decorated—because you've made it a tradition."

What a lovely daughter-in-law. How did she know what I needed to hear?

I have continued to do a lot of the same things that Grandma did at Christmas, but I think I'm going to have to make a few changes. Because every year when I clean out my refrigerator after Christmas, I end up throwing away a lot of holiday food. Some holiday treats can't even be considered leftovers because nobody ate one single bite—and nobody ever does. But year after year I keep buying them anyway. I guess it's just hard to break old habits. French onion and vegetable dips, a variety of cheeses, salami, and at least three kinds of crackers all displayed on a lazy Susan accompanied by an assortment of vegetables for dipping into those dips, eggnog, and pecan pie. Those were just a few of the in-between-meal snacks that Grandma always had in her house at Christmas time. But now there aren't even enough people in my family to eat all of those things, and nobody eats dip except me, and absolutely no one in our family eats pecan pie.

So why do I keep buying these things year after year, just to end up throwing most of them away? I don't understand it. I could buy these food items any time of the year if I wanted to, but I don't—not until they start piping Christmas music into the supermarket and then I head straight to the chip-and-dip aisle and off to the bakery in search of a pecan pie.

Maybe the reason I keep buying things that nobody eats anymore is because I'm missing the person who used to love to eat them. My Grandpa Hale loved pecan pie. His birthday was the day before Christmas and he'd start eating pecan pie on the 24th, and continue eating pecan pie right up until New Year's Day. It was his once-a-year treat. Years after Grandpa passed away, my mother was still making his favorite pie, even though nobody would eat it, and I've continued the tradition. I don't know if I'm quite ready to give up the pecan pie, but I am making a little progress. Grandpa Hale also loved chocolate-covered cherries. Usually I buy two boxes, but last year I walked right by them.

Holiday traditions are very comforting and I want to continue them, but I also leave a little wiggle room. For years I raised my right hand and took the oath: "I'll never ever have an artificial Christmas tree!" and I believed every word of it. But then a couple of years go when my husband and I walked by the almost-real Christmas trees on display, there was a moment when in unison we looked at each other and said, "This tree looks real." And we bought it! Let me tell you, when I fall, I fall hard. I blush when I confess that the artificial tree already had lights on it, too.

My new eight-foot evergreen Christmas tree came in three easy-toassemble pieces; all I had to do was style it. Imagine that, I'm now a pine-tree stylist! Pull this branch to the right, move that one a little over to the left, give it a little tummy tuck to cover up the wide-open spaces, and twenty minutes later my tree looked just the way it did the year before—only there was no need to water it and I wouldn't have to vacuum up those messy pine needles. My only Christmas tree worry from now on was going to be how to get the eight-foot evergreen tree back into the little box it came in.

There's a lot of stigma concerning Christmas tree etiquette. In fact, there seems to be an unwritten law that if you put your tree up before Thanksgiving, you might as well be wearing white shoes in January. Most tree sinners are hush-hush about their transgressions and they walk around silently carrying some pretty heavy pine-tree guilt. But for others the shame is just too much to bear and they feel the need to confess.

Three weeks before Thanksgiving my manicurist leaned over and whispered to me, "I've had three Christmas trees up in my house for a week already and they're decorated, too. What do you think about that?"

I assured her not to worry, that her secret was safe with me, and then I made my own confession about how I'd taken the oath: "I'll never, ever have an artificial Christmas tree!" Yet hidden away in my bedroom closet was an eight-foot tree stuffed into a little cardboard box waiting to be styled. Yes, I too was a Christmas tree sinner! And if only I'd fallen from grace a few years earlier, I wouldn't have ruined the brand-new light gray carpeting in my living room.

We'd just moved into a new house and I wanted our Christmas tree decorations to complement the soft, warm colors of my new sofa, rug, and drapes. So I didn't bother getting out the Christmas boxes with our old favorites that year, because they just wouldn't do. Instead, I spent hours, actually days (I got a little obsessed), looking for light pink, dark pink, and cream-colored ornaments and matching lights to make a perfectly color-coordinated Christmas tree.

Yes, indeed, when I finished decorating my Christmas tree it was breathtaking. An all-pink masterpiece—but only on the front of the tree. The tree stood in the corner of the living room and I neglected to decorate the backside. And one afternoon, plop! Over the tree went! Broken ornaments scattered everywhere and the water that had tree preservative in it spilled out onto my new light gray carpeting. I was so angry at the tree and myself that I just let the stupid thing lie in the middle of the living room floor for two days, which of course set a water stain in the carpet. My family thought I'd lost my mind. Looking back, I'd have to agree.

The decorations I traditionally put on our Christmas tree have been accumulated over the years. Every ornament hanging on my Christmas tree reminds me of a story, and every year when I decorate my tree one by one I remember.

I remember the day my son came home from kindergarten and hurried into the living room to put the Life Savers yarn doll on the Christmas tree. "Look, Mom, see what I made." A miniature roll of Life Savers in the middle of yarn arms, legs, and long locks of golden hair. It's still holding up after all these years.

Three red rocking horses—my daughter begged me to buy them when she was seven years old; it was the same year she asked me about Santa.

Two pink drum ornaments, remnants of that "almost perfect" all-pink Christmas tree. I gave the rest of the unscathed pink- and cream-colored ornaments away (it was too embarrassing to keep them around). But I decided to keep two of the pink drums as a forever, humble reminder that I need to keep some balance in my life, especially during the holidays.

I'd forgotten all about it, but there it was at the bottom of the Christmas box. I remember the day Mom gave it to me, she was so thrilled to find it—a clown popping out of a wooden children's block with a *V* initial on the front of it. (*V* for Virginia, my mother's name.) Mom used to be a clown in her hometown parade in Cuba City, and one year I flew back home to be in the parade with her. We even won a prize. She gave me the Christmas ornament the year before she died.

That stupid clown—there it is waiting for me to hang it on the tree, but all I can do is cry and the crying turns into sobbing, my knees give way, and soon I'm sitting on the floor in front of the Christmas tree, crying and remembering, because every ornament on my tree tells a story, a recipe from my life that I hope I'll never forget.

Candy-Cane Cookies

This is one of my favorite Christmas cookie recipes. You can make candy canes red-and-white or red-and-green. People will think you spent a lot of time in the kitchen, but they're really simple to make. It's fun to braid the dough for the candy canes, but since I do it only once a year, the first two I make are usually gigantic, because I use too much dough. The cookies expand when they're baking, so I would make only two at first, as kind of a test run to get your candy-cane-cookie bearings. But not to worry, big candy-cane cookies taste just as great as small ones.

3½ cups flour
2 teaspoons baking powder
½ teaspoon salt
2 sticks butter, at room temperature
1¼ cups sugar
2 eggs beaten with 2 teaspoons vanilla extract
Red food coloring

Stir together the flour, baking powder, and salt in a bowl. Set aside.

Cream the butter and sugar. Add the egg mixture, a little at a time, beating well after each addition. Gradually add the flour mixture, blending well after each addition.

Put half of the dough in another bowl. Add red food coloring to one-half of dough to make the desired candy-cane shade. Leave the other half of dough plain. Shape each portion into a ball. Flatten each ball of dough, wrap snugly with plastic wrap, and refrigerate for 30 minutes or until slightly firm. Don't over-chill because then you won't be able to work with the dough.

Dust your hands and working surface with flour. Roll a one-inch ball of plain white dough into a rope about 6 inches long. Do the same with a red-colored piece of dough. Take the red-colored rope of dough, along with a plain piece of dough, and cross the red over the white, to make a candy cane. Shape one end of the crossed ropes into the head of a cane.

Bake in a 350-degree oven on greased cookie sheets for 12 to 14 minutes. The cookies may be a little soft when they come out of the oven. Let cool completely before you handle them.

18. Did Somebody Bring the Cookies?

Chocolate-chip cookies have become part of who I am. My business card reads: Suzanne Beecher, Writer/Cookie Baker.

Fun in the sun, year-round flower gardens, and white sandy beaches. After a year of renting a house on the water, my husband and I wondered what's not to love about living in Florida. So we made it official. We bought a 1926 historical home in Sarasota and applied for our Florida driver's licenses, which meant we were no longer "snowbirds," but official Floridians.

Living in Sarasota felt like a dream come true—big-city amenities, yet a little bit of small-town Cuba City. Main Street was only a ten-minute walk from our house. In fact, almost anywhere my husband and I wanted to go was within walking distance: the marina, library, market, theater, dry cleaner's, French bakery, restaurants, two coffeehouses, bookstore, live outdoor entertainment on a Saturday night, my doctor's office, even the hospital emergency room. So theoretically if I were home alone, fell off the kitchen stepstool, and blood wasn't gushing out too badly, I could probably hobble to the emergency room in fifteen minutes, tops! And there's even a valet service out front, so I could tip some guy three bucks to carry me through the front door. What a city!

Well, there was one little thing bothering me.

I'm easily bored and life was beginning to feel too familiar. No doubt about it, my first year in Florida had been the kind of adventure people dream about, the stuff movies are made of, but even fun in the sun gets routine.

Managing my husband's software company kept me busy, but I missed the satisfaction and joy I felt when I was running Meals for Madison. Maybe Sarasota needed a free meal program? I'd always said if I could find a job that brought me as much joy as Meals for Madison *and* make money doing it, I'd be in heaven. But after three days of calling around, I discovered there were numerous meal programs in the city and they all seemed to be very well run.

So I kept nosing around, hoping for some kind of big sign: an airplane with one of those banners tagging along behind announcing in big bold letters THIS WAY TO SUZANNE'S NEXT BIG CHALLENGE would have been nice, but the skies were quiet—for months. Did I mention in addition to getting bored, I'm also not a very patient woman?

Eyes toward the sky, just in case, I spent a lot of time reading and I continued managing my husband's software company. All of the employees worked from their homes and most were women working part time, so they could be at home with their young children. Frequently one of the moms would mention when her children got older she wanted to go back to college. So one afternoon when I heard the frustration in Cathy's voice about wishing she could go back to school, I said why wait? "Your kids won't be going to school for three or four years, but you could start reading about whatever subject you're interested in right now."

Cathy's amused smile came through the phone loud and clear. "My dear Suzanne, I cook, clean, take care of my kids, help out at school, work part time for you, and you're suggesting I should sit down and read a book? I can't even find the time to shave my legs!"

I couldn't stop thinking about what Cathy had said. It was so true. I remembered when my husband and I were running two businesses, in addition to chauffeuring kids to soccer practice, music lessons, and after-school activities. What a crazy time! So that evening when I was preparing our daily company email, on a last-minute whim I started typing in the beginning pages of *Tuesdays with Morrie*, the book I'd just finished reading. The next evening, I typed in a little more from the book, picking up where I'd left off the day before, and the next night I sent another installment. Four days later, No Time to Shave My Legs Woman called. "I'm embarrassed to admit it, Suzanne, but I've been sneaking over to my computer late at night to see if company email has shown up yet, because I'm hooked on the book!"

Cathy wasn't alone. Later that same day another employee called to thank me. "I just wanted to let you know my husband and I turned off the television last night and we sat on the couch talking about the book you sent. It meant a lot to us because a friend of ours just recently died from Lou Gehrig's disease."

And then I received an email from another employee that must have been three pages long. "The book you've been sending us this week in the company email, thank you so much. My best friend died from Lou Gehrig's disease when I was only ten years old. I hadn't thought about her in a long time. None of the grownups would talk about what happened to my friend, and I was just a kid. Reading this book has brought back so many memories and a feeling of loss that I guess I've never had a chance to grieve until now."

I was stunned. If sending part of one book to a handful of employees could make such a difference in people's lives, what would happen if I sent daily book-club emails to millions of people?

You know that big sign in the sky I'd been waiting for? This was it! Sometimes you get what you wish for—in June 1999 I found my little piece of heaven when I launched DearReader.com.

(By the way, before I continue, I need to tell you that taking copyrighted material out of a book and emailing it is illegal, which my loving husband pointed out to me at the time of my new business revelation. I assured him it was for a small group of women and that's how creative ideas are born. But that still doesn't make it legal. All of the books I feature at my online book clubs are used with permission.)

I knew how to build a website and I could envision what the online book club would look like, but how do you get permission to use material from published books? I didn't know anything about the publishing industry. In fact, I was so naïve I thought if you called a publisher, they'd call you back. How amusing.

When publishers didn't call me back, I accepted the challenge and tried faxing, then sending a letter overnight via FedEx (hoping spending more money on getting the letter there would suggest it was more important), and I did a little networking, asking friends of friends to see if anyone had a name or a contact. Nobody did and nobody responded to my overnight letters, either. But finally, a couple of months later, my persistence paid off when an executive at Random House took my call. Excited, yet nervous, I realized this was my moment, so I took a deep breath and began explaining my new idea for marketing books. But after a few minutes it felt like I was losing the woman's interest on the other end of the line. "I have a meeting in five minutes. Send me some information about your company, outlining the concept you just told me about. Do you need my address?"

It felt like a brush-off, but on the other hand at least someone was talking to me. This must be progress, right? My letter went out overnight the next day. Two days later I followed up with a phone call—no answer, so I left a message. Three days later I tried calling again, left another message, but no response. No response for three weeks. Finally after dialing and redialing (caller ID turned off), my Random House contact answered the phone. "I'm on my way to a meeting. I like your idea, let's work out the details next Tuesday. Call me."

Yes! I did it! This was so exciting! Even though next Tuesday was only four days away, I felt like a kid waiting for Christmas. But Santa didn't show. When I called the following Tuesday, my Random House contact was gone. Literally. The recording on her phone said she didn't work there any longer. "Press one, if you need further assistance."

"So who would be taking her place?"

Nobody knew and no one cared about the agreement that was supposed to be signed, sealed, and delivered on Tuesday. Phone calls, letters, I'd spent all that time, finally made a contact, and now I was going to have to start all over again from the beginning? I couldn't bear to think about it, at least not right away. Friends describe me as persistent and resilient, which is true. I get a second and third wind when other people are ready to throw in the towel, but this time even I needed to catch my breath. So I took a two-week reprieve, regrouped, and started all over again.

Three months later after what felt like hundreds of phone calls, a little begging, and a lot of luck, someone at Random House finally agreed to give me permission to use material from their books. "But only one book a week, Suzanne, and I'll be on the mailing list monitoring what you're doing with the material."

It was a thrilling victory, but (looking back) it was a little humorous, too. This naïve, small-town girl from Cuba City had no idea what a huge accomplishment it really was—the largest publisher in the world had just agreed to work with her. But then again, if I hadn't been that naïve small-town girl from Cuba City, I might have been afraid to even try.

DearReader.com started out as one book club that I emailed to friends and family, but today there are eleven genres to choose from, and over

365,000 people read at the clubs every day. When someone signs up at the book club, they receive a daily email that contains a 5-minute sample from the book. The daily reads are consecutive, so by Friday readers have sampled two or three chapters, enough to know if the book is a good match for them. If it is, they can visit their local public library or bookseller. The concept is pretty much the same as the night I started sending part of a book in our company email, with a few extras thrown in: my daily column, free books, a recipe exchange, and other crazy giveaways such as bubble machines, pajamas, vintage aprons, and garage-sale treasures. I even bake homemade chocolate-chip cookies every month and ship them to four or five lucky readers.

In 2000 I partnered with libraries around the country, and now I produce online book clubs for thousands of libraries and even some publishers, too. I enjoy reading the books and producing the daily emails, but readers are the reason I'm so passionate about the book clubs. Every day I receive hundreds of emails from readers telling me how something they've read at the book club or in my column has made a difference in their lives. Readers don't just say thank you for my DearReader.com book club, they open up and share some of their lives.

Dear Suzanne,

Like so many of your readers, I think of you as a dear friend. My mother passed away this year after a long illness. My parents' home is four hours away from mine and almost every other weekend, for the past four years, my husband and I went to help Dad care for Mom. Many times my mother was hospitalized for several days and I went alone and stayed in the hospital with her.

The reason I'm telling you this is because I want you to know you were with me and helped keep my life more "normal" whenever I was away from home and my husband for long periods of time. Sometimes I was away for

three weeks. My husband and I talked every evening on the phone. We would
fill each other in on the events of our day and he would read me your column
from the book club every night. It became our ritual and he would say, "I
suppose you want to hear what Suzanne has to say today."

After I'd been working with Random House for a few months I assumed
I could name-drop to get other publishers on board with the book clubs. I
assumed incorrectly. But thanks to a marketing book I was reading at the
time, I discovered an easier way to reach publishers.

The author suggested that periodically we need to look back and review
what we "used to do" for marketing, because sometimes there are good
ideas that have been overlooked. Things that used to work for us, but for
some reason we stopped doing them and maybe it's time to try them again?
Reading those passages in the book made me remember how business-
people used to respond to the chocolate-chip cookies I baked for them as
a thank-you when they donated goods, services, or money to Meals for
Madison, my free meal program.

Whenever I gave someone a Ziploc bag filled with two dozen homemade chocolate-chip cookies, the reaction was amazing! The owner of a
silk-screening company had donated three dozen aprons with the Meals
for Madison logo silk screened on them. Not only did the aprons add a nice
touch when we served the meal, but the logos showed up boldly in photos.
It was great advertisement for the program.

As a thank-you for the silk-screener's generosity, I told him I'd be dropping off a bag of homemade chocolate-chip cookies. Using cookies as a
thank-you had become my trademark, and apparently word had gotten
around because the boss had left strict instructions with his secretary: "The
woman from that meal program is dropping off some of her cookies and I
expect the bag to be on my desk UNOPENED when I return!"

People might not remember my name, but they remembered my

cookies. The next time I'd asked for a donation: "We'd love to help, and will you be baking?"

Yes, I'd forgotten about the marketing magic of homemade chocolate-chip cookies. So I baked a batch of cookies and wrote a brief one-page letter simply stating that I had a new idea about how to get people reading again and how to sell more books. "I'm frequently in New York City and I'd love to stop in and tell you about my idea."

I realized a business letter and chocolate-chip cookies might seem like strange bedfellows, so I explained the cookies this way at the end of the letter: "The cookies? They're a hobby of mine. I hope you like chocolate chip. P.S. If you're a *dunker* you'll have to get your own milk!"

My letter and cookies went right to the top. Small-town girl Suzanne Beecher would have been intimidated to send cookies to a New York publisher, but author Anthony Parinello in his book *Selling to VITO* (Very Important Top Officer) convinced me otherwise. I had a fantastic idea, I could frame it up quickly in a meeting, but I wasn't sure who I should be talking to, so why not go right to the top?

I'd never met a publisher, none of these people had any idea who the heck I was, but they certainly loved my cookies because when I'd phone the day after they received my letter and cookies, the conversation would almost always be the same. When the secretary answered, I'd announce that I was following up on a letter I'd sent and could I please speak to Mr. or Ms. Publisher, and before they could respond with the standard "I'll take a message," I'd add, "Maybe you received the box I sent, too?"

"Oh, you're the cookie woman! I'm sorry we didn't get back to you yet. My boss is in the other room eating some of your cookies this very minute and she wanted me to find out when you'll be in New York City? You mentioned in your letter that you're here frequently."

Actually I wasn't in New York frequently (one of those little white lies), but whatever day was good for a publisher to see me was the day I'd be in the city. "When would be a good time? Name a day."

Obviously cookies couldn't guarantee a publisher would work with me, but cookies did open the door so I could tell my story. Once again home-made chocolate-chip cookies became my calling card: Suzanne Beecher book club woman/writer/cookie baker.

When I give someone cookies I've made from scratch, I'm giving them the best of me. Most people wouldn't believe it, but if I'm not in the mood to bake, yet I have to anyway, baking feels like a chore and my cookies don't turn out. They fall in the middle, or taste strange, like I forgot one of the ingredients—and in a way, that's what I did. For some reason, I wasn't able to add the joy I usually feel when I'm baking. Normally, when I'm mixing up cookie batter, I'm picturing the person I'm baking for, I can see the smile on their face after they open the bag of cookies, and I'm hoping they'll feel special.

Cooking is a powerful thing, especially baking. When most people think of homemade chocolate-chip cookies, they remember their mom or grandma—somebody who loved them—in the kitchen with an apron on, hands dusted with flour, counter all a mess, and something that smells good baking in the oven.

Baking chocolate-chip cookies is like writing. When there's joy, I'm into the task at hand, not thinking about anything else, giving it everything I have to give—giving my best to someone else.

Suzanne's Chocolate-Chip Cookies

Makes 36 cookies

2 sticks butter (make sure the butter is cold; slice it up before mixing)

¾ cup brown sugar

¾ cup granulated sugar

1 overflowing teaspoon pure vanilla extract

2 eggs

2¼ cups flour (plus an additional tablespoon if your kitchen is warm, or it's very humid outdoors)

1 teaspoon baking soda

1 teaspoon salt

2 overflowing cups good-quality chocolate chips

Beat together butter, brown and granulated sugars, and vanilla. Add eggs and combine well. In another bowl, mix together flour, baking soda, and salt.

Add flour mixture to butter mixture. Beat well. Add chocolate chips. Mix on low speed till just combined. Drop by teaspoons onto parchment-lined baking pans. Bake at 375 degrees for 10 to 12 minutes, until light golden brown.

Cool cookies on counter, then freeze immediately. I put the cookies into freezer bags. Freezing the cookies is an important step because it sets up the chocolate. When the cookie is thawed the chocolate stays firm.

Bake two batches, and give one away.

19. Seasonings: The Ingredients of a Small-Town Girl

My dog, Moochie, and me playing in the trailer lot. My parents and I lived in a trailer for a number of years while they were saving up money for a down payment on a house.

"It's better to be sad than happy. Too much happiness isn't good for anyone."

Years ago I heard a woman make that statement and it's stuck with me. Not because I thought it was something profound. In fact, at the time I thought the woman needed some serious help. But then a few years later, a friend of mine received some devastating news and as I was searching for words that might comfort her, I caught a little glimpse of what that woman might have been trying to convey.

Happiness is a wonderful thing and I definitely want my share. But if I'm really honest about it, the times in my life that have made me the person I am today have come from sadness. Knowing how to celebrate good news, how to hip-hip-hurray when the time is right, was standard equipment for me. Not much sorting needs to be done when the sun is shining, and I'm feeling great and problem free.

But finding the words to say to a friend who's going to have to shut down her business, or writing a note to someone whose younger sister just died from cancer, that kind of "knowing"—that kind of understanding—comes from the sadness I've experienced in my life.

I finally understood the woman's sentiments: "It's better to be sad than happy." No doubt about it, there's a purpose for both. I won't chase away the sadness; I might need it someday.

Yesterday when my husband and I were out for our morning walk, we stopped to read a poster that was tacked up on a telephone pole.

LOST CAT!

BROWN TABBY

MORRIS

20 YEARS OLD AND HARD OF HEARING

My husband commented that it was "that time of year," and Morris was probably just taking a romantic stroll around the neighborhood with a female companion. But the poster made me think about what happened to my dog, Moochie.

When I was five years old, Santa left Moochie under the Christmas tree. He was part terrier and part something else that must have had a very long tail, because when Moochie was just a pup, the veterinarian said we needed to shorten his tail or "the tail will grow longer than the dog." And so we had his tail nipped.

I was an only child, no brothers or sisters to play with except Moochie. Even when I'd dress him up in a pink dress and tie a ruffled bonnet around his neck, he was a real trouper. He'd ride in the side basket of my bicycle, barking nonstop—"Look at us"—and we'd go up and down Main Street. I loved that dog, but honestly I don't know how my parents put up with the pooch. Moochie loved to chew blankets. He never touched a shoe, sock, or a chair leg, but every single blanket in our house looked like a piece of Swiss cheese. Perfect little round holes—a real work of dog art—and every blanket, on every bed, was a Moochie masterpiece.

I never tied him up when he was outside, there wasn't any need to, because Moochie never left the yard. So it was strange one day when he just seemed to disappear. Everybody knew everybody and their pets in the small town I grew up in, but when I asked the neighbors, nobody had seen Moochie. Months went by, I was miserable, and I'd given up hope of ever finding him. The worst part was not knowing what had happened to him.

You know how things just seem to come together sometimes? There's no reason why a topic of conversation should come up, but it does when the time is right. That's what happened one day when I was waiting for my mother to get off work at the Dime Store.

It was almost five o'clock (closing time at the Dime Store) and Mom was behind the register ringing up the last customer when out of the blue, the woman she was waiting on, started telling a story about a dog who had wandered onto their farm a couple of months ago. It was a small brown dog, with a stump of a tail, and he just showed up one afternoon in their barn. He didn't look well and was obviously a very old dog, so the woman made a bed for him and tried to get him to eat, but he wasn't hungry. She'd been so worried about the dog that she got up in the middle of the night to check on him. The woman was in tears by that point in the story, and my mother and I were crying, too, because we realized who the dog was.

Moochie died in the woman's arms at about three in the morning.

Why did Moochie run away? I've always thought about it this way: Best friends never want to hurt each other, and I imagine Moochie decided it would be just too much for me—he wanted to spare me the pain, so he ran away from home to die.

LOST DOG!

BROWN, PART TERRIER WITH A SHORT TAIL

MOOCHIE

15 YEARS OLD AND THE BEST FRIEND I EVER HAD

I don't always recognize when I'm in the middle of a big moment, an experience that might change my life or someone else's. Perhaps it's a small gesture, a few simple words, or turning left instead of right. Maybe I was supposed to get lost this morning, maybe I was supposed to change my schedule and take a detour?

It's not an everyday event, but sometimes I feel an urgent tugging inside of me. Not a resounding call, rather more of a gentle nudge. In fact, if I ignored it long enough, it would move on and see if someone else was willing to help. I don't always know the person, nor do I have any idea what I'll be doing or saying when we meet, but it's clear from that little nudge that there's an opportunity waiting for me. The question is: Am I willing to listen and deviate from my comfortable routine? When I do find the courage, it's one of those perfect meant-to-be moments.

Years ago, I was headed home after a meeting and I noticed an elderly woman walking toward the bus stop, so I offered her a ride home. When we pulled up in front of her house, as I was helping her out of the car, I felt compelled to give her a hug. Without giving it a second thought I wrapped my arms around the woman and she held on tight, too. So very tight, yet the strangeness of our embrace neither one of us noticed.

"It's been years since my husband died, since someone has hugged me," she said, then she whispered a thank-you.

Who would have thought? The things I'm doing today. The words I'll say to someone tomorrow. Please, oh please, I want to remember they could be one of those big moments.

I'd stopped by a colleague's office for business advice and in the middle of a flurry of great ideas, he interrupted his thought midsentence. "I'm bipolar, did you know that?" He continued on with three or four more sentences about his bipolar disorder and how it affects him, and then returned to our original conversation.

I hadn't known about this man's disorder and I didn't mind hearing about it, but it seemed like a strange detour to take in the midst of a business conversation. But you know what was even stranger? Later, before I left his office, I detoured back. "Funny you should mention you're bipolar. My son is bipolar, too, and he's been struggling more than usual lately. Maybe it would help if he talked to you? Would you mind?"

The man smiled. And in that very moment I realized why we'd taken the detour. It was so obvious now, but in the beginning of our conversation, I hadn't a clue.

My mother told me the day before she died that what was really important in life was love. It was a strange sentiment to hear her convey because my mother had a hard time showing her love. But somehow at the end, she must have gotten a glimpse of what I saw and felt the other night.

It's four in the morning. Paul, my grandson, is in All Children's Hospital and I'm spending the night with him. There are four cribs in the room, each one has a baby in it, and there's a mom, dad, or grandparent like me sitting in the chair beside it. I've never been comfortable sharing a room with anyone, but this evening, even though we're all strangers, instantly there's a bond. Each one of us is hoping to hear good news when the doctors make their rounds in the morning. Each one of us is hoping nothing bad happens during the night.

There are curtains between the cribs, but there's really no privacy. You can't help but overhear. Across the room a husky man is leaning over a crib whispering to his four-month-old daughter, "Don't worry, honey, Daddy will always take care of you." And then he rings for the nurse, because Daddy's trying to figure out how to safely give his baby girl a hug. She just had a tumor removed from her brain and he doesn't want to hurt her.

It's hard not to hear and it's even harder to hold back the tears. A doctor is trying to help the mother next to me understand why her newborn baby's brain didn't develop like it should have and so her daughter will need a lot of special assistance when she's growing up. Then a nurse wheels the baby's crib out of the room, they need to do more tests. And the mother is left alone. I hear her crying.

Across the room from my grandson a mother is trying to sleep in the reclining chair next to her baby's crib. She brought her baby here from Michigan, because the doctors at the hospital where she lives kept telling her nothing was wrong. But she knew something wasn't right. And now she's been told that her new baby boy can't hear or see, and won't be able to do much of anything except "be." But simply "being" is plenty for this mother to love. She's hoping to be able to take her son home in a few days so his brothers and sisters can get to know him.

My grandson is finally asleep and I lay him back in his crib. I'm tired. The days and nights are long in the hospital. But tonight I'm at ease. The doctor says in a couple more days we'll be taking home a healthy boy. I felt a little guilty hearing such good news.

I've always thought my job, my purpose here on earth, certainly must be something more dramatic than simply loving and taking care of the people around me. So I've strived to be clever, artistic, and talented in business. But as I sit here at four in the morning looking around the room and looking at my grandson, I realize I've been looking at life all wrong. It's not complicated, there's nothing to prove. My mother was right. It's really very simple. What's really important is love.

20. Writing the Recipe for My Life

That's Rudy-boy, my eighteen-year-old cat, and the pillow he's leaning against was made for me by one of my book club readers.

I missed a soft place to fall when I was young, so I've created my own, but not without help. Reading and writing have been my mentors. People who read my daily "Dear Reader" column say I write about life and it's true. But that sentence is so boring, so simple, that in today's world it wouldn't entice anyone to spend time reading the things I write about.

I guess what I do is take the everyday, mundane things—the little things most people don't even notice—and bring them to life. Give them a voice so people can see the funny in a situation, or recognize the sadness they feel. I hate being preached to, so I'm not an advice-giver and I don't know all the answers. That's one of the reasons I write, so I can try to understand "why?" Like the day I started crying in the supermarket.

My husband bought me fresh tulips. It wasn't a romantic purchase, more of a rescue. We were at the market and after we picked out some strawberries, we walked through the flower section and that's when I got a case of the "remember when" blues. Looking at the spring flowers made me think about my father and our Easter tradition.

Every year on the day before Easter, my father would walk down to the florist, and when he came back home, he was carrying two small white boxes. Inside one was an orchid corsage for my mother, and in the other a pretty pink and white carnation corsage for me.

My father wasn't a sentimental man—far from it. He never said "I love you," but once a year when the tulips and daffodils of spring were peeking up through the ground—signaling a change in season—briefly there'd be a change in my father, too. I'm not sure how or where my dad got the idea, but buying a corsage for Mom and me became an Easter tradition.

"Look at what my dad bought for me." I wore my corsage all day long, even after I came home from church and changed into my play clothes, and I fell asleep with it on my pillow, too. When I was older and moved out on my own, my father stopped buying an Easter corsage for me. I missed it. Not just the flowers, but the way I felt every year when my father handed me the box from the florist.

Now here I was standing in the middle of the market, tears in my eyes, and my husband knew why. "I think you need some fresh flowers for Easter, Suzanne, don't these tulips look like spring?" And he handed me a pink and yellow bouquet of tulips—a new beginning and a new tradition of love.

Stories can kind of sneak up on me. When I'm writing, eventually there comes a part in the process where I become agitated and it's not clear what I'm feeling, but I plow through anyway and magically, twenty or thirty minutes later the story appears. I'm not quite sure where it came from, in fact, sometimes when I go back the next day and reread what I've written, I'm amazed I wrote it. Just where did these words, where did this ability to write come from?

Maybe I shouldn't be questioning my abilities. But as soon as I finished writing that sentence, I remembered what my mother said when I told her I was publishing a business magazine—I clearly remember the look on her face. It was a look of confusion and amazement, shock, really, and then she asked, "Just where did you learn how to do all of this?"

It was as if nothing great was expected from me, and my mother still couldn't believe I'd accomplished such a thing, or that I was successful. But truth be told, sometimes even today I stand back and look at what I do and I too wonder . . . just where and how did I learn these things?

Maybe my writing career started in high school, at least that's what some of my old school friends tell me. (They insist I used to rewrite their papers—though I have no recollection.) Then again, maybe it was the dozens of thank-you letters my mother made me write when I was a kid—I do remember those.

Guilt and my mother taught me at a very early age to always send a thank-you—immediately. Even to this day, as soon as I finish opening a gift, I hear my mother's voice: "Susan, sit down and write a thank-you note and do it this minute or you'll forget!"

A syllabus accompanied each thank-you writing assignment in our house; the thank-you needed to be at least twenty-eight words, including adjectives and sincerity. Not that I had to fake being genuinely grateful when someone gave me a gift, but when you're a kid, writing a thank-you note interferes with *actually* playing with the gift you're so thankful for. So it always seemed to me like a simple thank-you would suffice. "Thank you for the new doll. As soon as I finish this thank you note I'm going to play with it, so . . . gotta go . . . thank you. Susan Tindell."

There it was—twenty-eight words including my name.

But the toughest writing assignment I faced was a thank-you note for the white socks my aunt sent to me every year for Christmas. I realized it was the thought that counted—my mother had drilled that into me—but what could you say about a pair of white socks, year after year? At least "white" counted as one of my required adjectives.

"Thank you for the great white socks. I've never seen such bright, white socks. Those white socks will go with anything, and the handy thing about white socks is that you don't have to worry about matches. One white sock is pretty much like the next white sock. And if I forget to put my shoes on and run outside with my white socks on, Mom has a new bleach that will get the dirt out, and the socks will be white again. Thank you for the white socks."

Eighty-nine words—count 'em. More than I needed, and apparently the extra words were a little too encouraging and heartfelt, because my aunt kept sending those darn white socks.

Kid stuff aside, it's taken a long time for me to acknowledge my writing ability and actually call myself a writer. I wrote a monthly "Sorry We're Closed" column when I published *In Business* magazine, but I wasn't "really" a writer. Couldn't even bring myself to use my name and the word writer in the same sentence. Even when I decided to write a feature article about grief in the workplace, I still felt like I was pretending. Maybe with good reason. Because when I sat down to type up my notes from three different interviews, I realized I didn't know anything about using quotation marks.

Old-fashioned common sense is the first approach I try when I have a problem, and I admire other people who use the same no-frills approach. One of my favorite examples is how NASA spent bundles of money and time developing a pen that would write upside down in space. The Russians sent their crew up with pencils. So my commonsense approach for learning how to use quotation marks involved taking a bubble bath and reading *Time* magazine.

I couldn't go to the library and research the topic (my article was due in the morning), and since I needed a bath anyway and *Time* magazine was filled with oodles of direct quotes framed with those two little squiggles on each side, I filled up the tub with steaming hot water, added a capful of my favorite lavender bubbles, grabbed a yellow highlighter, and carefully skimmed the articles in my husband's copy of *Time*, noting the various placement of quotation marks. Then I matched the type of sentences I'd highlighted to the ones I'd written in my article and violà . . . I looked respectable, actually better than respectable. My final draft was barely touched by the editor's pen—and you can *quote* me on that!

In my mind I was just doing this writing thing for fun. Even when I started writing a daily column for the Dear Reader book clubs, I didn't think of myself as a writer, but other people disagreed. "Look out, Dave Barry," an executive from Penguin wrote after he finished reading a tale about my husband's boating escapades, and then a few days later he emailed again. My "Cashier for a Day" column had brought back memories of his first job in a supermarket. You might think I would have been grinning ear to ear from the compliments. I wasn't. Instead I was freaking out. *Oh my God, people are really reading this stuff, people think I'm a writer, and this guy works at a publishing house. How am I going to write tomorrow's column? This guy might be reading it!*

It took three weeks for me to shake loose the "writer" label, and just when things were getting back to normal, wouldn't you know it, a newspaper columnist contacted me. He loved my online book club concept at DearReader.com and wanted to write a story about it, and oh yeah, he loved the columns I wrote every day, too. In fact, he enjoyed my column so much, he suggested I should write it on the weekend, too.

These people were really messing with my mind. *Yes, I'm a writer . . . no, I'm not a writer . . . just pretending I'm a writer.* I thought I'd kept my multiple personality oddity pretty well camouflaged, but suddenly I felt so anxiety ridden and ashamed I could barely even write.

"When the student is ready, the teacher appears" is the wise old adage. My version: When the girl is ready to come out of the writing closet, but she needs a little coaxing, two teachers and a nosy guy at Starbucks suddenly appear.

A friend and I were sitting in Starbucks drinking coffee when a man walked over to our table. "I couldn't help but overhear your conversation, you were talking about deadlines. Are you a writer?"

The guy was looking at me, waiting for an answer. "Well, yeah, I kind of write this thing every day, um, I do these book clubs, I rarely write about books, it's kind of, well sort of, you see, I don't really (breathe, Suzanne, breathe) . . . why did you want to know?" By this time I'm sure the guy thought, *This is some weird woman*, because he slowly backed away from the table and offered a sympathetic good-bye.

People were staring—how embarrassing! This was ridiculous. What the heck was wrong with me? I really needed to work this out once and for all. *Are you a writer, Suzanne? What's the big deal? Why does this "writer" label bother you so much?*

The final confrontation came when the editor of *Working Mother* magazine called saying she'd read my column about Mrs. Creswick's Meat Loaf, "loved it," and "would I be interested in writing a monthly column for the magazine?" *Okay, Suzanne, this is your moment. Are you a writer? Can you at least tell yourself you're a writer so you can accept this project? Tell yourself you're a writer, start acting like a writer, and pretty soon even you will believe it.* And now, finally . . . I do.

My strength in life comes from my insecurities. Eventually I do find my way. It might take me longer than the average Joe, but I've never regretted the journey. Stumbling along through the uncertainty of it all, I learn so much when I'm not sure about anything. I write down the recipes from my life so I can reread them when I need confirmation. Even though the situation might look bad, I've trudged through before and I'll make it this time, too.

I have just enough confidence in myself and just enough doubt to write about my worries and fears, to make fun of myself, and invite people to laugh along with me. Wouldn't it be wonderful if we could all feel comfortable enough to laugh at ourselves when we screw up? A laughter that stays with us, tucked away inside, instead of feeling shame? Hopefully when people read the words I write they'll go easier on themselves and find that soft place to fall.

My father-in-law came over to our house for a barbecue, walked into the kitchen, said hello, and then out of the blue he commented, "You know, Suzanne, I've always wondered why you bare your innermost thoughts in the column you write every day, but now I think I understand. You make it all right for people to be themselves, whatever that might be. I imagine it's reassuring for your readers to think *Suzanne's been afraid and scared to death of life—I'm not the only one.* Or if someone feels like doing something a bit on the wild and crazy side, that's okay, too—because you've written about walking down Main Street with a bubble machine, so they know there's someone out there who's nuttier than they are."

I don't know if my father-in-law realized it, but his comments just about made me cry. Wouldn't it be wonderful if reading my column put someone at ease? Nothing would make me happier. I've spent way too much of my life worrying, *Am I doing it right?* and it was such a relief—such a big relief—when I finally accepted the fact that there *are* a lot of times when I don't do life the way most people do it, but that's okay. I used to spend so much time imitating other folks and trying to get them to like me that I forgot to spend time getting to like myself. I hope I never forget it's okay to be me—whoever that might be.

The more I write, the more I learn about myself. It's a love/hate sort of thing. Writing keeps me honest. Every day I hold up a mirror and force myself to look in it—sometimes I try to resist what I see. Sometimes I can barely breathe when I'm writing. That's when I know I've found the thing I need to write about. Interesting, isn't it? When I can't breathe and feel like I might pass out any minute, then I know I've come face-to-face with the boogeyman hiding underneath my bed. Learning about me is so exciting. Where else could I get this kind of thrill for free?

Writing has taught me that simpler is better. Take it easy, slow down, Suzanne, and simply say what's on your mind. Maybe I should use impressive words, sonorous adjectives, or make the sentences complex. But writing isn't really any different from other things in life. Too much eye shadow—what *was* I thinking? The first Dove Bar tasted divine, so I ate another—my stomach rebelled. The man at the deli thought he was doing me a favor when he put a little bit more of everything on my sandwich, but it was too much.

When life gets to be too much and I don't know where to begin, I start writing. It's not easy. Fear gets in the way, but if I keep at it, eventually one single line in the midst of my jumbled thoughts is staring back at me. It feels good to read it and I realize it's the comfort I've been looking for, my soft place to fall.

What will people think? used to be the first thing I'd think about when I sat down to write, but not anymore. If I want to give my best, I need to get to the place inside of me that's a little vulnerable. It can be scary. Give a lot, put it all out there, and someone may take advantage because some people take all you have to give and give nothing back in return.

But it's worth the risk—giving a little bit of myself—because readers give the nicest, most meaningful gifts back. Readers share a story, maybe one that hasn't come to mind for years. A story about the funny thing that happened when their grandfather was still alive, they remember—and I feel their laughter in between the lines they've written. Or maybe it's a confession, something they needed to say out loud, so they could ease their pain. I hear them crying and in a reply I reassure them there are times when none of us does the right thing, including me, and silently we cry together.

Years ago, Ann, a reader at my book clubs, sent an email, and before she signed off, Ann closed with these words: "You take good care."

I can't explain it, but those simple words continue to stay with me. Every time I think about them I feel loved and cared for and I'm right back in Mrs. Creswick's kitchen. I've never met Ann, but the words she wrote rescued me again just the other day. Everything I tried to do was a struggle. Nothing was going right and then I heard Ann whispering, "You take good care."

It's the kind of good-bye that's not an ending, but a blessing. I don't know where your life's journey is right now, or where it will take you, but I wish you well. *"You take good care."*

Thanks for reading with me. It's so good to read with friends.

It truly was a boy-meets-girl love story. The girl was in her early seventies, the boy in his late sixties. My mother and Ron had a magical first date and were married just a few months later. But the happily-ever-after part of the story lasted only a short time. One year and eight months after they were married, my mother died from lung cancer.

Ron never stopped loving and pining for my mother. Frequently he'd call to talk, reliving stories about the things they did together. Nothing fancy, just simple things like the time they sat together on a bench looking out over the water while a light mist of rain was falling, or the flower garden Ron planted in the backyard for my mother. A flower garden he still lovingly tended. "When I'm in the garden, it feels like your mother is right beside me." And each time Ron would call, before he'd say good-bye, the tears would flow. Oh, how he missed my mother.

In 2008, three years after Mom passed away, Ron also was diagnosed with lung cancer. He continued to call and reminisce about my mother, but he also started asking, "When is your book going to be finished, Suzanne? I don't know how much longer I'll be around."

On a Thursday afternoon in August 2009, Ron's son called to tell me that hospice was on the way and funeral arrangements were being made for his father. My book was still in production, so I carefully wrapped a copy of my manuscript in tissue paper tied with a ribbon and sent it overnight to Ron's home.

You don't die alone when you live in a small town. There was a steady flow of family, friends, and neighbors stopping by to say good-bye, and everyone who sat a spell read a little bit of my manuscript to Ron.

Sunday afternoon my phone rang and it was Ron. "Suzanne, I've called to give you the first review of your book. It's wonderful. Reading your book was the last entry on the list of things I wanted to accomplish, so now it's time to go and be with your mother."

Ron passed away early the next morning on Monday, August 17, 2009.

Writing it down this moment, it sounds a little like a fairy tale. But in a strange sort of way I do believe it was one of those true love stories, and that my mother and Ron are finally together again, happily ever after.

Ron's on the left, my mother's on the right, and that's me in the middle holding a big, ugly bowl. Just one of the many "finds" they came home with on their daily Florida garage-sale escapades.

Acknowledgments

I dedicate this book to my loving husband, Bob; I'm one lucky woman. The longer we're married, the more in love I am with you.

Writing a book was hard work and I never would have succeeded if it hadn't been for a group of friends and an agent who believed in me, even before I did. Thank you for hanging in there with me.

"Take as much time as you need." Those words gave me permission to grieve as long as I needed after my mother died, and those same words gave me permission to take as much time as I needed to write this book. Thank you, M. J. Rose, for being there every step of the way; I'm such a lucky woman. You've been a cherished friend and mentor since the first day we met in New York City.

"How can I make the transition?" I'd been a daily columnist for ten years, so in the beginning, when I'd sit down to start writing this book, I'd end up writing a column instead. "You can do it and I'll help you." Thank you, Sully (Thomas Sullivan), for the long-distance tutoring.

The message on my friend Linda's answering machine says, "Leave a message. It may take a day or two, but I'll call you back." You can hear the smile in her words. Linda understands the flow of life. Every few weeks we sit together on a bench, drinking coffee, blowing bubbles, and watching the people walk by. Our bench-sitting keeps my heart where it needs to be in order to write.

My friend Blaize Clement assured me that when you're writing a book, the end just kind of sneaks up on you. Suddenly one day when you finish writing a sentence, you realize you're at the end, yet the day before you didn't have a clue. Blaize, you were right.

Bill Duncan sent an email years ago telling me how much he loved my daily column. In fact, he enjoyed it so much, could I please write a column on the weekend, too? Bill, Jack, Prince William (he's a friend with many names), you've been a cheerleader from way back. Thank you so very much.

Jessica Keener knows how impatient writers can be, since she's a writer, too. Thank you for reading my first drafts—in a hurry.

Perhaps one of these days we'll actually meet and I can thank you in person, but in the meantime, thank you, Stephen Barr, for periodically talking me down from the rafters.

"How's the book coming along? If you need any help, call me." Thank you, Roger Cooper. You took me under your wing since the beginning. You're a good friend and you know how to pick great restaurants in New York, too.

When there's joy in my life, there's joy in my writing. Thank you to all of the readers and librarians at the book clubs and to everyone on staff at DearReader.com: Linda Kotopka, Diana Ziegler, Jean Dahl, Tiffany Yelk, Amber Beecher, Susan Cole, Tina Tine, Mary Shelden, Bob Russell, Patrick Casey, Lori Doerman, and Bryan Biggers. And a special thank-you to my everyday muse, Valerie Farman, a woman who sees me at my worst and envisions my best.

It was a picture-perfect meeting. "I love your voice," she told me. Thank you so very much, Sulay Hernandez, for falling in love with my book. Every writer should be blessed with such an inspiring and creative editor. (And I've heard through the grapevine that you're becoming quite a good chocolate-chip cookie baker, too!)

Small-town girl meets big-city agent. She learns about the business of writing and selling a book, and also makes a kind and patient friend in the process. Thank you, Dan Conaway.

"I don't know what I'm doing."

And he would ask, "Are you still writing?"

"Yes, Dan, I'm still writing."

"Then everything is fine, Suzanne."

Muffins and Mayhem

In *Muffins and Mayhem*, Suzanne Beecher, creator of DearReader.com, combines her life stories with 30 of her favorite recipes. With striking candor, Suzanne takes readers on a journey from her lowest moments to her greatest joys and personal victories. Suzanne writes about personal successes and failures and what each taught her about life, love, and her capacity to persevere.

Scattered throughout Suzanne's memoir are favorite recipes, and each is accompanied by a personal anecdote. Suzanne believes that recipes are more than just a mix of ingredients: They're food for the soul, and she doesn't leave readers hungry. From humorous tales about avoiding her mother's liver dishes as a child (and Mom's Thanksgiving meals as an adult!) to a reverent account of how a childhood hero touched her life through Frosted Meat Loaf, Suzanne's food-filled memoir warms the heart as well as fills the stomach.

For Discussion

1. In "Pretending My Way to Success," Suzanne writes, " . . . when you have to *convince* people you're in charge, it doesn't work" (page 46). Her solution was to change the way she dressed in order to change the way others perceived her. The result was an inner self-confidence that eventually led her to shed the "power suit" without losing any authority. Do you agree with Suzanne's belief that clothes can, in a sense, make the person? Have you ever had a similar experience where your outward appearance caused an inner metamorphosis?

2. In chapter one, Suzanne writes about her mother's "truths" and quirks and how, despite her best efforts, every now and then when she looks in the mirror she sees her mother looking back. Is adopting some of our parents' idiosyncrasies inevitable? Why or why not?

3. From failed marriages to unsuccessful business ventures, Suzanne journeys through many "live and learn" experiences. Even situations such as her restaurant folding ultimately lead to personal growth and insight. Would you consider her unsuccessful endeavors failures? Why or why not? How do you define failure? Did any of Suzanne's stories make you reconsider the value of some of the failures in your own life?

4. There's an old adage: "Dance like no one's watching and sing like no one's listening." In the story about Suzanne's hotel room performance of Irene Cara's "Flashdance

(What a Feeling)," she does just that—except she accidentally winds up with an audience. Have you ever experienced a similar situation? Was it comical like Suzanne's, or more embarrassing?

5. When describing her own quirky personality, Suzanne quotes Leonard Cohen's "There's a crack in everything. That's how the light gets in." How do you think Suzanne's embracing of her individuality and pride in being "a little strange" (page 74) has affected the way she interacts with others? How can embracing one's uniqueness help overcome life's obstacles?

6. An illness or injury can be one of life's biggest setbacks. Suzanne experienced such a setback when she was diagnosed with benign essential blepharospasm, a rare, incurable neurological disorder. Determined to overcome her disability, Suzanne learned to love her illness in order to live with it. Do you think her "love the illness" strategy could help others suffering from chronic conditions? Have you ever experienced a similar situation? If so, how did you learn to live with your condition?

7. In talking about the meaning of life, Suzanne writes, "I've always thought my job, my purpose here on earth, certainly must be something more dramatic than simply loving and taking care of the people around me. So I've strived to be clever, artistic, and talented in business. But . . . I realize I've been looking at life all wrong. It's not complicated, there's nothing to prove. My mother was right. It's really very simple. What's really important is love." Do you agree? Why or why not?

8. After her mom passed away, Suzanne discovered a short poem that her grandmother had given to her mother. The poem is just a silly anti-theft ditty written on an index card, but she cherishes the keepsake and makes an index card of her own because, as she says, "[S]ometimes a little bit of silliness is the recipe I need to get me through the day" (pages 78–79). Of all the values Suzanne carries, why do you think maintaining a sense of humor is so important? Are there any special pick-me-up tokens or rituals in your life that you use to help you through rough patches?

9. One of the book's main themes is family traditions. Holiday traditions are particularly important to Suzanne, so much so that she has trouble parting with antiquated rituals like buying pecan pies at Christmas. She also recognizes the importance of maintaining traditions now that she's responsible for holiday dinners. How important is tradition in your family? Did you experience a similar "passing of the torch" when you became an adult?

10. For a long time Suzanne was ambivalent about going home to visit her parents, even to the point of becoming physically ill. But through Mrs. Creswick's meat loaf and other recipes and stories from her recipe box, Suzanne discovered a way to go back home. What does going home mean to you? Has it been an easy journey or, like Suzanne, have you had to find a way to give yourself the home you never had when you were growing up?

11. Suzanne recounts the day when she was sitting in Starbucks and a man came over to her table and asked, "Are you a writer" (page 224)? After stumbling through an

awkward and embarrassing response, Suzanne realized it was finally time to face her moment of truth. Was she going to accept and acknowledge her writing talent, or let self-doubt continue to steal it away? The words in an old folk song proclaim, "This little light of mine, I'm going to let it shine." Have you been able to freely acknowledge the talents you've been blessed with, or do you hide your light under a bushel?

12. Toward the end of the book, Suzanne writes about having the courage to "deviate from my comfortable routine" in order to discover new opportunities to touch other people's lives (page 216). So many of her projects required her to trust her instincts and take a chance. For example, when she took it upon herself to essentially create her own job description at Sunny Hill Nursing Home. Have you ever found yourself in situations where you had an opportunity to take similar chances, and how did you react? Do you regret your decision?

A Conversation with Suzanne Beecher

You end your book with the same line you end your blog posts and website entries, "Thanks for reading with me. It's so good to read with friends." Is there a special significance to this phrase?

When you grow up in a small town like I did, the feeling of belonging to a community of friends comes naturally. Whenever I'd go for a walk, or ride my bike down the street, frequently I'd stop to say hello to a neighbor. So even though more than 365,000 people read at my book clubs every day, when I'm working on my column it feels like I'm writing to one single person. Just sitting at the kitchen table, drinking coffee, and chatting with a friend. The ending for my column, "Thanks for reading with me. It's so good to read with friends," wasn't planned. It's simply the sentiment this small-town girl feels in her heart each day when she finishes writing her column.

In the preface of Muffins and Mayhem, *you write about how you have only four childhood memories. Did writing your book help you recapture any additional memories, or do you still draw a blank when the topic of childhood memories comes up in conversation?*

Writing *Muffins and Mayhem* definitely helped me recall other childhood memories. Antique stores have become another trigger for helping me remember the past. Whenever my husband and I walk through one, he's amazed at how many times I'll see something and comment, "Ah, look at that! It looks just like the one Grandma Hale used to have in her kitchen." Every old cookie jar, potato ricer, or serving bowl for sale, reminds me of another childhood memory that I'd tucked deep away.

You've had a range of jobs, from publisher of In Business *to volunteer coordinator at Sunny Hill Nursing Home. Which one of your past jobs is your favorite? Why?*

That's easy. Meals for Madison, my free lunch program in Madison, Wisconsin. My life was in crisis when I started the meal program. *In Business* magazine was losing huge amounts of money, so in a way it was kind of crazy for me to start a program that gives away free food.

Yet I knew in my heart I was doing exactly what I was supposed to be doing. The lesson I learned from the meal program is that helping other people with their problems also helps me with my own. Meals for Madison didn't solve my financial problems with the magazine, but the experience of helping someone else brought joy and peace into my life. Now, whenever I'm consumed with my own problems, I'm reminded it's time to do something for someone else.

In Muffins and Mayhem *you talk about the importance of role models and the impact Mrs. Creswick, one of your role models, had on your life. Can you think of another adult figure from your childhood who was as influential as Mrs. Creswick?*

Two people immediately come to mind: Grandma Hale and Andy Griffith. I realize mentioning my grandmother probably doesn't come as a surprise, but why Andy Griffith?

Mayberry, the town depicted in the Andy Griffith television show, was much like the one I grew up in, and Andy Griffith was the father I wished I had. To this day, watching reruns of the *Andy Griffith Show* while I'm cooking is one of my favorite pastimes. I think I know the story line of every single episode by heart, but that's okay, because it makes Mayberry feel even more like home to me.

I spent a lot of time at my Grandma Hale's house when I was young, and even though Grandma was on the quiet side, she cared for me as I always wished my own mother would have. It's the little things that stand out in my mind. At my house when I wasn't feeling well, my mother actually got angry with me, sort of suggesting somehow it was my fault that I was sick. So I was pretty much left to take care of myself. But if I wasn't feeling well at Grandma's house, things were different. I remember one time when I was visiting Grandma and I was up in the middle of the night sick to my stomach and throwing up, Grandma Hale loved me anyway and never left my side all night long.

You and your husband have collaborated on numerous projects and business endeavors throughout your relationship. Do you still work closely together now that DearReader.com has become so successful? How have the time demands of running the online book club and blog affected your business partnership?

My husband and I continue to work together, and we couldn't imagine it any other way. But we don't work on the exact same project—that's a bit too close. I think my husband and I work well together because we trust each other completely. Consequently, we never feel like we're in competition, but rather a working team. Of course, sometimes our relationship does get off course, and when that happens the sentence that brings harmony back into our conversation is, "We've been here before, let's start again." It's our cue to reevaluate the dynamics of what's really going on.

You talk very candidly about learning to live with benign essential blepharospasm, and how you learned to love your illness. Do you still have a good relationship with BEB? Can you offer any advice for others who are currently learning to love their own illnesses?

Yes, my disorder and I are still buddies, but we continue to discover new things about each other's personalities. In some ways my eye disorder is kind of like living with a roommate. I'm an only child who still prefers her own space, so periodically my BEB and I get into a disagreement. My eyes get tired, my nervous system needs a nap, but Suzanne wants to keep going. I'm upset that I can't do what I want, when I want, so I say some unkind words about how my stupid eye disorder slows me down. But my "roommate" doesn't appreciate my choice of words, or my stubbornness. So my disorder retaliates with a one-two punch in return, which completely drains my energy, and then I have no choice but to rest in bed for a couple of days. Eventually we both come to our senses and negotiate a way to live peacefully together again.

If there's one personality trait that readers of Muffins and Mayhem *learn about you, it's your entrepreneurial spirit. Do you have plans in the works for any future projects outside your DearReader.com program?*
I've never planned any of my new business ventures; opportunities just seemed to show up and I simply jumped on board. So I don't have any plans at the moment, other than to continue creating new ideas for my online book clubs, and I'd like to become more personally involved with libraries around the country. I do have plans for a second book. But as far as launching another new business venture, I think I may have exchanged some of my entrepreneurial spirit with the desire to spend more time with my four grandchildren. I'm amazed at how they've affected me. I have such fond memories of the time I spent with my Grandma and Grandpa Hale, and I sure hope I'm creating those kinds of memories for my grandchildren, too.

You run multiple websites, including the DearReader.com book club and your own blog. Have you always been so web-savvy? Do you have any advice for someone just starting a blog or web-based business?
My website is one of the survivors from the early Internet boom, when folks had the attitude, "If you build it, they will come—and you don't have to worry about making money." That kind of thinking remains a mystery to me. I guess I'm old-school, because to me it doesn't matter where the business is located—you need to have customers and you need to find a way to make money. If you're going to start a web-based business, don't quit your day job until your new business is bringing in income. Having said that, I do believe if you love what you do, the money will follow—at least enough money to live a joyful life.

What's your favorite recipe in Muffins and Mayhem*?*
Skunk Beans. This is going to sound a little strange, but whenever I make Skunk Beans, I remember as a kid singing this little ditty:

Beans, beans, the musical fruit
The more you eat, the more you toot.
The more you toot, the better you feel,
So eat more beans with every meal!

Pork 'n' Beans were frequently on the dinner table when I was a kid. After saying grace and before we started eating, I'd sing the bean song out loud. Each line with a little more emphasis than the last, so by the time I reached the crescendo at the end of the song, my arms were waving high up in the air and I'd be laughing. There wasn't a lot of laughing in my house when I was a kid, so the little girl inside of me loves the Skunk Beans recipe the most. But not to worry, these beans are toot-proof! That confirmation comes from experience, because I've served these beans to my family for years and we've never had a toot outbreak yet!

How different was the process of writing Muffins and Mayhem *from your online writing? Do you prefer book writing to writing your daily blog column?*
There's an art to writing a column for the DearReader.com book clubs because space is limited, and in my case there's a daily deadline. The ideal number of words is 360. That's not a lot of words when your goal is to tell a story, including a laugh or a tear that you hope will touch someone's heart, and then wrap it all up neatly in the end. I love what I do, but it's a pretty big assignment every day. Since I only have a few words to tell a story in my column, there's not much sauntering allowed. I have to stay on track with my original idea. But in a book, there's room to wander, as long as it's an interesting journey. I don't know how most authors approach a book, but since it was all new to me, I had no choice but to let the book take charge. I can honestly say that I never knew for sure what I was doing until it was all over. Looking back I'm amazed at where some of the chapters took me. Writing a book was a magical journey for me and I'm ready to begin again.

Enhance Your Book Club

1. Plan a book club smorgasbord! Have everyone prepare his or her favorite recipe either from the book or from Suzanne's recipe blog (DearReader.com) and bring it to your book club meeting. Or prepare one of your family's favorite recipes and share the story behind it.
2. One of the most inspiring experiences Suzanne writes about is her role as volunteer coordinator. Give back to your own community by volunteering in your neighborhood.
3. Visit the author's website, DearReader.com, and see firsthand how Suzanne's free online book clubs work!
4. Visit Suzanne's website MuffinsandMayhem.com, and create a cookbook of recipes and stories with your reading group or family members, or make one for yourself.